010 Publishers

The Enclosed Garden

History and Development of the Hortus Conclusus and its Reintroduction into the Present-day Urban Landscape

Rob Aben and Saskia de Wit

Foreword

On entering a space with thick walls through a heavy door, you would logically expect to find yourself indoors. All the more surprising, then, when that indoors turns out to be outdoors. An external 'room' with unlimited scope and many guises: an alpine meadow, a flower-filled paradise, a primeval forest. And right in the city centre too, behind a busy car park or between officeslabs. This tranquil place, this enclosed garden, is where you can give free rein to your imagination or become lost in thought.

The divide between architecture and landscape is a rewarding area of research. In the enclosed garden the two disciplines are amply represented; the landscape has become interior, its dimensions tamed with architectural means. This book about the enclosed garden is therefore also about space and spatiality, about landscape and about the city.

What for us began during our landscape architecture training as a research into the architectural side of that discipline steadily evolved into this study that seeks to contribute to the current discourse on landscape architecture, urban design and architecture. Our knowledge of the historical backgrounds of the hortus conclusus (the archetype of the enclosed garden) grew and with it the sense of just how important this forgotten type could be in the spatial and cultural context of today. Our enthusiasm proved remarkably in step with the ongoing issues informing urbanism. The dynamic and caprice of our round-the-clock society is calling with ever greater urgency for a counterweight, for time and space, for peace and quiet. A typical contemporary notion in this respect is that of 'speeding down' (rather than up) and the enclosed garden has all the prerequisites for this condition. The enclosed garden is a means of finding, in Nietzsche's wonderful phrase, 'the sublimity of self-communion'.

The hortus conclusus has been described as the Ur-form of landscape architecture. Since 1985, research into the fundamentals of the discipline has been proceeding apace at the Architecture Faculty of the University of Technology in Delft. Among the fruits it has borne is *Architecture and Landscape*, a book by two pioneers of this research, Clemens Steenbergen and Wouter Reh. In it, they examine the garden design of the Renaissance, Baroque and Enlightenment with the aim of laying bare its meaning for garden design today. Regrettably, there are no surviving examples of medieval gardens. We have to make do with descriptions and illustrations passed down in book-form. The study we have made of these medieval sources and our design analyses of enclosed gardens from that time to the present day give, we hope, a picture of and a degree of insight into this most elementary form of landscape architecture.

Rob Aben and Saskia de Wit

A room with no ceiling

'We create designs in the belief that gardens only begin to live
when they express a feeling of landscape.'

Michel Desvigne and Christine Dalnoky, 1995

The enclosed garden

Gardens are by definition havens of peace and quiet, order and pleasure in a chaotic and hostile world. Places where nature is at once excluded and brought into view in water and coolness, fertile ground and a fine prospect. At times these two worlds – that of the 'unworldly' ideal and that of the real landscape – come together, as in the enclosed garden, the *hortus conclusus*.[1]

Etymologically, *enclosed garden* is a doubling up of the original

left: Alvaro Siza, Centro de Arte Contemporanea de Galicia, Santiago de Compostella, 1994. Bounded space in the city.

right: Farmstead garden, Arosa Valley, Switzerland. Bounded space in the landscape.

meaning. The Old-English 'geard' means (woven) fence and thus enclosed space.[2] The garden shows the landscape its containing walls, and in the garden the natural horizon is shut out and replaced by an internal horizon: the upper edge of its surround. Inside it, a *paradise* is depicted.

In architectural terms by contrast the garden is very much related to the landscape beyond it and is 'the most condensed unit in which the historical, functional and spatial complexities of the landscape are made manifest'.[3] So 'enclosed' and 'garden' would seem to be primarily in opposition. The garden *gathers* the landscape around it (garden) and at the same time shuts itself off from it (enclosed). The enclosed garden is as broad as the landscape, in that it incorporates the expansiveness of the sky, and as contained as a building. Thus it is an intermediary between man and landscape.[4] It is both inside and outside, landscape and architecture, endless and finite. How is this paradox rendered, how is the expansiveness of the landscape materialized in the seclusion of the garden?

Gardens are one of the oldest expressions of civilization. Three thousand years ago the inhabitants of Egypt, Babylon, Mesopotamia and Persia constructed walled places containing fruit trees, pools and places to sit. The medieval hortus conclusus took over these traditions and transformed them, translating the Oriental archetype of paradise into the European context. Centuries of garden tradition were anchored in the garden experiments of the Renaissance, Baroque and Enlightenment, taking a significant step towards shaping an

1. By the term landscape is meant the physical, visual-spatial dimension of the built and unbuilt surface of the earth with the distinctions to be made therein between natural, cultivated and urban landscapes. Nature is construed as that which is not made or influenced by man and as processes uninfluenced by man.

2. The Dutch word for garden, 'tuin', derives from 'teen' (twig), and means an area bounded by a wickerwork fence of willow twigs. In her doctoral thesis *The Garden as an Enclosure* (1986) Anne van Erp-Houtepen holds up to scrutiny the etymological origins of garden and allied words and meanings.

3. Steenbergen 1990, 13.

4. The architectural historian Christian Norberg-Schulz describes the fundamental quality of landscape as 'extension' (what we have chosen to term expansiveness) and the fundamental quality of the man-made place as enclosure. Norberg-Schulz 1980, 32, 58.

5. The innocence often attributed to the profession of landscape architecture has its roots in the hortus conclusus. It creates its own harmonic context from which disruptive factors are excluded. But the garden is more than just a place to withdraw to.

image of nature that still determines the way we see it today.

Although this book is about the enclosed garden, it will only make passing reference to flowers and trees.[5] It seeks rather to expound the ideas underlying a centuries-old, ever rejuvenating tradition in which man tries to reconcile himself with his surroundings by bringing these within the closest proximity. It is a report on the ever changing vision of nature, though one which essentially has remained the same. Awe at the grandeur of nature translated into architectural space – not to trivialize it, but for man to be able to relate to it.

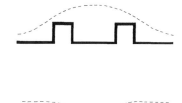

Inside and outside, earth and heaven converge in the enclosed garden. The building is, so to speak, erected out of the mass of the earth, with the garden a cavity in that mass. The boundless space of the sky penetrates the garden and absorbs it.

Acceleration and deceleration

'An insight is needed (and that probably very soon) as to what is specially lacking in our great cities – namely, quiet, spacious, and widely extended places for reflection, places with long, lofty colonnades for bad weather, or for too sunny days, where no noise of wagons or of shouters would penetrate ... : buildings and situations which as a whole would express the sublimity of self-communion and seclusion from the world. ... We want to have ourselves translated into stone and plant, we want to go for a walk in ourselves when we wander in these halls and gardens.'

Friedrich Nietzsche, 1882

So what is the situation as regards today's landscape, city and *urban landscape*? What role does the enclosed garden play here, what are the problems it identifies? In the fragmented urban landscape of today spatiality is replaced by objectness; the fragments add up to a collage devoid of scale. Inner cities, suburbs, shopping malls, business parks, agricultural areas and sports grounds are juxtaposed, separated only by residual spaces and tied together by infrastructure. The contemporary city is subjected to ever greater densification, spatial levelling out and fragmentation. Open space – whether in or out of the city – has to cede to built development and urban facilities. The breached boundaries between city and landscape offer boundless opportunities to colonize and these are seized on avidly. Our urban landscape is growing although exactly where and how is difficult to say. In the urban landscape density and void are replaced by objects and infrastructure set in an undefined field where identity and orientation can only be achieved artificially. Both the material landscape and the way we experience it are getting more and more fragmented and superficial.

In an age where all corners of the earth have become accessible to us, where the computer opens up worlds whose possibilities we can only hint at, multiplicity, speed and information seem to preside over society. Places falling outside

Collage of motorway intersection (Prins Clausplein, The Hague).

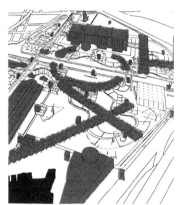

Bernard Tschumi, Parc de la Villette, Paris, 1990. Celebration of the urban landscape.

Jardin des Bambous. Reacting to the chaos around, Alexandre Chemetoff designed this enclosed garden as an oasis of tranquillity.

this sphere of influence appear at first irrelevant yet in their apparent aimlessness can offer a counterweight to the hectic world. Countermanding the acceleration of other urban activities is the need for a strategy of deceleration in which these oases of peace and moments of quiet can figure.

The contemporary city as an impenetrable chaos where urbanites must deploy every ounce of creativity to survive, is a familiar metaphor as much in a positive (excitement and adventure) as in a negative sense (individualistic, antisocial). In medieval times man had to contend with the might of nature and it was during this period that the hortus conclusus was born: the enclosed garden from which nature was shut out. If the natural wilderness is the model for today's urban wilderness, the hortus conclusus might serve as the exemplar for landscape-architectural spaces that exclude the city.

What is at the basis of the hortus conclusus, the introverted space that shuts itself off from the outside world to create away from it the image of an ideal paradise far from workaday reality? What ideas of space and time, of nature and culture, does it present and where do these come from? What are the archetypes of the garden, the original visual and spatial experiences that have come to converge there? What form and content can be given these smallest units of public landscape?

In this book we will be looking at the proportions, limits, construction and materials of the enclosed garden. In its measurements and refinement the enclosed garden has the character of an interior, which only makes this component of the public domain all the more interesting. The spatial unity of the enclosed garden is able to draw together the fragments: a 'stabilizer' in a landscape subject to change. Our point of departure is to make this operational as a landscape-architectural prototype for inward-looking spaces that introduce the expansiveness of the landscape into the urban tissue, or conversely, *enclosure* into an open landscape.

The tradition of landscape architecture is processed and actualized by reintegrating landscape and nature at the lowest scale of urban public space. Just this compactness and scale makes the enclosed garden suitable as an 'outdoor room' where one can engage with nature. How can the qualities of the landscape's expansiveness and those of the natural processes at work there, be represented at the smallest scale, and within what limits and with which design tools and techniques can this visual-spatial inversion be achieved?

In recent decades landscape architecture has been reconsidered as a design discipline in its own right. This coincides with its renewed deployment in planning issues born of urban restructuring, the design of public urban space and the formation of metropolises.

Research into the lower limit of landscape architecture – the smallest measure able to accommodate a visual-spatial representation of the landscape – and into the interface of objectness and spatiality, enables us to sharpen the conceptual definition of the area covered by the profession and add to the instruments at the designer's disposal. Within this smallest of landscape spaces the various layers of landscape design – geometric, spatial, visual – can be distinguished. The hortus conclusus acted as the stepping-off point for the Renaissance gardens, where the relations between architecture (building) and landscape were formalized and the foundations for the profession laid.[6]

6. In this sense the present study complements the research done by Clemens Steenbergen and Wouter Reh into the theoretical principles of landscape design and documented in *Architecture and Landscape*, their book on the rational, the formal and the pictorial.

The enclosed garden as paradox

What method should we use to get an understanding of the enclosed garden? For our research into the enclosed garden we must go back to the chaotic Middle Ages when city and landscape were spatially condensed. With the medieval ideas on nature, space and time as a backdrop, the various manifestations of the hortus conclusus are disclosed as the basis for a formal – spatial and visual – dissection of the enclosed garden. The type is then analysed with the aid of literature and engravings, the only sources that still attest to their existence. By closely following the development of the enclosed garden we can expose and identify each of the contradictions intertwined in the hortus conclusus.

After unravelling the formal aspects of the hortus conclusus we will look at how the type can be deployed in the current urban landscape as both the generator and the counterpart of urban processes. Assisted by four design experiments we will examine the feasibility of the enclosed garden today. Analyses of existing examples illustrate which form this might take. The method of analysis developed to this end takes the paradox as underlying principle. Herein lies the key to an understanding of the enclosed garden. The analyses are predicated upon literary research, extant visual material, topographical maps and ground plans and upon our own observations and measurements in situ.

Generator of forces
Transmitter of force

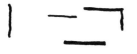

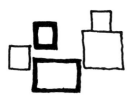

Spatial division
Spatial addition

Endlessness and enclosure

'Take off your shoes and walk along the beach through the ocean's last thin sheet of water gliding landwards and seawards. You feel reconciled in a way you would not feel if there were a forced dialogue between you and either one or the other of these great phenomena. For here, in between land and ocean – in this in-between realm, something happens to you that is quite different from the seaman's alternating nostalgia. No landward yearning from the sea, no seaward yearning from the land.'

Aldo van Eyck, 1978

The particular attractions of the beach derive partly from the duality of land and ocean, both of them present in the 'thin sheet of water gliding' across the ripple marks in the sand. The ocean is boundless; freedom, awe and the appeal of the distant horizon are attributes of the 'oceanic' sense of space: universal, timeless and unrelated to place and perception by the senses.[7] Against that we can pit walking barefoot along the beach and feeling the grains of sand, the palpability of the earth or the 'erotic' sense of space: physical sensation, feelings of finitude, safety and individuality and an awareness of both place (*topos*) and time (the moment).

In the enclosed garden this polarity emerges as its most distinctive quality: the paradox of the infinite in the finite, two extremes heightened by being present simultaneously.

ARCHITECTURAL ANALYSIS. At the beginning of the twentieth century the art historian Paul Frankl analysed architecture with a system of categories by describing it in terms of *polarities*, in the hope of being able to define, without normative ideas, the inherent qualities of architectural objects.[8] He distinguishes four aspects of form: matter, space, light (appearance) and intention, which he defines in terms of the following polarities.

CORPOREALITY	generator of forces – transmitter of force
SPACE	spatial addition – spatial division
LIGHT	one image – many images
INTENTION	freedom – constraint

Corporeality, space and light fix the form and the form is the expression of the intention. Intention in this case does not mean functionality, use, or fitness for purpose of the construction, but whatever meaning that the designer wishes his building to disseminate. Frankl distils the above into the polarity of freedom-constraint.

The four polarities together form a whole in the sense that the concepts of generator of forces, *spatial addition* and one image relate to freedom, and transmitter of force, *spatial division* and many images to constraint. A building informed by constraint, for example Mies van der Rohe's German Pavilion in Barcelona, enjoys a bilateral relationship with its surroundings. Several spaces or spatial components are tied together (spatial division), the spatial form crystallizes round structural lines running through the building (transmitters of force) and the image forms part of a coherent sequence. A 'free' building by contrast presents an autonomous unity (spatial addition), crystallizes round a focal point (generator of forces) and has one complete image, i.e. it is independent of its setting.

LANDSCAPE-ARCHITECTURAL ANALYSIS. The critical system wielded by Frankl is concerned with the architecture of a building, an object with a *spatial form*, a plasticity (matter) as container of the spatial form, and an *appearance*. The enclosed garden can likewise be construed as an architectural object. There the polarities are enacted within a single space with a containing shell, able to be taken in at a glance. But the enclosed garden is not just an architectural object, it is a *garden* in which the *landscape* is made manifest.

On closer examination this datum of landscape reproduction divides into three aspects: visualizing, complementing and symbolizing.[9] Just about every garden – from Versailles to the plastic gnome variety – is recognizable as such in that it reflects the landscape: there are water features, trees, lawns, flowers. In the enclosed garden, however, it is just this aspect that is often conspicuously absent or reduced to a minimum. In the *patio* of the German Pavilion, for example, the reference to nature in the travertine-clad walls is only present in the background. It is partly through this restraint in the visual rendition that the complementary aspect is all the stronger in the enclosed garden. Emptiness and enclosure in the garden make manifest the many images and the spatial expansiveness of the landscape. It is not merely that the landscape is symbolically present in the enclosed garden, the garden is itself symbolic of the landscape.

In order to dissect this relationship with the landscape we can resort to a method developed by Clemens Steenbergen et al. This divides the landscape into four architectural layers or treatments comparable with Paul Frankl's critical system. These layers are basic form, spatial design, visual structure and programme.[10]

The basic form relates to the treatment of the geomorphology and topography and is a rational (geometric) system of measures and proportions, a compositional system that examines the interference between the plan and the natural givens of the site. At issue in the spatial system is the visual-spatial relationship between the design on the one hand and the panorama and the plan's boundary on the other, in other words the dynamics of the landscape continuum. The visual structure relates to the (visual) representation of nature, expounded in the

7. For more extensive treatment of the concepts *Eros and Oceanos*, see Polak 1984.

8. Paul Frankl, *Principles of Architectural History*, The MIT Press, 1968 (Translation of *Die Entwicklungsphasen der neueren Baukunst*, 1914). Polak critiques this system at length in Polak 1984, 179-187.

9. Norberg-Schulz 1980.

10. The basis of this method is set forth in his dissertation *De stap over de horizon* (The Step over the Horizon – 1990). In it he treats basic form, spatial form and visual structure. In *Architecture and Landscape* (1992) written later with Wouter Reh he adds a fourth category: programme form.

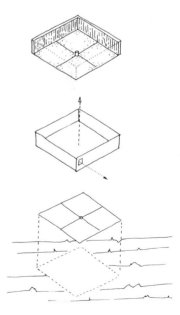

Appearance
Spatial form
Plan configuration and geomorphology

garden in a multiplicity of image-types such as water, rocks and greenery. Knowing just how the cultural-recreational and productive programmes in the garden are formed, simultaneously gives us a picture of the ideas on nature and culture at that time.

Analysing the enclosed garden

'There is no freedom in the desert.
Though there are no fences, no posts.
It is better – if you wish to be free –
to elegantly wander through a labyrinth.'

Gerrit Komrij, 1984

The hermetic world of the *labyrinth*, where the very limitations imposed by the space offer freedom, is the same as that of the enclosed garden which in its finitude admits infinity, freedom in constraint. The enclosed garden can be conceived as a *microcosm* (from the Greek 'mikros' (little) and 'kosmos' (world-order); a philosophical term that describes man (the soul) as a world in miniature in which the macrocosm is reflected. The whole and its parts are analogous. In that sense the enclosed garden represents a completeness, not least because from it emerges an accumulation of meanings. The garden as 'mirror of the soul', of man, the *cosmos*, paradise.

In order to relate the concept of the enclosed garden as microcosm, as architectural object, to the concept of landscape a strategy has been developed that effects a synthesis of the methods of analysis described above. There is a stratification that has to do not only with polarities within the garden, but equally with the relationship between the garden and the landscape of which it is part. It is as much a microcosm as a landscape space which is place-defined, open and changing over time; at once free and constrained. How are 'constraint' (translation of the geomorphology, representation of the landscape) and 'freedom' (seclusion, representation of an abstract concept of nature) able to relate?

The dialectic between the enclosed garden as free space and the many ways it makes the visitor aware of the world beyond it, finds expression in the reciprocal relationship between the different scales and the different layers of the plan. The garden is regarded in relation to the landscape, in relation to the building and in independence as a box, with the three planning layers – *plan configuration*, *spatial form* and *appearance* – each time in evidence.

This brings the number of categories of the object to be analysed up to nine. The *route* threads the scales of landscape, building and garden together, the planning layers (the form) together express the programme. The ambivalence of the

enclosed garden is rendered in the intermingling of multiple layers of meaning and qualifications, in the simultaneous occurence of the two poles. This ambiguity is created by, say, transparency, synchronicity and reciprocity, so that the space – or part of it – is both inside and outside, open and enclosed, extravert and introvert. The aspects then interact at the various scales and can even become each other's polar opposites.
A number of considerations informed the selection of examples for this book. One was that they should be in Europe, so as to be able to consider them within the development from the hortus conclusus. Another was that the garden should be a space in its own right. But the principal consideration was the relationship between landscape and garden and so also the paradox of the enclosed garden. In the first instance we assessed the measure of the design's impact at the scales of landscape, building and garden.

11. Topos is a concept deriving from Greek mythology that refers to the mythical landscape, the natural landscape as the dwelling-place of the gods. The term locus referred originally to the rational basis of Roman cultivation, the templum or mythical cross defining the city plan.

	LANDSCAPE	BUILDING	GARDEN
PLAN CONFIGURATION	locus – topos	centralized – decentralized	centre-periphery
SPATIAL FORM	enclosed – open	spatial addition – spatial division	zenith – horizon
APPEARANCE	natural – artificial	unity – diversity	sensory – abstract

	LANDSCAPE – BUILDING – GARDEN
ROUTE	introduction – negation
PROGRAMME AND MEANING	emblem – function
SYNTHESIS	freedom – constraint – microcosm – fragment

PLAN CONFIGURATION AND GEOMORPHOLOGY. The geomorphology of the landscape, the ground plan of the building and that of the garden – each has its own internal logic. But are there links to be discerned between them? The relationship between the central point and the periphery of the garden lays the basis for its ultimate *alignment*. Does the garden have an architectural system of its own or is it part of the landscape?

The concepts of *locus* and *topos* both refer to a fixed point in the landscape, a defined place, but each gives it a different meaning; topos regards it from beyond, from the landscape, and locus from within, from an internal order: a rational, geometrically determined concept of place. Topos embraces the local aspect whereas locus has a universal charge that erases all sense of the local.[11]

SPATIAL FORM. The landscape is determined by the horizon. This *horizontal alignment* is transmuted in the enclosed garden into a *vertical alignment*. The box in the landscape can contain a

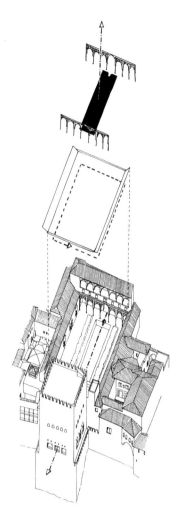

surprising inner world: 'The inside is bigger than the outside'.[12] The vertical alignment can find a counterpart in that box's relationship with the landscape, in the visual axis to the horizon, in the transparency of the space, in an emphasis on the periphery, in a horizontal sequence or subdivision of spaces.

The enclosed garden can be described in terms of open and closed on the one hand and the relationship between vertical and horizontal alignment (or expansiveness) on the other. The garden is closed with respect to the landscape, open with respect to spaces inside a building. Open and closed are played off against one another in the relationship between the scales of garden, building and landscape. The space is open to the sky, and it is this link between garden and sky that is decisive for the garden in its entirety – as though a tangible axis existed between its central point and the *zenith*.

APPEARANCE. The look of the landscape is determined by the characteristics of the natural landscape and the degree of human intervention there. This relationship between man and landscape (natural, cultivated or urban) is reproduced in the garden.

The garden is a formal representation of nature. How is this representation brought to bear? Sight, touch, smell and hearing all contribute to an integrated appearance in which abstraction and sensuality are brought face to face. The impressions gained by the senses together can indicate one or more image-types, such as a wood, a plain or a river.

ROUTE. The route bridges the gaps between scales. It also introduces a temporal aspect by its ability to accelerate, decelerate or cease movement altogether. The garden may be included in a sequence or it may be ignored. It may be announced or just suddenly appear. It may terminate the route or be merely a random station along the way.

PROGRAMME AND MEANING. Plan configuration, spatial form and appearance are an expression of the programme of the enclosed garden. The emphasis may be on social activity or on individual experience. The garden may be first and foremost a reflection of use or of a universal meaning. What does it say about nature and culture? The form of the garden can have a semiotic or a symbolic meaning; it can refer to the function or to the underlying idea. The meaning is also the layer behind the formal reference of the appearance: for example, a garden referring to a wood (the appearance) thereby also refers to the abstraction attendant upon it: endlessness, or nature (the meaning).

SYNTHESIS. If the garden is a totality complete in itself,

Patio de los Arrayanes, Granada, 13th century. A design laboratory in which to materialize infinity by the following means: a visual axis to the horizon, a perambulatory walk, eaves all round, mirrored heads and a reflecting pool.

12. See C.S. Lewis 1950.

unbound by context, if it illustrates an abstract idea, if it crystallizes round a central point, a locus generated from within that leaves behind an impression of unity – then the garden is a microcosm. If, on the other hand, the garden brings out the landscape, is related to the landscape's underlying structure, part of a composite space, aligned with the horizon, with a wealth of impressions – then the garden is a fragment. Thus, the synthesis of the planning categories is the relationship between freedom and constraint, and between microcosm and fragment.

Garden catalogue or design challenge

This book can be regarded as a catalogue illustrating the rich diversity of enclosed gardens in Europe. It can also be read as a manual for designing urban space. Aided by the analyses, readers can redesign and experience the enclosed garden themselves and thereby gain fresh insights. But it was chiefly written as a challenge to address a task whose importance is only now just beginning to register, an almost forgotten task linked with the decline of architecture in the city, namely giving shape to the urban landscape as a *spatial* constellation. The issue is not designing just gardens but also their context. Contrasts – flowers versus business parks – are brought out by skipping the 'medium scale'. Completeness is pitted against fragmentation, space-defining against spatial indeterminacy, intimacy against exposure, order against heterogeneity, immutability against transience.

Enclosed gardens could contribute towards visualizing, complementing and symbolizing today's fragmented landscape. The ideas underpinning the hortus conclusus can be wrested from the small scale of the garden and magnified and translated into the formgiving of the urban landscape itself. Discoveries made at the lower limit of landscape architecture are thus manoeuvred into the centre of the metropolitan debate. The garden as spatial laboratory for landscape design.

Hortus conclusus. Woodcut, 1520.

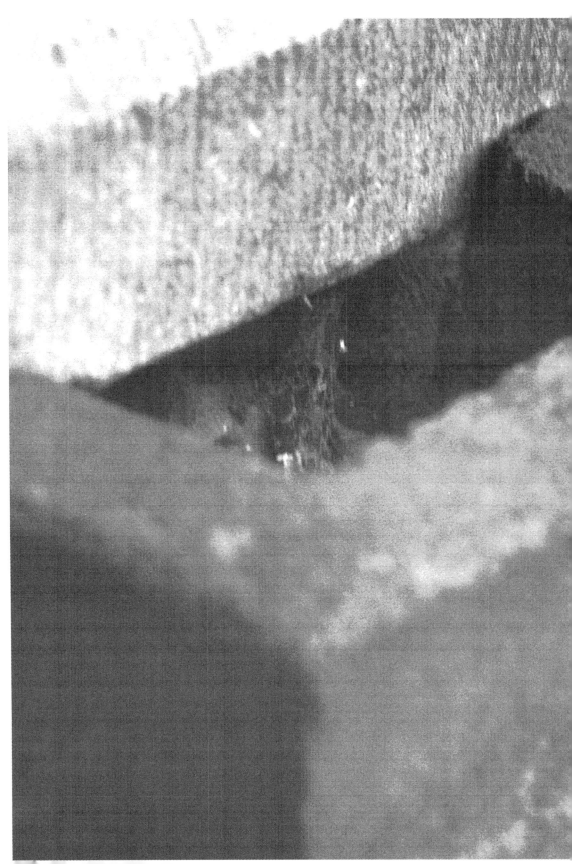

The hortus conclusus as landscape-architectural model

'The hortus conclusus is a veritable stage where "the immeasurable wealth of relationships between things" is enacted. A distilling flask in which spiritual and bodily love, church allegory and alchemy – under high pressure or in a vacuum – engage first in one way and then in another, the intention being to relieve God of the key of wisdom.'

Gerrit Komrij, 1991

Exploring the field

The hortus conclusus unites within itself a marvellous assemblage of disparate aspects. It seeks to understand the landscape it denies, explain the world it excludes, bring in the nature it fears and summarize all this in an architectural composition. The ingredients of this newly-appointed space laboratory for landscape architecture are to be found in its architectural, literary and landscape archetypes. The literary archetype of paradise presides over the interpretation of its landscape and architectural imagery, generating a tensionality between representation and reality.

The hortus conclusus in the Middle Ages: a sanctuary in an inhospitable world

Monastery garden of the Cathedral of Gerona, c. 1100.

THE EARLY MIDDLE AGES. The birth of Europe was a chaotic affair. With the collapse of the Roman Empire and the endless flood of nomadic barbarian peoples came war, famine and plague. Trade had become all but impossible so that the urban population left for the country and the remains of the Roman population merged with an unremitting stream of barbarian tribes. With its traditions and customs virtually unchanged, the countryside came to replace the towns as the factor determining society, thereby eradicating the explicit distinction between the town as embodying culture and the landscape as visible nature. Towns were enclaves in an immense landscape, a landscape to which monasteries, castles and settlements turned their backs. After centuries of enforced wandering, landownership became the summum bonum and the first medieval fields, meadows and gardens made their appearance. The world was seen as immutable, a stabilitas loci, with standards and values related to one supreme value only. This was no peaceful status quo but a fatalistic acceptance of chaos.

The Church, the only guardian of culture and multifaceted leader in a turbulent world, combatted the chaos with strict religious ideas regarding morals and duty, a severe doctrine of atonement and ethics that was to save mankind. In 529 AD St Benedict drew up the Holy Rule, his regulations for monastic life interweaving spiritual and physical labour into a strict daily routine. In a society that was at once anarchistic and conservative, the work ethic and the ordering of time and space were ground-breaking advances. This innovation, then, mainly originated in the monasteries, places of retreat able to develop with little danger of being attacked. In view of the limited opportunities for trade they were almost entirely self-supporting A whole range of gardens evolved there: orchards, cemeteries, herb gardens, flower gardens, vegetable gardens and the cloiste garth. These gardens, set within the introverted ensemble, represented the landscape. By placing work and contemplation on equal footing St Benedict, as it were, set the garden free. Elevated above its role as production unit, it was now a permissible source of pleasure.

THE HIGH MIDDLE AGES. The contrast between the dark early Middle Ages and the height of civilization attained by the Roman Empire weighed heavily on the minds of medieval folk and they looked back with yearning to Mediterranean antiquity or even further, to the bosom of Abraham and the *Garden of Eden*. An initial attempt to revive the Roman Empire was the so-called Carolingian Renaissance from the eighth to the tenth century. Under Charlemagne independent farmers developed a hierarchic system of vassals and serfs, with landownership the basis of power and fidelity the basis of ethics. The structure of society was predicated on free-ranging units organized round castles or monasteries and possessing a strong hierarchical structure. Fierce rivalry between such units made it essential to fortify the castles. The nobles were often themselves gentleman farmers, so there was no great distinction between cultural and rural life. For example, the hunt was a key event, being both an expression of cultivation and a means of sustenance. Here nature, farming and castle life cannot be considered distinct from one another.

Medieval man managed to glean snippets of information from travellers and traders, from manuscripts preserved in monasteries and later by way of the Crusades, about the refined civilizations of the Greeks, the Romans, the Byzantines and the Muslims. Despite their hostility towards these foreign cultures the semi-barbarian population had a profound admiration for them. Following the collapse of Charlemagne's empire a change overtook the world of knights and kings, when a Christian Europe emerged with an identity of its own. Between the tenth and fourteenth centuries new production techniques evolved in a big way. Farming and trade took a back seat as the economy burgeoned, the population doubled and building took place on a massive scale, most particularly the construction of bigger and more sumptuous churches. Crusades served to keep the quarrelsome peoples from each others' throats and gave shape to longings for the eternal kingdom of God.

THE LATE MIDDLE AGES. Little by little, urban society shifted towards centre stage in Western Europe, though at first still controlled by the feudal landowners and the Church.[1] The latter furnished the credit that the merchants were not yet able to yield themselves and glamourized the labour so looked down on by the nobility. The towns were principally trading centres that supplanted the political power of the small autonomous dominions with international networks.

These towns were sturdily bounded by ramparts, moats and walls, dykes, rivers or mountain ridges. Beyond these lay farmlands, for the towns were still almost entirely dependent on their own food production. As a rule, the surrounding fortifications encompassed a wider area than the actual town. This was to accommodate eventual expansion but equally to be able to grow food within the walls during long sieges as well as to house farming-related functions. These intramural margins were given over to more meadows, orchards and kitchen gardens. As time went by, trade put an end to the self-containment of the towns and these interstitial areas were filled by the expanding built development.

A number of towns sprang up round castles or monasteries whose gardens ultimately were given over completely to buildings. The later merchant towns were likewise compact and predominately of stone, with kitchen gardens, orchards and public areas directly beyond the ramparts and within them tournament fields, shooting ranges and cemeteries which had replaced the original farmlands. The gardens, both inside and outside the ramparts, were ambivalent as to use: cemeteries and orchards were as much places for music and dance.[2]

It was only at the end of the Middle Ages around 1400, when society became stabilized to any degree, that gardens took on a prominent place in cultural life. The monasteries had swelled into wealthy complexes with landed property and gardens where a mystical spirituality and Romanesque art rose to a climax. Castles were no longer fortresses but fortified houses with much of the social life taking place outside them. Already small gardens laid out by wealthy burghers were arising sporadically on empty patches of land in the towns. The garden moved from the periphery of the town to deep within it. With the coincidence of production unit and mythical place the garden achieved new significance as an architectural-spatial whole.

Landscape archetypes: counterpoints in the wilderness

Until the eleventh century Europe was shrouded in a mantle of forests and heathland, with only here and there an occasional cultivated spot. To resist the forces of nature was at that time deemed pointless. Society was still deeply embedded in a semi-mythical nature where natural and supernatural phenomena such as angels, miracles, devils and dragons existed side by side. It was wholly dependent on the whims of the mysterious powers of nature and in complete awe of the signs read in eclipses of the sun and moon, stellar configurations, sandstorms and earthquakes. The fear of nature and of death were inextricably linked with daily life, a state of dependence that

The month of July from *Les Trés Riches Heures du Duc de Berry* (Chantilly, Musée Condé). Typifying the medieval conception of nature is this book made for the Duke of Berry cataloguing time, in which the landscape acts as a stage set for the round of the seasons. In this miniature the cultivated landscape is the backdrop for activities symbolizing the month of July: harvesting and sheep-shearing.

brought with it an ambivalent attitude to nature. The forest was a wilderness peopled with real and imagined dangers but at the same time it provided a ready source of income; there you could gather honey, wood, resin and acorns for the swine, and hunt game.

For medieval man, the landscape had no aesthetic or spatial qualities in itself but gained its value from whatever took place there. The forest was the horizon of the world and the things of real value were enacted at isolated clearings. Again, the selective medieval image of nature was determined not by the wilderness but by cultivated open spaces. These were spatial entities that could be comprehended, as opposed to the terrifying endlessness of wood, heath and marshland.

CLEARING AND OASIS. In the dense, dark forest it was the glade or *clearing* that formed a natural inner world. Its meaning derives from its state of openness: the physical absence of the forest, where that which is hidden in the forest is brought into view.[3] There, light and clarity complement the darkness and complexity of the forest. The great depth of the forest is visible between the tree trunks, of which the clearing is a constituent component. In spatial terms, this free region is as much a part of the labyrinthine totality of the forest as a simple spatial unit. The gap in the leafy vault gives a view of the sky above, drawing an imaginary line linking heaven and earth. Where this line touches the earth, the undifferentiated ground plane acquires a virtual centre.

In the inhospitable openness of the desert, an *oasis* is a natural inner world where abundance and shade prevail. Against the spatiality of the forest glade we can pit the sensuality of the oasis, the palpable presence of water, nourishment and shady trees. Both oasis and clearing spatially and visually complement their context as *counterpoints* in the landscape. The oasis, an entity in a horizontal plane, visualizes the line linking earth and sky and constitutes the centre of the unbroken circle that is the horizon. The vertical alignment of the axis and the connection between oasis and horizon – the horizontal alignment – together give the coordinates of the space.[4] The oasis is a microcosm, a complete world in itself. At its centre is the source, the condition

2. The public spaces were often fenced-off areas of grass, possibly planted with fruit trees. Because of the lack of open places churchyards were often exploited for profane activities. The area just within the city walls was an amusement ground where fairs, trade and cattle markets and town festivities were held, but was also a place for walks and playing games. Elongated lots planted with trees and sometimes marked out by bushes were used as shooting ranges for longbows and crossbows.

3. Heidegger 1927/1962, 133. Heidegger uses the metaphors of the forest, the forest path (Holzweg) and the clearing *(Lichtung)* for 'Being', through which one must make a hazardous journey off the beaten track and beyond the boundaries of the familiar (Holzweg) to gain insight. The actual existing 'being' is not the fundamental Being (the forest) but the way it appears to us (i.e. as clearing).

Clearing and oasis.

4. A fundamental given of every space is the opposition between the unlimited mass of the earth and the unlimited natural space above it, which meet at the earth's surface. Added to the horizontal earth's surface (whose vertical orientation materializes in the oasis) are vertical walls with a horizontal orientation resulting from interaction between the walls, or between the wall and the horizon. The walls define the horizontal and vertical measures. In the oasis the two extremes exist together without transition. The unbounded natural space stands alongside the bounded internal space, and the horizontal plane linked by a vertical coordinate with the sky stands alongside the volume joined by a horizontal coordinate to the horizon. (Freely adapted from the architect-monk Dom Hans van der Laan's theory of nature and architecture. Van der Laan 1977/1983, 1-6.)

5. The garden as metaphor for the soul can be traced back to these natural archetypes. The oasis as the central point of boundless space accords with the traditional image of a meaningful core. Just like an archaeologist at the excavation site, the psychoanalyst has to expose the patient's psyche layer by layer before reaching the most deeply hidden and most valuable treasure. 'This metaphor of a human built up in layers, the deeper the more core-like, endlessly breaking open as they near the surface to blossom in an "un-corelike" excess of concealing superficialities' (Bekkers 1991). There is a general contempt felt for the periphery (surface, outward appearance, pretence, lies) and what amounts to epistemological veneration for the centre (depth, inner self, essence, truth). And so there emerges a new man with a periphery having nothing core-like about it and a centre that is all core. This new creature is an introvert. With his back to the world (its space makes him giddy) he searches for his own central point. The clearing archetype gives us quite another illustration of this metaphor: Sigmund Freud takes off his wedding ring and looks through it to an illuminated wall beyond: 'In its centre there is nothing, and yet its appearance is such as to suggest that the middle is the only thing about it that matters. ... A human built up of layers is an optical illusion. There is just a periphery about a void, and this periphery contains not just the un-corelike but the core-like as well. Depth and surface, pretence and essence, inner and outer, conscious and unconscious – all these are in the exterior, in close proximity to each other and to the world.'(Translated from P. Bekkers 1991)

6. Sacro bosco means literally 'holy wood'. A *labyrinthine space*, it was a part of the Renaissance garden that deviated from the rational geometry of the garden ensemble. A nymphaeum is a natural *grotto* dedicated to the nymphs.

necessary for life on which the entire oasis depends.[5]

The enclosed gardens of Egypt, Persia, Mesopotamia and Babylon were modelled on the oriental archetype of the oasis. For the hortus conclusus the eastern garden was transported into the western context, taking as model the archetype of the clearing, itself a product of the European landscape. Just as the oasis is a haven in the desert for the nomad, so the clearing was a refuge in the wilderness for medieval man.

ANGER AND TEMENOS. As the landscape became colonized it was the oasis and the clearing that were seized upon to be cultivated and given meaning. Grazing cattle transformed the open space in the woods into a meadow. This so-called *anger* offered space in which to enjoy and spend time in the landscape. Items of furniture such as a chess table and a turf seat were set

above: Anger. Meister der Leibesgarten, *Der große Liebesgarten.* Copper engraving, mid 15th century.

below: Temenos.

down in the meadow to make one's stay there more pleasurable and to define the place.

At the opposite end of the spectrum to this cultivated area were the places which one showed a healthy respect and held at a distance, places where the gods resided: the *sacro bosco,* the *nymphaeum*, or a holy tree, mountain or island.[6] Such sacred spots have the name *temenos*. The exceptional nature of the temenos could be felt in its physical enclosure, within which the altar of the deity, the temple and sacred objects – such as a holy olive tree or a spring – would have a place. Originally temenos meant an isolated piece of land, or domain, derived from *temnein*, to cut off. But the word is also allied to *temenios*: out of the holy forest. Cut off from their surroundings, such places took on a sacred air, dreadful and deserving of a respectful distance.

ORCHARD AND FLOWERY MEAD. A next step was to reproduce the natural spot in the orchard and flower-filled meadow, the oasis and clearing of the cultivated landscape. Food no longer came primarily from the forest but from the fields and meadows. The orchard and flowery mead, like their natural antecedents, were pleasant places of sojourn. They exhibit similarities with the anger, being tilled, manured, trimmed and weeded but lacking a legible order.

Architectural archetypes: ways of defining space

EXPERIENCING SPACE. So as not to be overwhelmed by the horror vacui – fear of the void – medieval man regarded the landscape as if it consisted of well-defined spaces. He sought no confrontation with the horizon of his world. Both literally and metaphorically he had no interest in the periphery, of which the horizon is an extreme expression. His world-view was introverted, centralized. Boundlessness was a quality attributed to God alone, the created world was finite. The divine infinity was beyond the mental grasp and matter could be understood only if it were conceived as finite. The only comprehensible space was the finite space, a cavity surrounded by walls, a *vacuole*. Medieval society was characterized by the tug-of-war between the restricted horizon of the open space and the infinite reaches of the world of Christian thinking. The horizon as we understand it today had yet to make an appearance. On the one hand there was the horizon as a real border of contained space, and on the other, the horizon as something infinitely far away, an idea charged with fantasy and mystery.

In the Middle Ages, the cultivated landscape of antiquity became more and more reclaimed by nature, and in this dense wilderness the ancient image of landscape as an assemblage of discrete objects lost its credibility. Man was steadily driven back into

above: Orchard. From the Bible of Wenceslaus IV (Vienna, Österreichische Nationalbibliothek).

below: Flowery mead. Meister E.S., c. 1460 (Berlin, Archiv für Kunst und Geschichte). Chess was one of the best-loved games of skill played in the open air.

7. Reh 1993, 14.

8. Steenbergen 1990, 25.

9. Comito 1935, 27.

enclaves enclosed by walls of greenery. The notion of space evolved together with this process into an idea of mass and volume, in opposition to 'depth'.[7] The medieval conception of space can be read in paintings of those days. There, the hierarchy is based on the symbolic anecdotic relationship between people, with space a monolithic, cohesive backdrop. There is as yet no perspective link between spaces and objects; these paintings deny the observer the fortuities of optical space.[8]

THEORIES ABOUT SPACE. Aristotle was one of the philosophers of antiquity who heavily influenced medieval thinking. Space for him was not distance with which objects were made to relate, as in the Renaissance, but an attribute of an object with its own border. Space existed not as an autonomous aesthetic category, not as emptiness (spatium) but as the concrete specific locus surrounding that object. This place was generated by the object expanding within it and forming its own cavity. For medieval man emptiness was an incomprehensible phenomenon. A cavity was quite a different matter. This is the space belonging to a central point, that like a grain of sand has been smoothed down to the extent that layers of mother-of-pearl have formed around it and it has itself become a pearl. Without the grain of sand the pearl would be unthinkable; similarly, without a centre space, to medieval man, is unthinkable too. Everything is enclosed and has its proper place, implying a relationship of appropriateness between container and contained object.

The total space is an aggregate of all these places. In this train of thought there is nothing of 'distance' but rather of 'circumstance', of 'being somewhere'. The concept of motion proceeds from a stable universe fixed about a real centre and bounded by a real border. Each space is *cosmic space* and as a reflection of the heavenly spheres can be defined as an objective form with an objective boundary. Such space is comprehensible to the human mind and has an order like that of a temple. 'The imagined coherence of space implies, indeed, a whole cosmology.'[9] Within this thinking the earth is construed as the centre of the universe, an immobile globe surrounded with nine concentric circles; seven heavenly bodies, the stars, and finally the 'crystal sphere' (primum mobile, the First Mover, i.e. God).

The universe as originally intended by God was exhaustively described in the fifth century AD by St Augustine. Everything that man made, he reasoned, was based on the *divine model*, which did not consist of 'natural' matter, although it could be found 'contained and hidden in the secret bosom of nature'. The physical world is temporary and fleeting and only the structure underlying it is stable, unshakeable and incorruptible. By ordering the designed surroundings according to measure, number and weight and fixing the limit, species and durability of each of its parts, the divine model took on visual attributes and the design gained a certain solidity and permanence. Everything has its own place in the divine order of things, and anything that deviates from it is the work of the devil. 'Design is combatting evil by giving back to the man-made environment the missing "limit, species and order". The more man and his creation, the man-made environment, remain at a distance from God, the less they resemble the divine model, the more "nothingness", "darkness", "degradation" and "death" threaten them.'[10]

The elements too have their own corresponding qualities. Upper and lower differ not just in position but also have their own properties. Each element seeks its natural place or locus. Fire tends to rise upwards and tries to escape from the central point, earth falls in a straight line to the ground plane, air and water have their locus between earth and fire. Regarding this idea of the correct place Copernicus would write that 'nothing is so contradictory of the order of the universe as a thing that is not in its own place (locus suum).'[11]

BUILDING SPACE: FROM TEMPLE TO PERISTYLE. The spatial form of the enclosed garden can be traced back to Greek architecture and can be seen as an inversion of the outgoing architecture of the temples. Ancient Greek culture was marked by community, democracy and the city. The temple, the place of communal worship, occupied the central position, and the Greeks concentrated on perfecting the visible construction: the combination of column and base. The importance of the architecture was dictated not by interior spaces but by the exterior. All the fun and refinement was accorded the exterior, in that men and gods interacted in the open air. Greek temples were composed of a containing box (cella) surrounded by a colonnade or series of columns as an intermediary between inside and outside.

Greek urban life was enacted in the 'agora' or market place. The surrounding range of columns was detached from the temple and transmuted into the *stoa*, the covered promenade round the agora. With the existing means of column and base a new spatial form was created, a shady place to sit and walk, to discuss and to sell wares. So it was that the haphazardly scattered shops, workplaces and offices were fused into a monumental unity. With the stoa came autonomy for the range of columns, rendering them more than just an edge; the boundary became a place of sojourn.

With the Roman tradition came the following transformation. Roman city houses turned their windowless walls to the hot and dusty streets and looked in onto the cool open garden at the centre. This garden – the *peristyle* – was surrounded by a colonnade.[12] Whereas the space around the temple was still

10. Tzonis 1972, 20-21.

11. Zilsel 1940, 115.

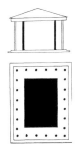

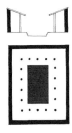

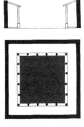

Evolution of the type:
Greek temple, stoa, peristyle, hortus
contemplationis.

undefined, the stoa succeeded in fixing the open space. In the transformation to peristyle this went a stage further in making the colonnade part of the open space (the garden). The columns once again formed an attached circle, but with the enclosed space functioning as exterior and the edge as interior.

The domus, the Roman city house, occupied an entire city block in the orthogonal street pattern based as this was on a north-south and an east-west axis, within which the houses lay side by side.[13] The house was constructed round an *atrium*, originally a room with a smoke hole in the roof that later developed into an inner court for receiving guests. The hole let in light as well as rain which was collected in a square basin or impluvium. Behind the atrium was the peristyle, a derivative of Greek temple architecture where it originally meant an external colonnade. The Roman peristylium, the centre of the private rooms for the family, is an internal colonnade enfolding a garden. To make the house look bigger than it really was, the walls of the atriums and peristyles were painted with idealized landscapes and mythological imagery. A central (visual) axis tied the two spaces together, sometimes with additional rooms in-between or in front.[14] In the peristyle was a recess containing an altar for the family deity. Worshipping the gods had by now become a private matter. The outward-facing sacred space of the Greek temple was now turned inwards.

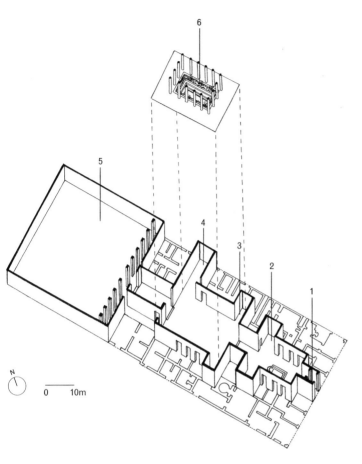

above: Andrea Palladio, Villa Rotonda, Vicenza, 16th century. The inversion of temple into hortus contemplationis is now reversed. The building organizes the landscape as the Greek temple had done. Four identical porticoes formalize the four winds, proceeding from the open hall at the centre.

left: Peristyle. The House of Pansa, Pompeii, 2nd century BC. A domus of asymmetrical composition. Most spaces, probably accommodating cattle, slaves and servants, were open to the street. Only one or two emerge at the central access. The spaces on the axis present a sequence from the small vestibule to the relatively large, likewise contained kitchen garden behind the house. At the centre of the peristyle court is a pool, around it a gallery where one could sit and eat, converse and make music.
1. vestibulum (entrance) / 2. atrium / 3. ala (recess for undisturbed conversation) / 4. tablinum (open living room) / 5. garden / 6. peristyle

Literary archetypes: heavenly paradises

'In the beginning, God created a garden called Eden. Before the Fall, Eden was a fertile, fragrant oasis of delight, magically calm except for the sweet sounds of water and laughter. Since the dawn of civilization, humankind has ceaselessly endeavoured to recreate this mythical paradise.'

Gabrielle van Zuylen, 1994

The idea of paradise as a garden is one of the oldest ideals of humanity, shared since prehistoric times by societies with nothing further in common. The blessed paradise, a garden of eternal spring, is the reward in the hereafter. The image of a place of peace and abundance can give meaning to a wretched existence on earth and make its transient nature acceptable.[15]

12. With the introduction of the peristyle the garden gained its place in the city. The peristyle, for that matter, is not just a Roman tradition but is also the essential hallmark of Islamic architecture, the two ultimately converging in the hortus conclusus.

13. We can distinguish two types of urban house, the domus described here, and the insula, a tenement building in three or four levels with a light court at its centre.

14. The country houses or villas are organized along comparable lines, though they are more spacious in design and consist of discrete volumes as often as not linked by promenades. The relationship between house, garden and landscape figures prominently in the villa, some descriptions repeatedly referring to the view to be had from it.

15. Moynihan 1979.

16. There is every indication of the reverse too: the city as paradise as opposed to the wretched landscape, with the church as central point, its spire an axis mundi making the connection with the heavens. The Dutch word 'tuin' (garden) and the English word town are related etymologically.

17. The oldest known Persian garden was laid out some 2500 years ago on the Iranian plateau, a bowl-shaped desert some 1400 metres above sea level in an inhospitable climate (harsh winters, baking summers, little precipitation). Lying at the foot of the rocks lining the plateau, the garden was geometric in plan, with a decorated stone water figure drawing together the various palaces; trees and bushes were planted symmetrically in compartments.

18. Koran 47:15.

Literature, poetry, paintings, miniatures and garden carpets gave medieval man a whole range of images of the garden as paradise. Images that in the hortus conclusus gel into a single hybrid image of paradise, at times with the accent on order, at others on an ideal image of nature. The descriptions of an idealized *Arcadian* landscape handed down from ancient times were no longer seen as a foil to (urban) culture but now formed part of it. The Arcadian landscape is a human invention, and as such forfeits its relationship with the landscape as it really is. This heavily distorted the image of paradise. In seeking to adapt to the cultivated landscape in the West, its distance from the natural landscape and the attendant archetypes of oasis and clearing increased steadily. The garden as representation of paradise went urban. It became a city enclave with walls, gateways, channels and pavilions.[16] This medieval picture of paradise is seen to derive from three mutually influential archetypes: the Persian Pairidaeza, the classical Arcadia and the biblical Garden of Eden.

PAIRIDAEZA. It was in the Persian desert that the model of an ordered paradise emerged, with walls around it to keep out the unpleasant world.[17] In its centre is a spring, from which irrigation channels convey water to the north, east, south and west, dividing the garden into four. Each quarter is subdivided into smaller paradises, which are divided up again. Clumps of trees and pavilions afford protection against the scorching sun, fountains cool the air, flowers give visual and aromatic delight. Birds compete in colour with the flowers and in song with the sound of the water. The gardens contain pavilions with galleries around them so that one can admire the garden from the shade of the galleries.

Paradise is derived from the Persian word Pairidaeza, literally meaning 'surrounded by walls'. The garden is a reproduction of the garden described so many times in the Koran: 'Such is the Paradise which the righteous have been promised: therein shall flow rivers of water undefiled, and rivers of milk forever fresh; rivers of wine delectable to those that drink it, and rivers of clarified honey. There shall they eat of every fruit, and receive forgiveness from their Lord.'[18] The mysticism of water, trees and mountains – a legacy from the pre-Islamic nature worshippers – and the symbolic division of the earth by four rivers determine the image of the garden. It is as much a pleasure garden as a *cosmogram.*

The four rivers of paradise depict the world's rivers which divide the earth into four continents (Europe, Africa, America and Asia) or the four winds. This is the cosmogram, the emblematic depiction of the world or the cosmos. The universal symbol of the ordering of the world has a whole range of meanings attached to it: the four elements (water, fire, earth and

Pairidaeza. Carpet with depiction of paradise, Persia, 17th century.
'Baffled by monotony and mocked by phantoms delirious, / Beset by stalking Death in guises manifold; / The dreaded jinns, the beasts ferocious, / The flaming heat and the exploding storms, / From all this peril here at last set free, / In the garden all find security.' Ode to a Garden Carpet by an anonymous Sufi poet, c. 1500. The four world rivers meet in the centre, with cypress and fruit trees as symbols of eternal life and rebirth.

above: Arcadia. Claude Lorrain, *Coast View of Delos with Aeneas*, 1672.

below: Garden of Eden. Antoine Verard, *The Temptation of Adam and Eve*, 16th century (New York, Metropolitan Museum of Art).

19. Whenever cities were founded in the Roman Empire, first there would be a ritual whereby the priest would draw on the ground the arrangement of the heavens as two lines bisecting at right angles: the templum. The 'cardo' ran from north to south and represented the axis of the sky and the 'decumanus' from east to west, illustrating the path of the sun.

20. Theocritus, *Idylls* 22: 36-42.

21. This idealizing of the shepherd's life tied in with the Christian symbolism of Jesus, the good shepherd.

air), the four temperaments (choleric, melancholic, phlegmatic and sanguine) related to the human organs, the four colours (yellow, white, red and black).[19] In the Middle Ages these 'heathen' symbols became absorbed by Christian thinking and tied to the symbol of the cross of Christ, turned to face Jerusalem in the East (the cruciform floor plan of the church). Besides depicting the cosmos, the axial cross is a two-dimensional abstraction of the landscape. All directions converge at the intersection and are related: it gathers the landscape together.

Universal symbolism, depiction of the social system and the landscape come together in the way water is given shape. The Middle Eastern settlements were dependent on an ingenious system of tunnels and reservoirs that was regulated by an extensive system of laws. The irrigation system represents society and the world, and the garden, irrigated with raised channels, is at once the pinnacle and the symbol of this system. The king, as head of the irrigation system, was directly responsible for the welfare of the entire country. The fountain symbolizes the hand of the monarch who defeats his enemy and defends his people.

ARCADIA. In the third century BC the Greek writer Theocritus described a sylvan landscape far from the civilized world. '[Castor and Polydeuces], wildered both, / Searched through the boskage of the hill, and found / Hard by a slab of rock a bubbling spring / Brimful of purest water. In the depths / Below, like crystal or like silver gleamed / The pebbles: high above it pine and plane / And poplar rose, and cypress tipt with green; / With rich flowers that throng the mead, when wanes / The Spring, sweet workshops of the furry bee'.[20] It was with this image as starting-point that Virgil created the pastoral world that he situated in Arcadia, an isolated hilly region of the Peloponnese, the southern peninsula of Greece, and the favourite haunt of Pan, god of pastures, flocks and woods.[21] Between 42 and 37 BC he wrote his *Eclogues,* a collection of ten pastoral poems.[22] In his *Bucolics* he introduces the *locus amoenus* – literally, 'delightful spot', a glittering field of flowers surrounded by trees and graced with a limpid stream.[23]

A major concern of the Greek and Roman cultures was the decadence and corruption of what was once an exalted urban culture, in comparison with which they regarded unsullied nature as good. Remarkably enough, this idealized image of nature was taken over by medieval man as a foil to the real nature which since the Fall had become degraded to a wilderness.

THE GARDEN OF EDEN. 'And the Lord God planted a garden eastward in Eden; and there he put the man whom he had formed. And out of the ground made the Lord God to grow every tree that is pleasant to the sight, and good for food; the tree of life also in the midst of the garden, and the tree of knowledge of good and evil. And a river went out of Eden to water the garden; and from thence it was parted, and became into four heads.'[24] Man had been driven out of the Garden of Eden for his sins. Earthly life was purely a temporary phase between the paradise lost and the promise of a new World of God, which in fact was paradise all over again. 'In medieval thinking redemption meant above all liberation from the world, that is, the raising of man above his sensual, earthly existence.'[25]

To be deserving of this new paradise one had to foreswear all pleasures and lead a humble life. Not everyone was in a position to search for the lost paradise (which was still deemed to exist somewhere, surrounded by a ring of fire), but one could always construct an image of what was to come. In contrast with the idea of nature as a wilderness, this Garden of Eden was conceived to be a sublimation of the ground developed by man: a garden with flowers, trees and water. The word Eden has a double meaning: an irrigated, well-watered place, and the Hebrew derivative of the word for pleasure and enlightenment. It was not just to be enjoyed, but to endow one with refinement and an attunement to higher things.

Ingredients of the enclosed garden

The fundamental principle of the garden is a contained territory for the purpose of growing plants. Each garden is an interpretation and reworking of nature and consequently a reflection of culture. To unite nature and culture man needs order, and so he makes boundaries. On the one side there is an image of flowers and birds, the tinkle of water and the scent of nectar. On the other side, enclosure, the physical separation of a particular space from space in general. In order to hold one's own in nature one must be able to orient oneself.

In the enclosed garden there are palpable references enabling one to orient oneself in space, time and society. *Cosmic orientation*, the primitive experience of being on this earth, is provided by the opposition between earth and heaven, high and low, vertical and horizontal, light and dark. The sun's path and that of the stars aid orientation and give a sense of direction. *Temporal orientation* is gained from the rhythm of the seasons, of day and night with their utterly different effect on our experience of space, and from the tangible presence of the past. *Territorial orientation* proceeds from the visible topography, the simultaneous presence from close to and far off, the references to the far distance from out of the enclosed space, and the dualities of centre and periphery and inside and outside. These various aspects of orientation take on architectural shape

22. '... escapist literary excursions to the idyllic pastoral world of Arcadia ... They convey in liquid song the idealized situations of an imaginary world in which shepherds sing in the sunshine of their simple joys and mute their sorrows (whether for unhappy love or untimely death) in a formalized pathos.' *Encyclopaedia Britannica* 1990, Volume 29, 499. The fourth Eclogue prophesies the birth of a child that would return to us the golden age, drive out sins and restore peace. It is a vision of universal harmony.

23. Virgil's *Aeneid* mentions Elysium, a place of sublimated delight for the souls of the blessed, located below the earth as a counterpart to Tartarus, the dungeon of retribution. Aeneas has to travel here where the purpose of life is to be revealed to him in a vision of the future, when he will be taken up among the 'blissful seats of happy souls' on 'plains of pleasure' (amoenus).

24. Genesis II: 8-10.

25. Van der Marel 1985, 61.

Temporal orientation. Patio de la Acequia, Granada, 13th century. Fruit trees, flowering annuals and permanent planting set in opposition the passing of time and timelessness.

Cosmic orientation. Dom Hans van der Laan, Mariavall convent, Mariavall, 1994. Every detail is omitted, so that all attention is drawn to the theatre of the sky.

Territorial orientation. Alvar Aalto, Säynätsalo Town Hall, Säynätsalo, 1950. An opening in the wall brings into view the relationship between garden and landscape. The enclosure marks the distinction between inside and outside.

in the physical enclosure, a structure introduced into unspecified natural space: organizing the surface on the one hand, and giving spatial form on the other. The world is made comprehensible, enabling us to interact with the surroundings.[26] Universal space is overwhelming, terrifying even. Which is why it is chopped up into clearly arranged and structured pieces with boundaries to distinguish between them. The interior is particularized with regard to outside, generating a magic threshold between two worlds that is rendered visible by the physical boundary.[27] Passing this boundary makes one aware of this magic border. The first such enclosures were constructed to protect places appropriated for use and to stop cattle from straying, ordering the landscape in the process. The enclosure marks the distinction between inside and outside, between clearing and wilderness, cultivated and uncultivated.[28]

The most pronounced form of enclosure is the wall. It restricts the exchange between inside and outside to manageable openings so that entry through it is consciously experienced. A sense of security prevails within the walled enclosure through the palpable presence and solidity of the walls and the balance between space and mass. The outermost limit of the visible is shifted from the horizon to the wall and the visible world splits into an internal and an external world.

left: *The battle at Nancy*. Woodcut, 1477. The town is bounded by a fence of stakes.

right: Rose garden, from a manuscript of *Le Roman de la Rose,* 1481. The garden is surrounded by a wickerwork fence of willow twigs.

Herb garden. Woodcut, 1557 (Berlin, Bildarchiv Preussischer Kulturbesitz). The raised beds are held in place by planks.

26. According to De Jong this interaction takes place through a sequence of interfaces, beginning with the skin. Touching is the most direct contact we can have with our surroundings and every stimulation of the skin evokes a primary form of consciousness without which there is no self-awareness. When this boundary is crossed we experience our existence in a state of tension: 'Birth, eating, aggression, sex and death are biological moments of boundary-crossing, which in all cultures have led to various crucial concepts, traditions and rituals. It invariably concerns a transition from a more natural state to a more inter-human, cultural state, or vice versa. Every border-crossing therefore has the Janus-faced character of nature and culture.'(Translated from De Jong 1994, 9)
'"Existence", a word of Latin origin, means the same as the Greek-derived "ecstasy", that is, standing forth. It is the active variant of the more passive "moving outward", the literal translation of "e-motion". In the Middle Ages, Thomas More wrote in his *Utopia* that all human pleasures consist of taking in that which belongs in the body and expelling and voiding that which does not.'(De Jong 1994, 35)

27. Such as in the enchanted garden in *Erec et Enide* by Chrétien de Troyes (ca. 1170): 'Neither wall nor moat, nor fence, water or hedge', but a magic circle, where no-one can enter or leave.

28. The only being to largely ignore this boundary and feel as much at home in the wilderness as in the village was regarded by the population with suspicion and named 'hag' after this official barrier (the hedge) that she was reputed to have deliberately transgressed.

Typology

Within the walls of the hortus conclusus the landscape is cultivated, isolated and ultimately eliminated. The garden creates its own context: an interior of fountains, flowers, herbs and furniture relative to the landscape. Against the scale of the landscape it sets the scale of the 'room'. In the hortus conclusus the containment of the space is stressed by the directly visible presence of the limitless sky. Limited dimensions against endless space, the mass of the walls against the space of the garden, the invisibility of the world outside against the view of the sky.

Three types

'Three things are necessary for beauty: first, integrity or perfection, for things that are lacking in something are for this reason ugly; also due proportion or consonance; and again, clarity, for we call things beautiful when they are brightly coloured.'

Thomas Aquinas

Hortus conclusus. Woodcut, 1487.

The three aspects of beauty identified by Thomas Aquinas find their expression in three types of the hortus conclusus that during the Middle Ages crystallized in the monasteries, the castles and the cities. These three types are clearly distinguishable by their form and programme, a distinction that simply did·not exist in the literature until now. Each programme, it transpires, that of knights, citizens and monastics, was given shape in its own way. So to differentiate between the formal types we have accorded them names that reflect the programmes: *hortus ludi*, *hortus catalogi* and *hortus contemplationis*.[29]

HORTUS LUDI. The aspect of brightness or beauty (of colour) is rendered in the expressive tableau of the hortus ludi, the pleasure garden, paradise as a place of delectation. Intended as a pleasant social space for games or play (ludus), the hortus ludi is the garden of courtly life.

HORTUS CATALOGI. The aspect of due proportion takes prominence in the geometric arrangement of the hortus catalogi. In the Late Middle Ages so much was already known of the natural diversity that the arrangement and classification of plant species took on a role in the depiction of paradise. This garden, consisting of rectangular beds and a wall, expressed knowledge and riches for the well-to-do citizenry.

HORTUS CONTEMPLATIONIS. Integrity or perfection can be found in the spatial completeness of the cloister garth or hortus contemplationis, the garden of reflection, which depicted the hierarchy of the Universe with God as its centre. This was a space surrounded by a *gallery* and with the sky for a ceiling, and the monastery was organized around it.

Hortus ludi: the garden as spectacle

'Ther sprang the violet al newe
And fresshe pervinke rich of hewe,
And flowers Yelowe, whyte and rede:
Swich plantee gres ther never in mede,
Ful gay was al the ground and queynt
And poudred, as men had it peynt,
With many a fresh and soundry flour
That casten up a ful savour'

Guillaume de Lorris, 1230

A garden full of flowers forms the setting for *Le Roman de la Rose* and this was the ideal place for courtly love, a delightful spot shut off from the outside world. Courting but also rhetoric, philosophy, music and sport took place there against a backdrop of widely spaced trees, on *turfed seats*, in and around the fountain, all of these seemingly placed at random on a fresh green lawn. Play (ludus) in the double meaning of the word – as dramatic performance and as activity – was the raison d'être of this garden.[30] The garden of delights was a profane interpretation of paradise.

In *Le Roman de la Rose* the leading role is played by a rose garden, symbol of earthly love in all its contradictory facets. The story is written in the form of a dream, populated by allegorical figures. The hero cum narrator wanders along the bank of a river until he reaches a high wall enfolding a garden. The description of the landscape acts as a frame for the garden which attracts notice through the trees rising up above the wall and the warble of birds. He enters the garden, and this is where the entire remainder of the story is played out. Seeing a rose bush reflected in a spring, he falls in love with one of the buds whereupon he kisses it. Lady Jealousy then shuts the rosebud away in a castle in the garden, leaving the grieving hero behind. The garden where this all takes place is a perfect square and contains all the known local and exotic fruit trees of the time. Besides these there are flowers, herbs and animals, and various springs, fountains and rills.

In a part added later the castle is attacked and the rose set free. To encourage the army to make the assault Lady Nature's chaplain fervently tells of the reward for being a good Christian, namely the heavenly paradise. The garden he describes is compared with the rose garden. Just as the rose garden is square to symbolize the earthly and ephemeral, the paradise garden (described as a park) is round as a symbol of perfection and eternity. On the wall there are depictions of hell, earth, the four elements and the firmament and there is but one spring. Whoever drinks from it will never suffer ill health and will never die.[31]

The great distance between the idealized nature represented in the hortus ludi and the landscape in reality has a lot to do with the siting. The garden is fully unhitched from the surroundings, whether in the natural landscape, the cultivated landscape or within the castle walls. The rose garden in *Le Roman de la Rose* lies as a discrete walled edifice on the river. Paradise in this case is a walled fortress with turrets and battlements pitted against the natural landscape. The analogy with a fortress derives primarily from the surrounding walls. The 15th- and 16th-century castles seem to consist of a vertical skeleton with walls spanned between its components; the heavy donjon and the low, narrow wings. Likewise, the hortus ludi often has four towers with lower walls or *berceaux* (covered walks) in-between, as we can see in Cerceau's engraving of the Château de Bury in France. Even the *archer's walk* behind the battlements sometimes returns in the hortus ludi, to protect those using the garden against invaders. From this path one can take in both the garden scene and the landscape beyond.

The garden from *Le Roman de la Rose*, 13th century (London, British Library).

29. Because this typology is based purely on form and programme, there is no historical link between the types. Thus, for example, the hortus contemplationis probably existed much earlier than the hortus ludi, as monasteries were the first 'designed' buildings, but only gained its typical spatial form in the Late Middle Ages. The hortus catalogi changed little formwise over time, but the accent shifted from production to ornament. The hortus ludi was most prevalent in the early castles which later would transmute the hortus catalogi into the castle garden. Because the sources from which we know of the three types are so disparate it is impossible to make a historical comparison.

30. Ludus means 'play' or 'game'. The plural form ludi not only means 'games' but also 'public games', 'ridicule', 'madness', 'child's play', 'bagatelle', 'primary school' and even 'barracks'.

31. Stuip 1992, 143-151.

Queen Eleanor's Garden, Winchester, Reconstruction of 13th-century garden with a berceau, stone seats, turfed benches, a fountain crowned by a falcon, a lean-to and a herber surrounded by hornbeams with a stone chess table at its centre.

Winchester Castle

In the thirteenth century, there lived in Winchester in England a queen and her daughter-in-law, both named Eleanor. They laid out gardens in the grounds of Winchester Castle, of which the present Queen Eleanor's Garden is a reconstruction. This garden ensemble is organized *heterotopically,* typical of a hortus ludi. The Great Hall is the social and spatial hub of the castle, a chaotic clutter of buildings stitched together by a network of alleyways and oddly shaped leftover spaces where gardens are screened off as green oases amongst the mud and waste. A triangular space contains various garden elements, a covered walk, a turfed seat (a long raised bed containing flowers and plants), and a fountain, each with its own surrounding space. The *herber* in the north-east corner is a modest space bounded by *trellises* (frames for supporting climbing plants) with a turfed seat around it and a lawn of aromatic camomile: a garden within a garden.

'La Teseida' from *The Decameron* (Boccaccio, 1460; Vienna, Österreichisches Nationalbibliothek). Herbarium consisting of a lawn, turfed seat and rose-grown trellis.

Woodcut, c. 1500. The hortus ludi as external room.

The elements of nature form the background for amatory lyrics and epics alike, influenced by the classical paintings of nature and landscapes, depictions of Christian teachings of salvation and Oriental fairy tales. But nature's great powers of attraction were most particularly a result of poor living conditions indoors. The longing for nature is more than anything else a practical sensory longing for light, air and space.

The wealth of meanings ascribed to nature is evident from the double role of the hortus ludi. Against the terrors of nature it pits a safe haven, like a walled city, against the disadvantages of cultivated life an idealized rendition of nature. Selecting the pleasing aspects of nature, it then placed these together as elements in their own right.

In the hortus ludi, space can be understood in two ways: the place occupied by an object such as a fountain (determined from the inside) and the space shaped by the walls (determined from the outside). Curiously enough, these generally fail to coincide; the walls include both the place – as an attribute of the object – and the residual space around it. The place itself is established by an extra enclosure of trelliswork or fencing; the space between fence and wall seems not to be recognized as such and is not given shape.

The hortus ludi is inspired by classical literature which has handed down to us the image of Arcadia, a rolling pastoral landscape that provides the archetypal image of nature for the epics and amatory lyrics of the medieval culture of knights and chivalry. The Western European landscape of the Middle Ages, however, consisted of impenetrable forests, swamps and

32. The Song of Solomon iv:12. This paean of love meshes with the symbolism of Jesus as gardener of the heart: 'in that heart the lilies of chastity and the roses of martyrdom need planting, and the unruly tree of sin needs pulling out roots and all'. Translated from Komrij 1990, 36.

33. The ambiguous symbolism of the garden is given prominence in many ways such as illustrations that include the unicorn, where the combination of woman, garden and this mystic animal designates both chastity and sinful love.

meadows, where great space was merely a source of fear. Closer to medieval man's perception of his environment was the translation of Arcadia into the seclusion of the *'locus amoenus'*, an idyllic flowery mead with clear running water. In the locus amoenus nature was rendered without the intention of giving a complete, all-embracing image. The fragment of landscape was representative of the whole. The exotic image of the locus amoenus was projected onto the enclosed place familiar from the cultivated landscape – the *anger* or forest glade created by grazing cattle. To protect the locus amoenus from the wilderness it was then walled off; these enclosed spaces could now accommodate activities that were formerly tied to the home. To this end they were furnished with *turfed seats*, fountains and tables. This 'delightful place' transmuted into a hortus conclusus was at the basis of *Le Roman de la Rose*.

The hortus ludi not just represented paradise but also symbolized woman, predicated on the Song of Solomon in which the bride is compared to the hortus conclusus: 'A garden enclosed is my sister, my spouse; a spring shut up, a fountain sealed.'[32] The knight is the hero who has all sorts of adventures but whose ultimate goal is the lady, the point of crystallization in courtly society, the axis round which thought and poetry revolve. Hence she is central to the hortus ludi. The meaning given this position ranges from the highest platonic love to vulgar eroticism and this tension establishes the deeper significance of the hortus ludi.[33] The physical nature of this paradise finds expression in the emphasis placed on sensual aspects. Here the earthly beauty of woman, courtly love and the reality of life interweave.

PLAYGROUND OF KNIGHTS AND LADIES: THE TYPE. As a type, the hortus ludi is a pictorial arrangement, and consequently best-known from paintings and miniatures and from evocative descriptions of gardens. The elements and the relationships between them in particular are determined by their symbolic context within which aesthetic and functional aspects also have a place. So, for instance, fruit trees and herbs were grown and a large part of social life was enacted here as an alternative to the noise, stench and oppression of the dark, dank castles.

The hortus ludi was the scene of dining, dancing, conversing, playing, bathing, courting, frolicking and music-making. It is an outdoor room, the playground of daily life where the qualities of the open air join with the safety and ease of the home.

The hortus ludi is a tableau, a spectacle. The stage is a fresh green lawn with sweet-smelling flowers and aromatic herbs, the stage set the surrounding walls and the props a turfed seat, a stone table, a spring and widely spaced trees. The props and stage scenery have no connection spatially, but are held together by the lawn. The players are the principal element and

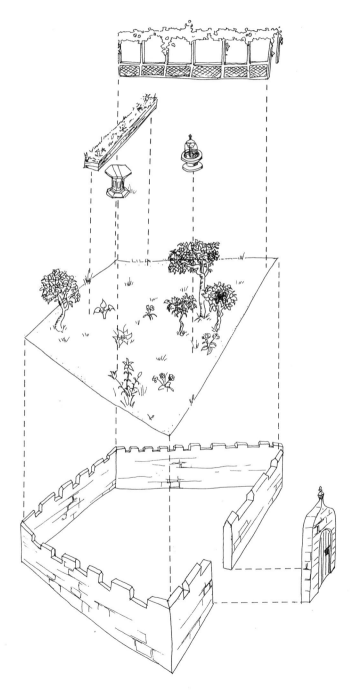

Component parts of the hortus ludi:
stone walls and a gate, flowery mead,
fruit trees, fountain and stone table,
turfed seat and berceau.

these bring unity to the garden, as in the 'Paradiesgärtlein' where the tableau's composition is decided by the positions of the personages.

The space is isotropic (comparable to today's urban landscapes). Seldom is there a sense of alignment or a principal element to be discerned, let alone a link between ground plane, enclosure and built mass.

In the garden various scenes are enacted. A berceau grown with roses running like a gallery along the wall is a shady place, more enclosed than the garden itself and creating distance between it and the spectacle in the garden. A turfed seat along the edge acts as a spectator's stand. In the centre, the stage is divided into a foreground and a background by trees placed on one side that generate a division into a shaded and a sunny place. The position of the trees is such as to create shade and to encourage a breeze. The centre of the garden is left open and ideally trees stand on the southwestern side only. There is no geometrical concept informing the hortus ludi, rather a pragmatic reworking of the local landscape.

The hortus ludi is a place of delight, a pleasure garden in which smells, sounds, taste and touch play a role alongside the visual aspect. Often the turfed seat is planted with herbs that become bruised when sat upon thereby spreading their aroma. The trees are fruit-bearing, and the tinkle of the fountain is often supplemented with birdsong and music.[34]

Hortus catalogi: ordering the plane

'A thing is good when it lacks nothing of measure, species and order'.

Thomas Aquina

Measure or proportion, distinguishing between species, and order representing nature before the Fall – these are ever recurring themes in the Middle Ages. The Latin word 'catalogus' means enumeration and so the hortus catalogi is a garden consisting of an enumeration of plant species to illustrate order in nature. The various species are contained in an orthogonal grid. Originally the sequence of rectangular beds and the separation into plant species came about because this made tending simpler; later the arrangement took on a formal and expressive character.

The hortus catalogi first made its appearance some 5000 years ago in the garden culture of Ancient Egypt, as a walled vegetable and herb garden. In Ancient Greek and Roman times the type reappeared unchanged and still exists to this day in medieval monasteries, in castles and in towns. If the hortus ludi has largely come down to us in illustrations, the hortus catalogi has been immortalized above all in inventories and descriptions.

34. Albertus Magnus prescribes species sweet to both taste and smell such as the vine, the pear and the apple-tree. Others such as the walnut he rejects as being harmful.

35. *Liber de cultura hortorum*, translated in J.P. Le Dantec and G. Le Dantec, *Reading the French Garden: Story and History*, MIT Press, Cambridge (Mass.) 1990 (transl. J. Levine).

36. His hortulus is inspired by classical descriptions of gardens such as those of Columella, the Roman author of the twelve-volume *De re rustica*, which gives detailed instructions for planting vegetables and herbs.

From a manuscript of *Le Roman de la Rose*, 15th century (Berlin, Archiv für Kunst und Geschichte). The hortus catalogi in the town, with herbs being picked, dried and collected.

In the eighth century, for instance, Charlemagne, in drawing up a statute for the administration of his landed property, provides a catalogue of seventy-three species of vegetables and herbs. Five centuries later, Albertus Magnus in his scientific treatise distils the many preceding descriptions of gardens into an overarching recipe for the ideal garden, one half hortus ludi, the other hortus catalogi.

'Having cleared the ground, we try small vegetables, shoots taken either from seedlings or from older plants whose first youth we try to restore. The first growth is then sprinkled by the rain of spring, then the moon caresses the shoots with her tender warmth. But when excessively dry weather refuses to help with dew, my love of gardening and my fear that the frail fibres will succumb to thirst push me to hard work, and I make sure to provide a flow of pure water.'

Walahfrid Strabo, 9th century[35]

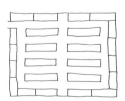

Walahfrid's hortulus (reconstruction drawing). From a manuscript of *Le Roman de la Rose*, 15th century (Berlin, Archiv für Kunst und Geschichte). The hortus catalogi in the town, with herbs being picked, dried and collected.

The original hortus catalogi is the herb garden vividly described at the beginning of the ninth century by the young Benedictine abbot Walahfrid Strabo in his poem *Liber de cultura hortorum*.[36] In it Walahfrid tells of the climate and the landscape of the Swiss island of Reichenau and of the soil, eminently suitable for cultivating for those willing to work hard and tend their plants lovingly. The hortulus (little garden) lies before the door of his cell on the east side of the monastery, protected against wind and rain by the roof. When the abbot first set eyes on it the garden was a wilderness. He describes his efforts to transform this wilderness into a garden with raised rectangular beds separated by wooden planks, and his joy when the first crops sprang up. His description of the plants leads straight into their symbolic connection with Christian doctrine. Beauty, smell, true and imaginary beneficial effects and uses, such as the use of pumpkins as wine casks, follow in rapid succession.

The hortus catalogi can in many respects be traced back to the Muslim garden which had a firm scientific basis. It was via Spain that Islamic conquerors brought to Europe botanical, medical and cultural knowledge of the garden, and seeds, bulbs and living plants were imported from Africa, India and Syria. Influenced by Arabian doctors, the herb garden changed into a hortus medicus and in the Renaissance – when scientific research became a discipline in its own right – into a botanical garden.

Particularly in the towns, the garden's relevance for production dwindled along with the importance of the hinterland for providing the towns with food. Inside and outside the towns gardens sprang up as places of representation. Through the division into public and private life, which was now much more in the home, these gardens were not primarily places to linger such as the hortus ludi, but ornamental gardens intended to show just how prosperous, well-travelled and learned their owners were. They were sited alongside the house but separated from it spatially. The garden was still very much an autonomous unit.

In the hortus catalogi it was the plants that took centre stage. Each had its own place, to best show it off visually and as a product, and the relationship between plants was anecdotic and symbolic. The enclosure drawing the plant collection into a unit was in the first instance protection against wind, cold, marauders and wild beasts.

The medieval meaning of the hortus catalogi transcends the desire to give an image of nature, and gives insight into God. The totality of the universe was beyond the grasp of the medieval mind. Nevertheless it could be broken down into recognizable units or 'species' – intermediates between the objects and the mind. By understanding these species one could obtain knowledge of the universe in its entirety. Medieval man tried to recover the Garden of Eden by carefully collecting and piecing together all the fragments scattered across the earth after the Fall.

Placed in a rhythmic order, the elements of nature could be distinguished by sorts or species with the aim of bringing man nearer to the divine. Nature was conceived as a catalogue or enumeration of sorts with iconographic, aesthetic, healing, culinary or scientific value, as a representative slice of the Creation as a whole. Science, intuition and tradition intertwined in the process of attributing meaning to and classifying plants.

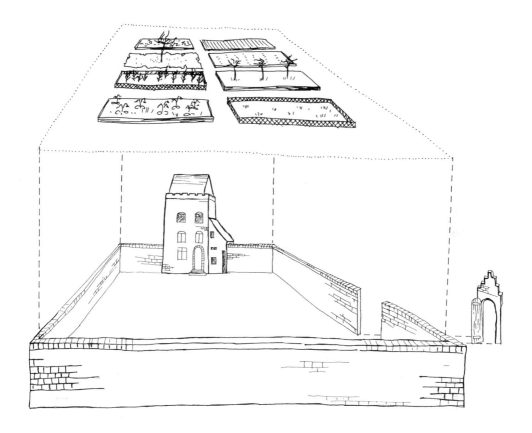

For example, the beauty of some plants was enough to attribute magical and healing properties to them.

By working hard one could earn a place in the forthcoming paradise, a glorification of work that is reflected in the hortus catalogi. In this garden, with its plan organized to illustrate production and efficiency, work and repose meshed together.

Component parts of the hortus catalogi: stone walls and a gate, rectangular bounded or raised beds.

THE GARDEN AS TREASURE HOUSE FOR THE ERUDITE: THE TYPE. Whereas Walahfrid laid his garden before the door of his cell, the productive garden was usually directly linked to the kitchen, as close as possible to the place where the vegetables and herbs were prepared and cooked. The garden was located between the orchards and fields as a haphazard element in the totality. Its rectangular plot lay loosely within the spacious, irregular enclosure of the ensemble.

The division and measurements of the beds was such that they could easily be worked by hand. The herb garden was organized as eight oblong beds laid in a north-south direction, sometimes encircled by a further eight beds. The beds were roughly two arm-lengths broad (150 cm) and twice as long. They were raised and framed with stones or strips of wood, with unpaved paths in-between. Running through the garden was an axis of symmetry though this was not determined architecturally. The entrance was the only element to be formalized. This was often a decoratively framed door to show on the outside that there was something special to be found behind the otherwise plain wall. As the Middle Ages progressed the raised beds steadily ceded to beds laid flush with the ground, sometimes surrounded by low wide-meshed fencing, stones or shards. We see a more differentiated pattern emerge, for instance a checkerboard pattern or an arrangement around a fountain or central bed. Aesthetics took over from practical considerations.

The image is one of great unity in that it is predicated upon a repetition of the same elements (the compartments of plants). Within these the various plant species are composed to give a representation of nature. The ground plane is now under control but the relationship with the third dimension (the walls) is absent as yet. The plan configuration of the hortus catalogi is universal and can in principle be continued beyond the garden; the ongoing pattern is at odds with the spatial enclosure. During the course of the Middle Ages the hortus catalogi would be increasingly deployed as an ornamental garden to replace the hortus ludi as a place of delight or pleasure garden. In the ornamental garden the neutral plan gets a formal treatment, enclosure and plan are fine-tuned to one another and the house and the garden related spatially.

Hortus contemplationis: the abstraction of space

'Nihil praeter animum esse mirabile'
[There is nothing outside the soul worth admiring].

St. Augustine, sixth century AD

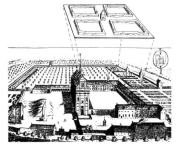

Brabant Abbey. The hortus comtemplationis as organizer.

With these words St. Augustine sketches the medieval spirit of self-examination and introspection. To make the unfathomableness of space workable, space had to be experienced from a point at the centre. The endless time was made understandable by experiencing it in terms of repetition: each year there is a summer, each week a Sunday, each day vespers.[37] 'Man manages to sustain himself in the endlessness of time and space by celebrating and by concentrating his actions.'[38] The incommensurability of God and the world is expressed by ascribing the infinite to God and the finite to the created world. We can find this relationship between space, time and coexistence in the hortus contemplationis.

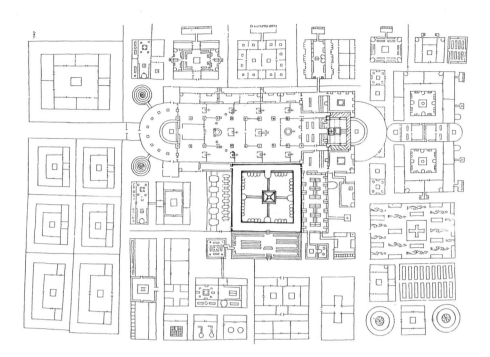

The first monasteries, no more than rectangular stone
edifices, were built from the 5th century onwards. In the 9th
century these were expanded into ensembles, organized round a
cloister garth.[39] These places afforded light, safety, clarity of
organization, coolness, shade and fertile ground in the midst of
inhospitable nature. The monasteries and abbeys are symbols of
the cosmic order, complete worlds in miniature. Hence all three
garden types are found in the realm of the monastery. In the herb
and physic gardens (horti catalogi) the monks perpetuated the
Roman horticultural tradition and adapted the old axial
organization with rectangular beds, for practical reasons but
also from the need for a structured living environment. The whole
ensemble of gardens for use was contained by a high outer wall
beyond which were the fields and meadows. Also inside the
walls were the orchards (horti ludi), themselves enclosed by
trelliswork fencing or a thorn-hedge. These gardens within the
walls clearly belonged to the inner world of the monastery and
the entrance gate was accordingly locked and guarded by a
gatekeeper.

Of those medieval monastery gardens there have been few
manuscript illustrations or paintings passed down to us. The
most important extant document is the plan of the monastery of

Plan of St. Gall monastery, c. 820.

37. Lemaire writes about oriented repetition in
his book *Filosofie van het landschap*, 1970,
89-97.

38. Lemaire 1970, 89.

39. The Late Middle Ages saw the emergence
of both the Dominican order of friars who tried
to convert the swelling number of heretics and
the Franciscan order of mendicant friars who
preached absolute poverty. Their monasteries,
unlike those of the much older Benedictine
order, were situated in the town and were a
reflection of town life.

40. Ezekiel XL:47.

St.Gall in Switzerland. Founded in the year 610 or thereabouts, it served for centuries as an ideal model for the Benedictine monasteries. The church is cruciform in plan, its principal axis pointing east towards the Holy Land. Parallel to it – on the south side of the church owing to the position of the sun – is the central point of the plan as a whole: the cloister garth. The buildings surrounding this garden are two storeys high, with around them an unbroken ring of less-tall buildings. The garth is square, an ideal plan based on the description of the Temple built by the Israelites: 'So he measured the court, an hundred cubits long, and an hundred cubits broad, foursquare.'[40] Paths divide the garden into four; the text on the drawing says as much: 'Quator semitae per transversum claustri' (four footpaths intersect the cloister garth). The four main fields this produces are planted with grass or ivy and in the smaller square central field stands a juniper, a conifer that remains the same throughout the year, thereby ensuring the static aspect of the garth in temporal terms too.

The plan of the St.Gall monastery projects a hierarchic schema on to a haphazard landscape. The main church tower, visible from a great distance, orders the landscape and crowns the concentration of monastic buildings. The open space of the hortus contemplationis – counterform of the mass of the church – acts as the central point though lying hidden behind the layers of walls, the surrounding buildings and the gallery. As the organizer of the entire complex the hortus contemplationis is celebrated by its position in the sequence from outside to inside. The mood conjured up outside the building is one of expectation, inside it everything is shown in veiled form, and finally in the garden all is unveiled and explained.

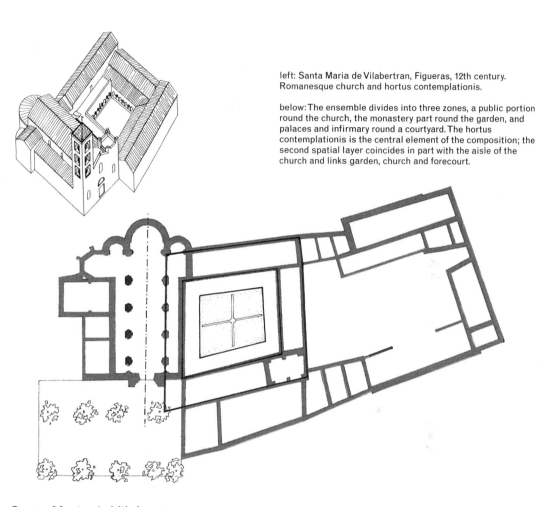

left: Santa Maria de Vilabertran, Figueras, 12th century. Romanesque church and hortus contemplationis.

below: The ensemble divides into three zones, a public portion round the church, the monastery part round the garden, and palaces and infirmary round a courtyard. The hortus contemplationis is the central element of the composition; the second spatial layer coincides in part with the aisle of the church and links garden, church and forecourt.

Santa Maria de Vilabertran

Near Figueras in Northern Spain, at a place where three roads meet, stands the 12th-century Romanesque monastery Santa Maria de Vilabertran. The church dates from the 11th century, the cloister from a century later. Parts were added on until well into the 18th century. The garden today is neglected, the well being the only remaining feature of the original layout. Erected from large sand-coloured stones, the building is sober and unembellished both inside and out.

The monastery consists of a piling-up of volumes grouped round the hortus contemplationis, an irregular trapezoid space.

The interior spaces are arranged like protective layers round the garden so that the trapezoid shape is adopted by the ensemble as a whole. The church ignores this arrangement by sporting an orthogonal organization of its own. In the corner is a square with two rows of plane trees welding the composition to the open landscape.

A series of partitions stresses the garden's introverted, secluded character, starting with the 45 cm thick gallery wall and ending at the outermost layer built for defensive purposes. The *centripetal* impact of the garden is borne out by an axial cross with a well at its centre.

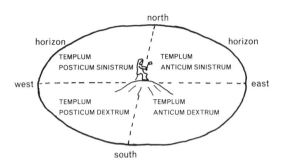

The imago mundi, the world-image as reflected in the hortus contemplationis. Roman settlements were divided into four quarters, a spatial order related to the central point. The horizon or 'finalis circulus' marks the boundary.

above: Bristol, 1479. In this illustration the town has four gateways and four streets with the High Cross at the centre. Bristol is here rendered in analogy with the ideal city of Jerusalem, itself a expression of the imago mundi or world-image.

below: Model of existential space according to Norberg-Schulz: the axis mundi links the earth's surface with heaven.

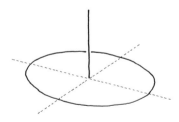

In the Middle Ages, Christianity took a dualistic position on nature. Chaotic nature with no system to it represented the aftermath of the Fall, while the cyclic motion of the heavenly bodies refers to the perfection of the original Creation. Nature as the result of God's Creation – the aesthetic conception of nature – gets pointed up in the hortus ludi. In the hortus contemplationis the objectionable side of the wilderness is featured as well. The anarchy of nature, like the anarchy of society, is the embodiment of Evil. Rules are the exception here, so to control nature and create order in the chaos becomes the ideal.

The hortus contemplationis is a void puncturing the compact mass of the monastery buildings. The walls of the garden are the buildings, the walls of the buildings the gallery of the garden. This unmistakable confluence of place and space within the organization of a larger ensemble is the spatial characteristic of the hortus contemplationis. Its finite space is a rendition of the infinite space of nature: the horizontal plane of the earth, fixed i the cruciform system of coordinates with which space can be measured, and above it the heavenly vault. The sky is the ceiling framed by the roof of the gallery. The earth's surface is depicted by a measurable plane, linked to the sky by the *axis mundi* or world axis. Horizontal plane and vertical axis together form the model of *existential space*, the diagrammatic rendition in coordinates.[41] This vertical orientation illustrates the sacred aspect of architectural space, and the horizontal the profane.

So as to represent the Garden of Eden and the geometric perfection of the divine, the medieval hortus contemplationis contained a cosmogram inspired by the gardens of Persian kings. For this purpose the Muslim symbolism of the latter was simply replaced by the Christian.[42] The *cosmogram* formalizes the relationship between heaven and earth imbuing the garden with a cosmic orientation. The spatial component and the notion of 'geometric harmony' as a reflection of the divine converge, determined by the idea of God as architect of the universe (elegans architectus) who has provided absolute rules. That which is harmonious and true is that which adheres to the prototype instead of proceeding from aesthetic and technical requirements. For everything that man makes, it holds that 'the Lord God has been the model, so to speak, seated on the throne in the centre of Paradise, with round the throne the four Evangelists as it is written in the Book of Revelations.'[43]

In the Middle Ages, the hermetic world-view of the ancients was broken open. A fleeting experience of the world via the senses ceded to experience related to the immutable spiritual notion of the divine model, with the individual a component of and subordinate to a higher supra-individual unit: the 'communio'. That same hierarchical character informed the sense of beauty, whereby that which approached the divine principle most closely was deemed the most beautiful. God's original intention with the world was the Creation as a perfect structure, a static whole of hermetic forms and rhythmic repetition.

The ideal is a proportionally ordered system from which nothing can be subtracted or added without disturbing the harmony. The square, the cube, the circle and the sphere were regarded because of their geometric harmony as reproductions of the divine model, which made it essential that they be applied in architecture. These elementary forms are based upon a central point, from which they radiate on all sides in equal measure. This radial symmetry represents perfection. The halved square was regarded as the correct form with which to organize the plan of a monastery because it 'agreed with the true measure'.

In the interests of harmony all artistic expression was seen as part of a greater whole, and this was expressed in the unity of architecture, art (most particularly sculpture), music and religious ritual in the monasteries in accordance with Benedict's Holy Rule, oriented as this was to concord between mind and body. All aspects of monastic life coincide in the liturgy which captures space and time in a rhythm that reflects the divine order. The rhythm of the seasons, of day and night, is visible in the division into tasks and the sequence of texts, chants and prayers in the masses and processions.

41. Norberg-Schulz 1972.

42. In the garden can be seen a representation of the city of Jerusalem which in turn is a reflection of the heavenly Jerusalem (the community of saints) and thus of paradise. Although its real form was familiar enough at the time, Jerusalem is rendered as a perfect circle, divided internally by two streets intersecting at right angles to form four districts. The form as it appears to mortal man is only part of the overall image, the true form being the circle with axial cross.

43. Ackerman 1949, 84.

'To see a World in a Grain of Sand
And a Heaven in a Wild Flower,
Hold Infinity in the palm of your hand
And Eternity in an hour.'

William Blake, ca. 1800

The miniature world of the hortus contemplationis is a reflection of the spiritual, harmonious world, a means of reconciling oneself with earthly existence. Here the medieval Christian thought constructs that brought order to nature converge in a square horizontal plane with a central point and axial cross, surrounded by a gallery. The autonomy, centric configuration and unity of the garden and the movement around it create a microcosm. The garden is an enclosed, finite space, organized round a tree or spring yet forming part of the infinity of natural space: the sky.

The monastery is configured as a chain of effectively independent spaces whose autonomy is underscored by the thickness of the walls and by the gallery. Its solid buildings are welded together by the unbroken rhythm of the gallery, a transparent length of columns and *arcades*. The gallery is the linking element that to the building represents the 'outdoors' of the garden, and to the garden the 'indoors' of the building. To this end the massive stone floor and rear wall present a contrast with the openness of the sky and the refinement of the columns. In the arcades the relationship between earth and sky is reflected yet again, with the floor representing the earth and the arches the heavenly vault. The gallery ties the 'earthly' to the 'heavenly' in a functional sense too. This is where the monks or nuns spend time after their daily activities, and prepare themselves for worship together in the chapel.

The garden offers a limited quantity of visual information: a fountain, four areas of grass, masses of columns. These are subject to a hierarchical composition and an unremitting repetition. The columns are decorated with sculptures which together tell a story. The building shuts out all sound and invokes a beneficent silence. Inside it is dark, with light entering the garden from above and percolating into the adjoining rooms.

ENDLESSLY CIRCLING. The entrances to the gallery are discovered in the corners – in a line with the gallery – and it is here that the circling movement begins. In the monastery the most important routes take in the gallery, a fact that underlines its central position. The circulatory movement (the physical relationship) is at right angles to the spatial relationship between building and garden permitted by the spacing of the columns.

The surface of the garden has emblematic significance and

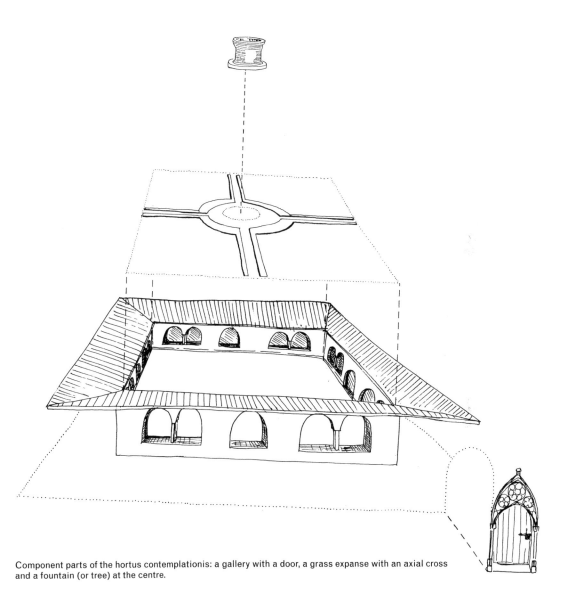

Component parts of the hortus contemplationis: a gallery with a door, a grass expanse with an axial cross and a fountain (or tree) at the centre.

the act of perambulation gives shape not to encounter but to contemplation. This is stressed by the ever repeated framing of the image by the arcade, while the rear wall is solid with its openings in shadow. The distance created between the gallery and the symbolically charged surface particularize the garden as a temenos, a sacred place forbidden to entry.

THE CONVERGENCE OF SPACE AND TIME. In this idea of repetition the finite and the infinite are brought face to face. The procession is the ritual re-enactment of an episode from the life of Christ, for example the way to Calvary. A single occurrence such as this becomes an unbroken process by joining the beginning and the end into the perambulation about a fixed central point: finitude of time and space coincide and are given physical form in the gallery. The paradox of this ritual of the procession round the garden is that on the one hand it has a fixed order with a beginning and an end (corresponding to melody), and on the other it is endless and cyclic *(rhythm)*. Time seems to stand still, motion and stasis being identical in scenographic terms: the choreography consists of a sequence of images of equal value rhythmically strung together. The march of time is manifested not in the changing of the image but in its repetition and is therefore not linear but cyclic. At the central point all movement seems to have come to a standstill.

Genealogy of the hortus conclusus

The image we have of the hortus conclusus is in the first place that of *Le Roman de la Rose*, the idealized image that acts as a backdrop to stories and fables. The literary strain of hortus conclusus – the hortus ludi – where image and meaning all but coincide is, however, only one moment in the genealogical series of the hortus conclusus. The question then arises as to the *architectural* moment in this sequence, the type that gave birth to landscape architecture and is still deployable today as a tool of spatial planning.

The pictorial and symbolic aspects presiding over the hortus ludi remain recognizable throughout the series. The medieval understanding of nature is determined by the double significance it possesses, the locus amoenus on the one hand and the wilderness on the other. In the garden, the theme of locus amoenus is developed, the wilderness is shut out and in-between the two all gradations are possible. The experience of nature is the projection of desires, an image that grew from studying the Greek, Roman and Middle Eastern sources and whose essence is found in the garden.

A subsequent moment in the series comes with the hortus catalogi, the objective type. Here the notion of a divine order is caught in a rational scheme primarily informed by practical considerations. The garden had to be for working in, and each element useful to man. The poetic image is replaced by the two-dimensional reality of the plan.

The hortus contemplationis marks the architectural moment in the typological series. Here, spatial considerations dictate the proportions within the three dimensions of the space and between the garden and the surrounding spaces: space and representation are the same. The hortus contemplationis is sealed off from imperfect nature and invites a search for the invisible, underlying beauty, the perfect nature as God intended. It is a reflection of this divine order: a spatially complete unity with harmonious proportions and symbolic references. This shutting out of the everyday world is resolutely achieved by the surrounding walls, within whose confines symbolism is uppermost. With this new arrangement, the medieval unity of symbolism, fitness for purpose and beauty was sundered.

The natural space is symbolized by that one imaginary line through the central point, the link with the infinite sky. The diversity of landscape is symbolized by that one basic ordering principle of the axial cross. Each enclosed garden is a transformation of this concept, up to and including the *Espace Piranésien* in Euralille, where the tangle of stairs illustrates as much the diversity of the urban world as the boundlessness of space.

As soon as a garden transcends the limitations of its walls it attains the realms of landscape architecture. At each planning level the garden suggests a larger entity. In terms of *image* the garden points to nature instead of imitating her. The *space* seems larger than it is. The absence of a ceiling and emphasis on the sky makes the endless space above a component of the finite space of the garden. Irregular spaced trees such as those in the hortus ludi suggest a continuity beyond the garden, and the gallery of the hortus contemplationis introduces a stratification to the walls so that the garden boundaries are ambivalent. The *plan configuration* of the garden does not merely enable the ground plane to be designed but forms part of the universal organization to which it refers. In the hortus contemplationis, for example, the axial cross binds not only the garden to the one central point but the entire surrounding landscape with it, and the grid in the hortus catalogi is a fragment of an implied endless pattern.

Each of the three types of the hortus conclusus gives shape to one of the programmatic aspects of the garden. The earthly paradise acts as a backdrop for play, instruction and contemplation: the hortus ludi as a stage for play and sensual enjoyment, the hortus catalogi as a showroom for nature, to work in and to learn from, and the hortus contemplationis as an

Contemplation, play and instruction:

right: Studying the heavenly vault. The medieval woodcut shows a seer observing the heavenly hierarchy beyond material reality.

centre: Titillating the senses. Jacob Marrel, *Vanitas*, 1637.

below: Nature under control. Collector's cabinet. Engraving by L. Vincent in *Wondertoneel der Nature*, Amsterdam 1706.

emblem, encouraging contemplation. Each type calls upon another human capacity with which to observe the surroundings sensory experience, intellectual understanding, mental abstraction.

In its growth towards a spatial form we can also discern a refining in the symbolic representation of nature and the way the means to this end are ordered. The first arrangement to be made was setting together and excluding, the second geometric control, with architectural control of the space completing the process. The reproduction of the world in the complete and closed-off microcosm of the hortus contemplationis is a ritual, the creating of space for reflection. In the abstraction of the geometry, the spatial form and the image, it is not the tangible aspect of paradise or of nature that is rendered, but the idea. 'The smaller the tree, the further away it is from nature. The less the resemblance to reality, the more magical the effect.'[44]

Together they give an overview of the sheer range of the hortus conclusus, but at the same time they lay the foundations for those components that would join forces in landscape-architectural designs from the Renaissance onwards, the three layers that determine the form of the garden: spatial form, plan configuration and appearance. Each type marks a phase in the controlling of these layers. The *rational gardens* of the Renaissance would not have existed without these experiments carried out within four walls.

There is a Utopia incapsulated in the hortus conclusus. It is a testing ground in which man tries to create a paradise on earth. There he experiments with seemingly irreconcilable objectives such as illustrating the divine, and sensual pleasures: 'the hortus conclusus as a focus and miniature concentration of the Civitas Dei, remains a closed circuit where man is invulnerable, full of magic-erotic potential.'[45]

44. Stein 1987.

45. Komrij 1991, 39.

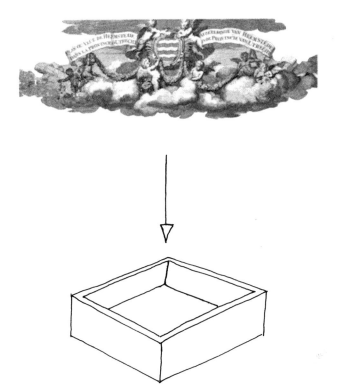

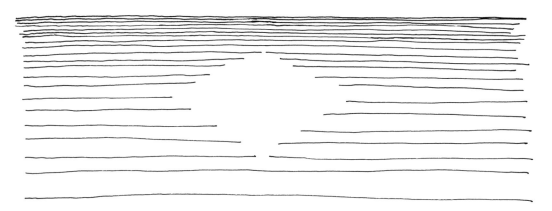

Model of the hortus conclusus.

Landscape transformations

'He leapt the fence and saw that all nature was a garden.'

Horace Walpole, 1780

Garden and landscape

'Things fall apart, the centre cannot hold.'

W.B. Yeats

The prototypical hortus conclusus is a closed system, a microcosm reflecting the macrocosm which for simplicity's sake is likewise conceived as a closed system. The paradox of the garden emerges when it is related to an external environment which can be experienced within the garden. These surroundings inevitably bring about a transformation. Lying in the landscape, the garden drinks in its most salient quality: the endlessness of the horizon. In the city, by contrast, the garden has evolved into a counterweight to the dynamism and variability of the urban fabric. The garden in the landscape and the garden in the city seem to possess utterly different raisons d'être. Yet one and the same type can be deployed that despite all the changes keeps its relevance. The two examples that illustrate this exhibit the same means and the same formal idiom. In the urban tissue of the Alhambra, a fifteenth-century citadel, the Patio de los Leones and the Patio de los Arrayanes are moments of repose; in the nearby Generalife the Patio de la Acequia brings in the horizon. In both examples the garden firmly engages with the surroundings, though without changing in the process. They illustrate the turning point between type and transformation.

The transformations we will be looking at below all derive from the same need to escape the limitations of the hortus conclusus and replace it with the unfolding of the world at large. The Islamic examples make it clear that it cannot be a case of replacing one thing with another. The medieval containment and the modern desire for the horizon are two ingredients of the same recipe.

In the enclosed world of the hortus conclusus the only expansive element is the sky, and the sky's endlessness the vertical link with the zenith. The suggestion alone was enough to inspire medieval man with awe for the boundless magnitude of God. But the tangible reality of the earth has its endlessness too: the horizon, where the sight line touches the surface of the terrestrial globe. The question is what happens to the introverted garden when it engages with the world outside, the landscape. What happens when the central point and the horizon meet?

This breaking open of the type not only involves the garden with the landscape, the very qualities of the type are called into question. For the envelope becomes visible when a hole is punched in it. The thickness of the wall is then made manifest, and space is set against mass. Equally, the interior only acquires meaning when made to relate to the exterior, and the visibility of the expansive landscape drives home the enclosure of the

Prospect. Caspar David Friedrich, *Wanderer above the Sea of Fog*, 1818.

garden. Only then does this spatial paradox of the hortus conclusus come into full flower. Whereas the hortus contemplationis used to present an external world to the cells of the building, now it is as much an internal world to the external world of the landscape.

We shall embark on the further evolution of the hortus conclusus using an example in the southernmost tip of Spain which enjoyed a cultural flowering through centuries of Moorish influence, when the rest of Europe was still in a primitive state. In the Generalife the view of the horizon, which would prove typical for the post-medieval history of the garden, is already one of the garden's principal themes. Also, in the Christian buildings of Northern Spain, where the Muslims had been driven out centuries before, the opulence of the Moorish culture can still be recognized. From this time on, revolutions in the history of the garden would increasingly be played out in more northerly climes, in France, England, Germany and then across to America.

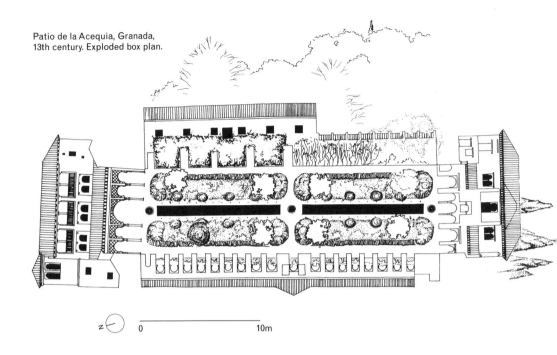

Patio de la Acequia, Granada,
13th century. Exploded box plan.

z 0 ——————————— 10m

Generalife, Granada, 13th century.
Enclosed garden and landscape.

Patio de la Acequia

In the Islamic tradition, just as in that of
Western Europe, the garden is a recreation of
the earthly paradise. But in the world of Islam,
much more oriented as it is towards pleasure
and sensuality, the paradisiacal aspect was
also seen on the earth itself. Here the pleasure
garden flourished to a greater extent than in
the more ascetic European gardens. The
delights of the garden are earthly ones and
there is always a link made to the landscape,
stressing the fact that taming the landscape is
a condition of life. Irrigating the dry, hot ground
and arranging it in terraces makes it fertile and
brings a prosperity expressed in the coolness
and shade and luxuriant growth of plants in the
gardens. These are places for living, for eating,
making music and conversing. They are the
central spaces of the house.

THE GENERALIFE. At the foot of the Sierra Nevada lies the city of Granada. Two rivers, the Genil and its tributary the Darro, converge here. Together they border a hill or spur, the Sabikah, on which the Alhambra and the Generalife are situated [see illustration on p. 112]. These enjoy a visual relationship across a ravine. In the fourteenth century the Generalife was built as a summer palace across from the Alhambra, complete with orchards, farmland, gardens, farm animals and horses for riding. In the villa complex can be found a pleasure garden, the Patio de la Acequia (Court of the Long Pool).

The spur is split into three by streams. The northeastern crest is the highest and this is where the Generalife is sited. Terraces were laid out on the western slope for orchards and gardens for vegetables and fruit. In this century the topmost terrace has been transformed into a *formal garden* with an amphitheatre. The siting of the three portions of the Generalife – amphitheatre, formal garden and the palace with the Jardines Altos – adhere to the gentle S-bend of the slope. The formal garden juts out balcony-like from the hillside between the palace and the amphitheatre.

The villa, rotated to follow the curve in the hill, is fully oriented to the Alhambra, a relationship concentrated in a sight line from the *mirador* (watch-tower) to the Puerta del Arrabal, the northern entrance to the Alhambra. The views towards the city, the river Darro and the Sierra Nevada are likewise formalized in towers and terraces.

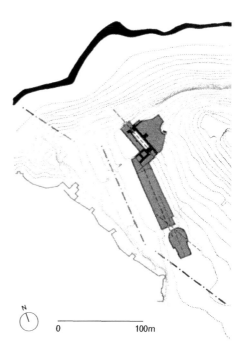

0   100m

above: Plan configuration and geomorphology. The S-bend of the spur is expressed in the placing of the components.

below: The villa is sited beyond the crest of the hill, so that there are views to all four points of the compass, each formalized in its own space: the mirador looks to the Alhambra; a second sight line, from the Torre de Ismail to the north, is oriented to the river Darro and the town beyond. A third viewing direction is introduced from the corner tower: across the garden to the Sierra Nevada in the south. A jutting terrace just beyond the palace formalizes the view to the Darro. 1. Granada / 2. Darro / 3. Sierra Nevada / 4. Puerta del Arrabal

Ranks of closely trimmed cypress separate the Generalife from the planted slope above and the terraces of farmland below. Lying it seems against the point of the hill, the ensemble of buildings with its white-plastered walls, red-tiled roofs and bowed windows accords with the white villas on the other side of the Darro.

Through the terraces, a path has been incised that rises up from the bottom of the valley. Aligned with the tower, the Torre de Ismail, it swerves midway up the slope so as to continue straight up and emerge in the western patio forming the entrance to the villa. (These days the Generalife is accessed via the formal garden which is linked by a bridge with the southeastern tip of the Alhambra.) This patio has a pastoral character. A second patio behind it draws together the various levels, and is much more cultivated. From a small white-rendered indoor space, a steep staircase leads up into the Patio de la Acequia presenting a view of the sky like a veritable stairway to heaven. The cool chamber at the bottom of the stair contrasts dramatically with the sunny and colourful garden. The Torre de Ismail, set at the end of the main axis and preceded by a gallery and a rectangular hall (the Sala Regia), can be regarded as the conclusion of the route.

A NECKLACE OF GARDENS. In the plan configuration of the Generalife, there is a shift in alignment among the three parts of the villa

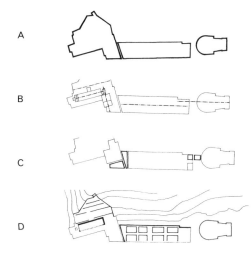

A. The villa ensemble consists of three components laid out along the hillside: the amphitheatre, the formal garden and the villa with the old gardens.
B. The principal axes of the amphitheatre and the formal garden are connected by a staggered link, which places the building and the old garden at an angle of about 15 degrees with the formal garden.
C. The crossover between the villa and the formal garden is effected by two wedge-shaped elements set at right angles that take up both the axial shift and the angle of rotation. Seemingly identical on plan, their roles in the spatial system differ. The one piece completes the villa portion to the valley, the other reconciles the formal garden and the entrance section. These wedges and the entrance patios present a complex entity with a great many changes in direction, differences in height and degrees of enclosure.
D. Originally the villa lay amidst farmlands. In the 19th century a formal composition was designed on the uppermost terrace and the villa slotted into it. In this composition the patio terminates a sequence of spaces. The sequence begins in the amphitheatre, a sunken static space dominated by a podium whose raised position makes the connection with the formal garden, which is set on the slope and is asymmetrical as a result. The garden contains a series of introverted green 'rooms' on the slope side and a series of open ones to the valley. The result is a tensionality that would later figure prominently in the Patio de la Acequia. The viewing direction to the valley, emphasized here by the distinction between open and closed, is set square to the main axis.

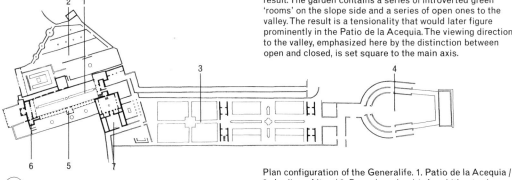

Plan configuration of the Generalife. 1. Patio de la Acequia / 2. Jardines Altos / 3. Formal garden / 4. Amphitheatre / 5. Mirador / 6. Torre de Ismail / 7. Entrance patio

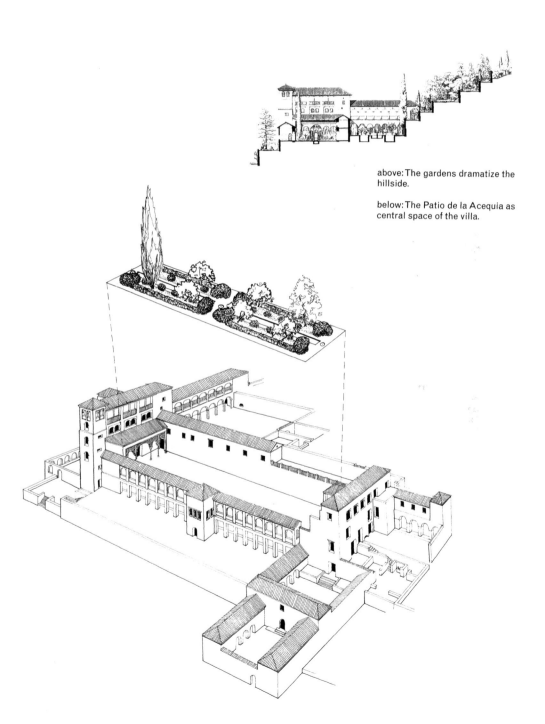

above: The gardens dramatize the hillside.

below: The Patio de la Acequia as central space of the villa.

that is summarized in the shift in the three main axes. This is a formal processing of the original situation, where the ensemble of buildings is rotated and set back in respect to the uppermost terrace, thereby responding to the bend in the slope. The access road arrives at the place where terrace and buildings meet to continue as a string of patios with a central axis set at right angles to the villa's principal direction.

On the steep slope above the villa lie the wooded Jardines Altos, contrasting with the large open terrace below the villa. The two garden complexes link the building with the face of the hill. The openness of the terraces and the containment of the Jardines Altos come together in the Patio de la Acequia which combines a view out with the shelter of the hillside. The patio and the miradors are confronted head-on with the panorama without the intercession of the garden complexes. At the extremity of the patio, the Torre de Ismail juts beyond the walls of the villa, anchoring the building to the steep slope and the view.

The regularity of the clipped hedges of the amphitheatre and the formal garden present a stark contrast with the luxurious, colourful planting, the irregular solid walls and the labyrinthine villa.

THE GARDEN: A PARADISE ON EARTH. The plan configuration of the Patio de la Acequia proceeds from the limitations of the oblong terrace. Its corners are not right-angled and the eastern wall is kinked. A symmetrical ground plane is adapted to the deviations of the building. The proportions of the garden are 1:4 (six by twenty-four metres) in which the axial cross breaks down into a longitudinal and a transverse axis. Of these the longitudinal is emphasized by galleries for heads and a canal boasting fifty-eight fountains. The transverse axis links the mirador with a door leading to the gardens above.

Lengthwise, the garden has a graduated structure with the galleries mediating between inside and outside, between garden and building. Although the galleries mirror each other, the extremities of the axis are

left: Spatial configuration of the central portion of the villa, with the dark entrance room and observation tower as polar opposites.

right: Prospect of the Alhambra.

distinguishable by a mirador with a view out over the Darro at one end, and a recess terminating the other. The long eastern wall is the side against the hillside and is blank, irregular and of unplastered brick. The western wall opens up as a double arcade, so that the garden is asymmetrical. This double arcade looks out on the Alhambra, which originally could only be seen from the mirador. So the four differently designed patio walls represent the position in the landscape. The views set at right angles are formalized in two parallel lines – the longitudinal axis and the open wall – which together define the space. The path running through the double arcade is geared to the views, the other extending before it is turned inwards. The closed corners of the patio and the shifting columns of the double arcade generate within the four walls an alternation between containment and views out.

Lying on either side of the longitudinal axis are beds surrounded by boxwood hedges and luxuriously and irregularly planted with flowers bushes and trees. Pitted against the severe geometry of the ground plan are the organic forms of the profuse planting. The orange trees the many colours, the fragrant flowers, the sound and cooling effect of the fountains all point to the eternal spring of paradise. In the double arcade can be read the confrontation between garden and view: Moorish arches for the refined artificial 'interior landscape', Romanesque arches for the landscape proper.

PROGRAMME AND MEANING. The Generalife was designed as a pleasure retreat and has an agricultural character, a counterpart to the political life of the Alhambra. In the patio the double arcade functions as a grandstand for a double performance: the reality of the landscape on the one side, and the idealized picture of the garden on the other, the two vying for the audience's attention. The 'acequias' – natural rivulets from high in the hills – are formalized in channels, cascades and fountains, so that the water supply for the entire villa complex can be controlled. The long straight canal represents the complete system of water figures and fountains with which the supply of natural water is cultivated. Thus the patio refers as much to the cultural achievements of the Moorish designers as to the value of the water, vital as it is in this hot and arid country.

SYNTHESIS. The central point of the patio is reduced to a barely visible juncture where two axes intersect but its presence is enough to steady the space, as a foil to the infinity of the horizon. The axial cross of the patio as an organizing principle and the walk surrounding it suggest completeness. Strong views from the double arcade and miradors put this completeness into perspective by confronting it with other worlds: the Islamic world of 700 years ago (the Alhambra) and the city of today. The double arcade in this respect is both a wall and a frame for views. It is this arcade that generates in the patio an exchange between enclosure and exposure that manifests itself in a balance between horizontal and vertical orientation.

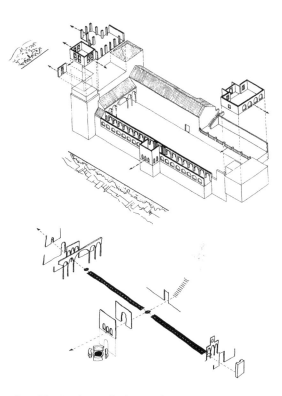

above: The visual-spatial cohesion of the villa.

below: Enfilade of spaces culminating in the framed view.

Patio de la Acequia.

The Patio de la Acequia contains ingredients that would keep returning in different proportions in the physical transformation of the hortus conclusus: the enclosing framework in which zenith and horizon – vertical and horizontal alignment – engage in a game together. In the Western world too, after the Middle Ages the tangible endlessness of the horizon had been discovered and would take the place of the immaterial endlessness of the zenith and the centric configuration this brought with it.

After the Middle Ages, the view of the world and nature changed, influenced by the revelations of science and the effects of trade and the crusades, such as improved agricultural techniques, the discovery of the unbelievable natural variety in exotic lands and the confrontation with more hedonistic cultures. The earth itself offered pleasure and beauty, comparable with what previously had been destined for the virtuous of spirit in the paradise of the hereafter.

The landscape of the Middle Ages was steadily being colonized by man and, from the Renaissance on, developed into an ever more rational and large-scale cultivated landscape. With the functional changes to the landscape the form and impact of the landscape space changed too. It was now possible to establish one's physical location and relate visual elements to one another. The need arose to control and manipulate space.

Petrarch writes that his Viletta (small villa) in France has two gardens, one dedicated to Apollo (self-control, rational thinking), the other to Bacchus (sensuality, following the instincts). In the two complementary gardens control necessarily takes chaos to task. Shut off from the chaos of nature, the sensual and unmanageable facet of the Bacchic garden could be kept in hand, but to integrate the unbounded space of the landscape in the garden Apollo's self-control would seem to be a prerequisite. It is then as if Bacchus's garden disappears.

Thus, the garden sought out the landscape and opened up to the horizon. This happened because of the views to be gained, but also to parade this taming of nature. To better relate the garden to the landscape (also in terms of dimensions) the garden became steadily larger, transforming the simple structure of the hortus conclusus into a complex spatial composition. Once a free agent, the enclosed garden became downplayed to a component of the landscape-architectural ensemble. The landscape architecture of the Renaissance, Baroque and Enlightenment represented and celebrated the natural and cultivated landscapes by imposing upon them an urban organization. The distinction between garden and landscape became less and less, until eventually the garden took over the scale of the landscape. In the contest between the central point and the horizon, in which the rules of play were constantly being researched and elaborated, the horizon would seem to have emerged the winner.

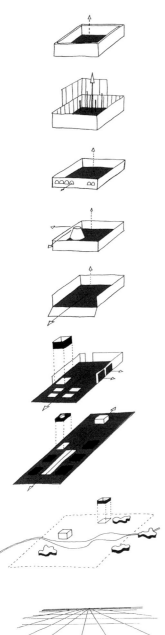

Opening

After the Middle Ages, man's sense of involvement with and awe of nature and the supernatural decreased in stages. No longer regarded as something self-evident that needed treating with respect, nature was now a subject to be studied and fathomed out. Its materials, structures and laws could be used to the greater honour and glory of God, and as a means of getting closer to the divine.

In medieval times, the heavenly vault represented the divine order and as such was at the centre of earthly life. This order was reflected in the contained world of the hortus conclusus, but the abstraction became less and less satisfying and medieval man went in search of a way of expressing it in concrete terms. The increase in knowledge and control of the world around brought with it the opportunity to make the endlessness of the earth (the horizon) visible in the garden and the hortus conclusus underwent an inversion. The garden was made to face outwards. Gradually the focus on the sky was replaced by a focus on the earth.

There are two forms this orientation to the earth could take. First, there is the horizontal alignment, the axis spanning between a fixed point in the garden (the house or a statue) and the horizon. This horizontal focus took shape in, say, the *Baroque garden*. The second possibility is *horizontal expansiveness*, the unbounded and non-hierarchical space as given form in, for example, the eighteenth-century *landscape garden*. The space is indicated by the horizontal surface of the earth alone, with the vertical dimension becoming insignificant.

Elaborating the vertical axis: the Gothic garden

'It is, indeed, utterly impossible that our human spirit should succeed in imitating and considering the heavenly hierarchies without using material means to do it, means capable of serving as a guide by adapting to our nature ... The material light stands for the revelation of the immaterial light, being its image.'

Pseudo-Dionysus the Areopagite, fifth century

The hortus conclusus itself contained the condition for its demise. Making a material paradise on earth and cultivating sensual pleasure are a first step towards enjoying the earth itself as a paradise. The Gothic garden tried to address the first doubts about the divine model by making it tangible in the intertwining of sensory and geometrical aspects.

Illustrating the divine had, since the early Middle Ages, been a theme that occupied those concerned with spiritual matters, aware as they were of the incapacity of the population to gain

Stages in the development of the hortus conclusus.

insight into the divine without being given a concrete image of it.[1] Architectural research evolved until it was almost a goal in itself: to fix the structure of the divine and develop the tools to convert it into formal artefacts and architecture. More and more, the perfection of geometry became a gauge to measure the degree of divinity of man and his creations and this reached a peak in Gothic architecture. With the results of the research – the pure geometry of square, cube, circle and sphere, and the 'ideal' proportions of the cube (the number of faces, corners and edges have a ratio of 3:4:6) – came the conditions which were also to realize an image of the divine in the Gothic hortus conclusus. The other means deployed to convince the sceptical was an appeal to the senses. Material beauty and shining light would help to make man more receptive to the spiritual glory of the Creator. The architecture became vertical and transparent, calling attention to the sky.[2]

Making the divine tangible and introducing a distinction between sacred and profane marked the beginning of the demythologizing of nature. God and nature were not the inseparable pair they used to be. God was only where scientific man could discern Him.

The vertical orientation of the gardens gained meaning through the contrast with the horizontal relationship between garden and landscape. Thus, the garden at the monastery of Santes Creus gathers the landscape around it in a series of leaps in scale, with the garden as the most condensed space. The garden of the Cathedral of Santa Eulalia is a hortus contemplationis gone urban, and presents an abrupt contrast with the narrow streets where the sky is scarcely visible at all. Though the hortus contemplationis is still the type, the space is at the point of imploding. A tensionality obtains between the space and the desire to break out of that containment.

1. Whereas Romanesque gardens were set on an isolated site beyond the town, Gothic cathedrals were built in the towns to impress the populace and remove any doubts they may have had about the existence of God.

2. The discovery of the rib vault enabled these geometric principles to be put into practice in Gothic architecture to illustrate in the cathedral the change in world-view. Thanks to the rib vault the divine on earth could be rendered by the lightness and transparency of the cathedral. Generating a diagonal direction, the rib vault made it possible to transform the basic form of the cube into a vertical space. The walls no longer had to be load-bearing and lost their inert surface to gain in spatiality and plasticity so that the spaces could flow into one another. The pointed arch, like the rib vault, expressed the force field thrusting up heavenward, an element which was lacking in the harmoniously round Romanesque arch.

The Romanesque garden of the Santes Creus monastery

At a fertile and well-watered spot in the arid mountain landscape of Northern Spain stands a monastery with two gardens in its midst. The monastery is linked to the plains by way of a spatial sequence culminating in a *glorieta*, a circle of cypress constituting the centre of the more hidden of the two gardens.

MOUNTAIN RETREAT. On the east coast of Catalonia lies a large plain hemmed in by mountains. The eastern edge of the northernmost part of the plain is defined by the River Gaià. At the place where one of the tributaries, the Barranco de Hort Gran, flows into the Gaià, there stands on the northern slope the monastery of Santes Creus (with below it the vineyards exposed to the sun). It looks down from a plateau thirty metres above the river onto the small village of the same name. The monastery was built at this remote spot in the twelfth century in accordance with the Cistercian values of sobriety, severity, personal poverty and isolation from worldly life.

below: The monastery nestles at the convergence of two river valleys, hidden behind a ridge of hills and lying along the edge of a large coastal plain. 1. Santas Creus hill / 2. Tarragona plain / 3. River Gaià / 4. Barranco de Hort Gran

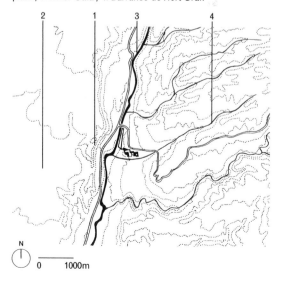

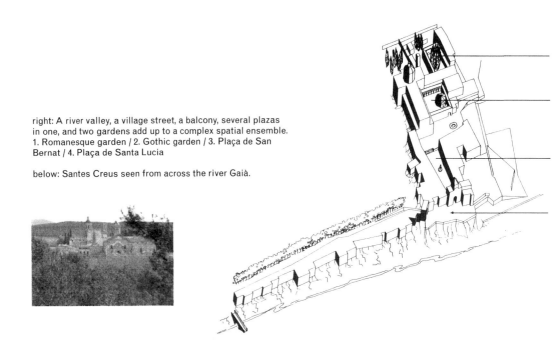

right: A river valley, a village street, a balcony, several plazas in one, and two gardens add up to a complex spatial ensemble. 1. Romanesque garden / 2. Gothic garden / 3. Plaça de San Bernat / 4. Plaça de Santa Lucia

below: Santes Creus seen from across the river Gaià.

Santes Creus is one of the royal monasteries along the pilgrims' route to Santiago de Compostela.

Moving up the hill, the spaces become smaller and more clearly defined, alternating grand views with framed *vistas* and thoroughly introverted features. The horizon, a strong presence in the plain, becomes increasingly hidden in stages as the series of spaces progresses.

In the dry expanse of the plain the Gaià valley is an oasis: white poplars and hazels grow along its banks, and where the valley opens up to the plain there are vineyards, gardens of almonds and olives, and woods. Towers pick out the monastery complex rising from the sea of trees. In the village, the road is shaded by the houses and sycamores, after which the successive layers of wall make for ever increasing shelter and distance from the inhospitable landscape. The form of planting gets more cultivated too as it approaches the end of the sequence of spaces: honey locusts on the Plaza de San Bernat, orange trees, clipped box and cypress in the garden.

At the bridge over the Gaià, the road through the river valley and the way out of the mountains converge. Here the difference in height between the deep gorge of the Gaià and the monastery set high on the plateau becomes clear. From the bridge over the Gaià onwards, the route leading to the monastery is accompanied by buildings and gateways. The ascent, the decreasing heat and increasing shelter and the rich growth together imbue the route with a chastening effect.

A MONASTERY WITH TWO GARDENS. The monastery consists of two parts lightly rotated from one another. Around the Gothic garden is an unbroken succession of buildings that includes the main church. The buildings are arranged round the Romanesque garden in clusters, including a smaller church and a royal palace. The gardens are spatially linked by two axes that slide by each other, thereby stitching the two parts of the ensemble together.

Measured against the ensemble the gardens are self-sufficient entities, with this difference – that the western portion is a compact mass out of which the Gothic garden is carved like a vacuole, whereas the framework of the Romanesque garden is a free standing arcade amidst the spread of buildings held together by the wall surrounding the ensemble.

The monastery is a melting pot of building styles. The messy street and the Baroque Plaza de San Bernat usher in the dark Romanesque church with its solid plain walls and alabaster windows. Each of the spaces round the garden reflects another part of the history of the monastery. Finely wrought Gothic arcades enfold the Gothic garden which is formally designed with hedges of boxwood, trimmed orange trees and a *lavabo.* The sober Romanesque garden has low solid walls and dark cypress, a reference to the cypress beyond its confines.

THE ROMANESQUE GARDEN. This trapezium-shaped garden has a concentric organization consisting of the gallery, glorieta, cruciform pool and fountain. Views through to the adjacent spaces lighten the sense of enclosure in the small garden with its heavy walls. The Romanesque part of the monastery is horizontally aligned by way of the heavy walls, the round arches, the horizontal building volumes and the flush ceilings. This horizontality continues in the garden, where the gallery presides over the spatial form. The glorieta was added later, so that in the middle of the garden the horizontal alignment is abruptly exchanged for the vertical. Enter the circle of cypress and the view of the gallery is gone, with the crowns of the trees framing a circular portion of sky. The fountain formalizes the reference to the sky.

Arcades scooped out of the tall solid wall present diagonal lines of action owing to the absence of columns. Here plantings consist of unorganized groups of oleander, laurel and the like, with only the glorieta as a compact, geometric form. The garden conjures up the image and sensory impact of a forest, with scented flowering plants, coolness, shade and damp. The glorieta is like a condensed hortus conclusus with at its centre a cruciform pool as a material version of the invisible axial cross. In its midst is a miniature landscape, a mushroom-shaped lump wreathed in moss and ferns and spouting skyward a stream of water.

PROGRAMME AND MEANING. The succession from plain to glorieta reflects the intentions of the Cistercian community: to retreat from the world, illustrated in a series of spaces much like the Stations of the Cross. The gardens together with the church offer space for contemplation: the church for the public

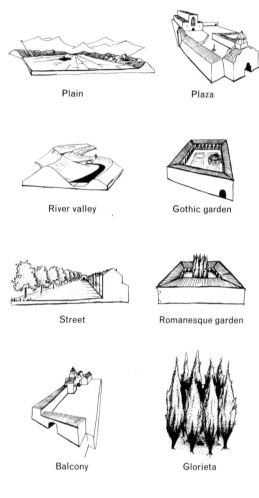

Plain

Plaza

River valley

Gothic garden

Street

Romanesque garden

Balcony

Glorieta

Each space can be identified with a landmark element: a hilltop, a cross, a chapel, a fountain, a lavabo and a glorieta. A low hilltop, the Santas Creus, marks the site of the monastery on the edge of the plain. The river crossing is marked by a wayside cross. The village of Santes Creus consists of little more than a steeply rising street that narrows constantly to end at a gateway accessing a 'balcony' overlooking the Gaià valley, the Plaça de Santa Lucia. A small chapel abutting a monumental gateway, the Portal de l'Assumpta, terminates the south side of the square. A second square is composed of the Plaça de San Bernat with the enormous Romanesque church at its head, and the Plaça de Jacob II with a view across the terraced landscape. A lavabo dominates the Gothic garden, linked by a dark passage to the smaller Romanesque garden. The glorieta at the centre of the latter garden terminates the sequence.

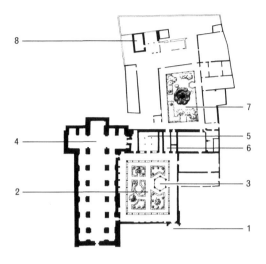

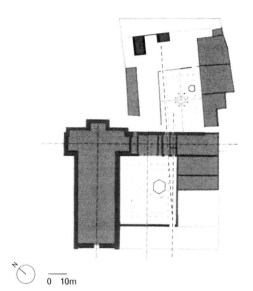

0   10m

service, the Gothic garden for processions and the Romanesque garden for individual prayer. In the Gothic garden the columns on the garden side and the succession of moments on the building side materialize the rhythm and the melody of the procession: church door, recesses with tombstones, church door, sacristy, chapter house on axis with the garden, stair to the dormitory, parlour and passage to the Romanesque garden, refectory, the Puerta Real to the square, a long blank wall, ending at the church.

If it is the endless circular movement that is stressed in the Gothic garden, in the Romanesque garden it is the central point referring to infinity that predominates. The circle of eight evergreen cypress in the Romanesque garden are a metaphor for eternity. The cross-shaped pool and the jet of water accentuate the coordinates of existential space.

SYNTHESIS. There is, then, an inversion in stages from the openness and horizontal alignment of the plain to the enclosure and vertical alignment of the glorieta. In the garden, the landscape is shut out but the sky is not yet subjected to architectural treatment. The glorieta brings out the verticality in a way that would also happen later in the Gothic.

left: Plan configuration of the monastery ensemble. 1. Puerta Real / 2. Gothic garden / 3. Lavabo / 4. Church / 5. Chapter house / 6. Locutorio and passage / 7. Romanesque garden / 8. Chapel

right: The Romanesque garden (14.3 x 21.7 metres) and the Gothic garden (21.1 x 25.4 metres) act as central points of the two parts of the monastery, which are slightly out of true.

The fountain at the centre of the Romanesque garden.

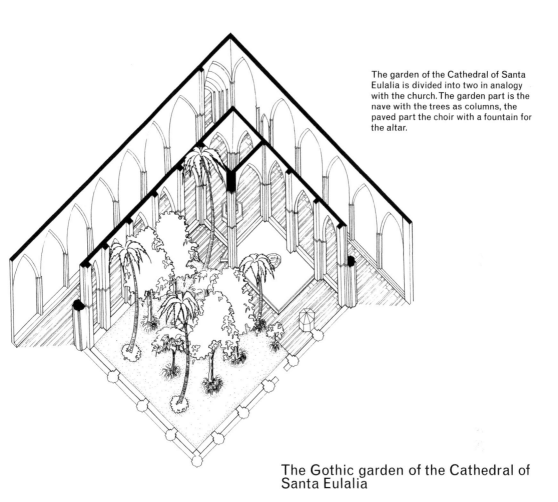

The garden of the Cathedral of Santa Eulalia is divided into two in analogy with the church. The garden part is the nave with the trees as columns, the paved part the choir with a fountain for the altar.

Cathedral of Sante Eulalia, Barcelona, begun 1298. The church is strongly vertical in its proportions and the subdivision of its wall planes. The nave is 28 metres high with a surface area of 1900 square metres, which means grand proportions despite the church's small overall surface area.

The Gothic garden of the Cathedral of Santa Eulalia

'Symbolic in its conception, mystical in its aim and calculated in its principles.' Thus Otto Van Simpson on the Gothic cathedral (1962). This description certainly fits the garden of the Cathedral of Santa Eulalia in Barcelona, as far as is known the only garden in perfect keeping with the design of the Gothic cathedral. It is set in the heart of the city, a hortus conclusus with palms and geese. These recall the geese kept by the Romans during the city's heyday.

THE CATHEDRAL AND THE GARDEN: ONE WORK OF ART. The garden and the church are organized according to the same orthogonal grid. It informs the distance between the inward-facing buttresses and the chapels these

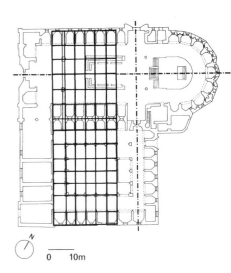

generate, as well as the distance between the columns of the gallery and the trees in the garden.

The distinction between spaces and subspaces, wall and ceiling, building and garden, is resolved in a game played with vertical lines. Differences in height, walls, columns, vaults, openings and differences in material, create a welter of edges, which together with the chapels, the arcades, the recurring vertical lines and the exuberant ornamentation erase boundaries, for all the solidity of the walls. One corner of the gallery folds inward along the diagonal, so that a separate space emerges, binding the garden with the church. This is the *lavatorium* with a second fountain at its centre.

The image this evokes is that of the clearing; the columns and the tree trunks create an illusion of a forest, sprinkled with daylight filtering down evenly through the perforated wall and the treetops.

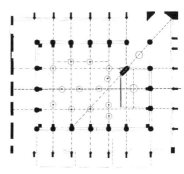

THE GARDEN: A HIDDEN DRAMA. The way this garden is configured can be traced to the division of the bays in the gallery (four and six respectively), the ever recurring (holy) number three and the parti of the church: a central axis with a head (the choir) and aisles. Three rows of trees stand in an orthogonal grid. The outer rows continue the line of the columns, the inner acts as a central axis with the fountain at its head.

The massive columns of the gallery represent the church in the garden. The trees on either side of the axis are larger and heavier than the three actually on it, a transcription of the open middle section of the church. An intermeshing of spaces and absence of a hierarchy mean that in the garden the emphasis is on the space as a whole, rather than on one or other stand-out element.

Filtered light, walls so high that they all but blot out the sky, sounds that reverberate in the gallery, a damp coolness, walls, vaults and floors of untreated cut stone; all the senses work together on the impression of a subterranean space (or a cathedral). Dates and oranges, magnolia and orange blossom, incense

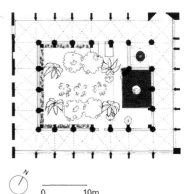

above: Church and garden are based on the same hypothetical system of measures.

centre: The uniting grid of trees and columns. One column emphasizes the diagonal linking garden, gallery, gateway and church.

below: Plan configuration of the garden.

and candles tantalize the senses of taste and smell. Because of the thick planting the entire space can not be taken in from one point, so that the visible portion seems to be a component of a larger whole. The trees (date palms, fan palms, magnolias) stand in large densely overgrown circles on a field of gravel. White geese waddle in the hard paved area. The large dark leathery magnolia leaves and the even larger feathery palm leaves contrast starkly: dark against light, rough against fine, hard against soft.

PROGRAMME AND MEANING. The sensory aspects of the garden together with the iconographical depictions in the gallery clearly refer to paradise. Besides illustrations from the Old and New Testaments the Catalan saint Jordi is depicted twice: on the fountain and on the keystone of the arch. On the day of Corpus Christi, celebrated with an impressive procession, you can admire the so-called 'L'ou com balla', (an egg dancing on a jet of water) in the lavatorium. Through this linking of rituals and symbols the garden's significance transcends its limited physical dimensions.

SYNTHESIS. In the garden, sensuality and reason link arms. The dynamic of the seemingly infinite grid of the floor plan, the suggestion of great space and the lush greenery are kept in check by the gallery. The unity of the cathedral is shaped by the diversity manifested at various levels: the historical stratification, the polygonal plan (orthogonal grid, radial pattern and triangular grid), the various horizontal levels, the exuberant detailing and the transparency of the walls. By these means, the underlying order is only discernible in the second instance. The seeming transparency of the walls and the flow of spaces into each other suggest an endlessness. The vertical lines of the tree trunks and the gallery give palpable form to a vertical alignment that was merely hinted at the Romanesque garden.

above: Filtered light creates a hallowed ambience.

below: The garden is populated by white geese.

The view across the wall: the French castle garden

'At first I stood there almost benumbed, overwhelmed by a gale such as I had never felt before and by the unusually open and wide view. Athos and Olympus grew less incredible... From there I turned my eyes in the direction of Italy ... . The Alps ... looked as if they were quite near me, though they are far, far away.'

Francesco Petrarch, 1336

When Petrarch climbed Mont Ventoux in 1336 he was overcome by the great space before him. His horizon shifted past the ancient, contained world. 'It is atop Mont Ventoux that a dramatic meeting takes place between St Augustine and Petrarch, between the spirit of the Middle Ages and that of the modern age, between introspection and expansion ... On the one hand the enclosure of reflection, in which the soul sought self-justification for eternity, on the other the opening up of the world and the onset of individual existence.'[4] Petrarch's leap into the void does not as yet mean an immediate break with the past. His curiosity is roused, yet in the first instance he regrets his daring ascent of the mountain and seeks to return to the medieval way of thinking.

THE MOUNT. This hesitation likewise marks the first attempts to draw the horizon into the garden. After the Middle Ages, when defence became a lesser issue, mounds of earth were erected so as to be able to look out over the garden wall. Once again we see the classic theme of the hortus conclusus expanded with that other classic theme of the prospect beyond the wall. But the fear of nature was still such that there was no question of doing away with the surrounding walls remain a certitude, and the *mount* became an incident within those walls without influencing the garden and without touching the landscape, just as Petrarch continued to interpret his experience in a way that left medieval thinking unaffected. It is particularly in the flat landscape of the Netherlands and the South of England that the mount became a component of the garden, due to the dearth of natural observation points. In the Middle Ages, mounts served mainly as places from where you could keep an eye out for unwelcome visitors, but even when the view out became important this aspect remained at loggerheads with that of protection. In his essay *On Gardens* (1625) Francis Bacon argued for a mount for the pleasure of looking out, yet the old fear of untamed nature persisted. Standing on the mount, the surrounding wall had to come up to chest height. 'The purpose of the mount was to give a prospect without sacrificing the sanctuary of the garden.'[5]

Mount. From Charles Estienne, *La Maison rustique* (1564).

4. Lemaire 1970, 13.

5. Appleton 1975, 193.

THE SECLUDED WORLD OF THE FRENCH CASTLES. At the end of the Middle Ages there was less reason for the castle to defend itself, which left more room for comfort. Castles became chateaux. Air, light, sensual pleasure and space came to replace the drab, dark fortifications. The organizing principles that since the early Middle Ages had manifested themselves visually in the hortus catalogi and the hortus contemplationis were a premonition of developments now affecting the organization of the French castles: elements set together apparently at random were contained in a geometric composition. Spatially too, the developments undergone by house and garden are closely linked. An early medieval noble house had just a large hall. Later the lord and his lady had chambers of their own, with the other members of the household, including the servants, sharing common rooms. The gardens were now construed more as an extension of the house and were divided into a number of 'green rooms' with paved paths: the kitchen garden, an orchard, a bowling green and often an ordered, regular wilderness or maze.

As a component of this larger composition the hortus catalogi continued to play a key role. The neutral geometric grid ordering the ground plane was applied in the *parterre* as a foreground from which to view the landscape. The hortus contemplationis saw its role as *organizer* of the ensemble translated into that of configuring the plan of the entire complex, while at the same time remaining virtually unchanged as a garden room within it. The contained space, enfolded by a gallery and organized by an axial cross, symbolized the world order.

The conditions for this release from the medieval enclosed garden were created by Charles VIII whose invasion of Italy at the end of the fifteenth century introduced France to Italian social and craft achievements though without abandoning feudal culture. There was an attempt made to shake off the psychological limitations of the past and find new organizing forms.

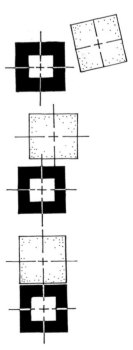

Development of the relation between garden and castle in France from the Middle Ages to the 16th century (according to Kask, 1971).

Château Amboise

These new insights Charles VIII deployed between 1483 and 1498 in Château Amboise, his solid if irregular medieval castle on the river Loire, which after his experiences in Italy he found difficult to see anything of value in.

Within the walls of the castle nestled a small castle garden on a raised terrace near the cemetery. The Italian priest and landscape gardener Da Mercogliano enlarged the terrace and enclosed the garden, which he designed to a basic geometric pattern of flower beds with fruit trees around, plus a trellis and pavilions. Later the trellis was replaced by a gallery with windows drawing into the garden a spectacular view across the Loire. Moreover, the net symmetry ceded to a simple bilateral symmetry, given shape by ten richly ornate parterres. The central point had been abandoned, but the garden kept within its limits.

Château de Bury

Unlike Amboise the castle garden at Bury was laid out at the same time as the castle was built between 1511 and 1524 also on the Loire. House and garden are conceived as a single entity, Italian style, although the complex still adheres to the idea of a medieval castle surrounded with towers, battlements and a generous moat. Compared with Amboise we can see a fundamental change here, namely that the Vitruvian theory of beauty and harmony has been applied to the garden. This ties in with the shift of attention from horticulture to architecture. The garden is made part of the overall plan for the castle. The ensemble presents a almost regular rectangle and is divided into quarters. Each intersection is marked by a round tower. A gate leads to the forecourt, itself divided into four and with a bronze copy of Michelangelo's David at the centre. The steady shift to humanism and a more anthropocentric world-view has replaced the supernatural power deriving from Christianity with an illustration of the beauty of man. The garden behind the forecourt is sunken

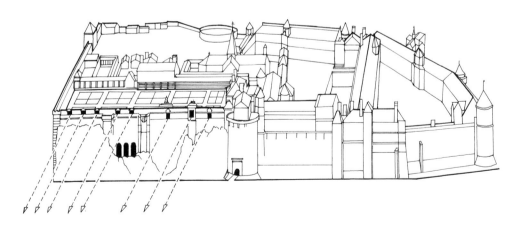

Château Amboise, Indre-et-Loire, 1498. A hortus conclusus giving a view of the Loire landscape.

Château de Bury on the Loire, 1524. A bronze statue of David in the forecourt: man takes centre stage. The axial cross organizes the entire castle ensemble.

so that it can be observed from the head of the steps. This garden consists of eight opulently patterned beds and a small chapel set at the end of the axis, against the external wall. As in Amboise, this chapel is moved away from the central point but at Bury its place is taken there by a fountain.

The hortus contemplationis and the hortus catalogi are used side by side and each have their own role to play in the ensemble. The former as the central point of the castle is now rendered as the forecourt, and the latter the intermediary between castle and landscape. Here the compactness and completeness of the hortus contemplationis seem to preside over the composition of the entire ensemble. Projected over this composition is an axis which – ignoring the division into four – introduces a new hierarchic order, causing wall, ground plane and landscape to relate.

The panorama as garden wall: the early Renaissance garden

The medieval sense of beauty, the way medieval man tried to grasp the divine order and beauty by translating them into mathematical truths and visible light, laid the foundations for Renaissance aesthetics in which geometric abstraction and proportion were welded into a new ideal of harmony.[6] But the closer one came to perfection, the more estranged one got from the mystical element and the visible came to replace the invisible as a subject for reflection.

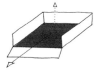

From the medieval premises of repetition, addition and orientation based on the four points of the compass there evolved a rational understanding of space. A space that assembled all forms into a single entity and, 'emancipated from the uniform medieval realm, evidently could no longer be caught in a definitive form, but – seeing that the principle of its unity had been lost – gained a countenance of many facets and many meanings.'[7] Whereas in the Middle Ages space had meaning as a place, with respect to a single object, space in the Renaissance took on the sense of distance, the relationship between objects. With the distance between objects, between here and far away, the concept of endlessness had become a fact, an imaginary

6. Reh 1993, 14.

7. Lemaire 1970, 22.

extension in which two parallel lines, past the short range of human sight, will never meet. And this is not the result of our limited optical capacities but is a quality of the universe itself: 'an immeasurable blank field on which the mind [can] describe all the perfect figures of geometry, but which [has] no inherent shape of its own.'[8] The relationship between objects, between cause and effect, between endless worlds of possibilities, literally stripped the universe of a central point.

The viewpoint shifted from the abstract heaven to the tangible earth's surface, a horizontal experience of space which unlike the vertical experience can be controlled optically, in that between the viewer and the endless distance of the horizon is the middle ground of the earth's surface, and this can be manipulated. With the developing of perspective there arose the possibility of controlling space by bringing the geometric plan into alignment with the optical space. The vantage point and the perceived proportions could be hitched together systematically so that space and objects enjoy a relationship that is independent of the position of the observer.[9]

The conquest of space also meant the conquest of the landscape as a subject for research and aesthetic appraisal. This emergence of the landscape entailed a certain estrangement between man and nature: man's bond with the landscape was no longer taken for granted. This new mode of thinking was largely the province of the nobility: enjoyment of unsullied nature in concert with an appreciation of town life. Their accommodations, the fifteenth-century Italian villas, were an expression of their appreciation and control of the landscape and forged a relationship between town and landscape. These houses were so comfortable that there was no further need to retreat to the garden. The *loggia* was an exterior room where one could sit, eat and converse, the garden an ornamental area to walk in and enjoy.

The relationship between house, garden and landscape was contained in an architectural system of formal rules. In this system the garden was an intermediary with the enclosed garden becoming a component of the ensemble. For example the hortus catalogi returned as a parterre and the hortus ludi as the sacro bosco. The landscape itself was left free of intervention but, viewed from the garden as if through a field glass, was drawn into the ensemble (integrazione scenica). The divine model made its reentry in the proportional system, in the company of such emerging humanist aspects as sensual pleasure, perspective, references to myths and natural images in the garden. Through this profanation of the garden the optical experience of space gained more and more ground as the principle underlying garden design.

8. Cornfold 1936, 219.

9. Steenbergen 1990, 24, 25.

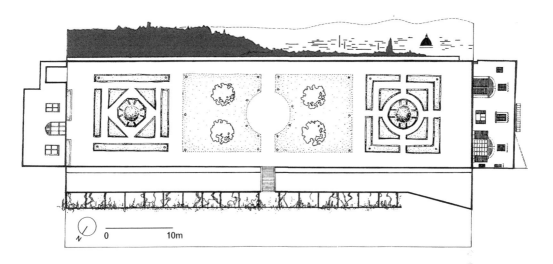

Villa Medici

The Villa Medici was built midway through the fifteenth century, as an urban enclave in the landscape with a panorama across Florence and the Arno Valley. The villa is situated on a south-facing hillside 250 metres above the river. In winter the slope protects the garden against the cold north-east wind and in summer the west wind is there to cool it. The location, which was determined by climatological, visual and representational considerations, is essentially different from that of medieval castle architecture, where agriculture and military strategy were major contributory factors.

The configuration of the garden plan can be traced back to the square with axial cross of the hortus contemplationis, which is here draped over the hillside to create two terraces. Folding away the wall of the lower terrace serves to draw the panorama into the garden as a backdrop. The gallery is tucked in, so to speak, and acts as the east-west axis, binding the two levels together and looking out across the lower terrace to the landscape. The axis running exactly from north to south formalizes the view which, owing to the angle the villa makes with the slope, is not aimed specifically at anything and includes both the wooded hills and the town. The overwhelming space of the panorama engages with the homely dimensions of the ensemble.

above: Michelozzo, Villa Medici, Fiesole, c. 1462. Exploded box plan of the southern terrace.

centre: Transformation of the type:
• The underlying principle is a square hortus contemplationis with an axial cross and a gallery.
• The surrounding buildings are concentrated on the east and west sides.
• The gallery is moved to the centre of the garden so that it coincides with one of the axes. A heavy retaining wall acts as rear wall.
• The other axis is enlisted to dramatize the hillside: a recess with a belvedere anchors the axis in the slope; the gallery (separated from the upper terrace by the retaining wall) has a stair leading from its centre to the lower terrace; and a pool with a fountain marks the central point of the garden.

below: The axial cross in action.

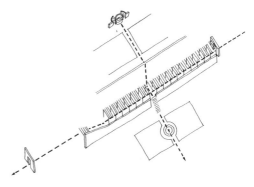

Integration

The trend had been set for inverting the enclosed garden. Now that the hortus conclusus had been well and truly opened to the landscape a development took place in two opposing directions. An inversion occurred in the garden, with alignment shifting from the central point to the horizon. At the same time, the enclosed garden was perpetuated as a component of a garden geared to the horizon. Containment and endlessness were thereby set up in opposition as distinct themes.

Giardino segreto and panorama: the Renaissance garden

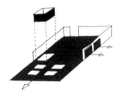

The *Renaissance garden* is dedicated to the mathematical control of space, from the *giardino segreto* to the horizon. The view across the landscape had become the hallmark of the garden, so that even the most hermetic garden space is in its thrall. In many respects, Mannerism is the antithesis of the High Renaissance. In place of harmony, clarity and repose this tendency is typified by affectation, complexity and innovation, decoration becoming more important than the logic of harmonic proportions. The Late Renaissance or *Mannerist garden* elaborates further certain themes from the Renaissance gardens, such as the route, the plan configuration and the perspective effect, yet emphasis is more on sensory perception that on the objective, rational aspect of the Renaissance garden. This has much to do with the shift from the universal to a subjective, topos-related world image.

GIARDINO SEGRETO. 'In a world from which divine and human law seem to have fled, it is only in such places as these [gardens] that the soul can recover its own poise between "licenza" and "ordine", "festa" and "ragione" [license and order, festivity and reason].' Terry Comito, 1935.

The gardens that figure so prominently in *The Decameron*, Boccaccio's celebrated Renaissance novel, are decked with a dazzling variety of scented flowers and the air is filled with music.[10] These gardens of plenty serve not merely as scenery but are part of the essential defining of human behaviour. Here the sensory aspect of the hortus ludi (Bacchus) and the order of the hortus contemplationis and hortus catalogi (Apollo) converge. In the self-assured opening towards the horizon, the medieval introversion remained present as an undercurrent: hidden worlds contained in the composition of the Renaissance garden. The enclosure of the hortus conclusus became condensed in the giardino segreto, pitted against the openness of the garden composition. The giardino segreto is as a rule closely connected

10. Boccaccio set his *Decameron* in the landscape of Fiesole and in the gardens of Naples under Angevin rule. The main protagonists, a party of young men and women who flee plague-ravaged Florence, take refuge for ten days in a country villa outside the town. The gardens provide the backcloth to the tales they tell each other, but also dictate the content and form of the stories so that these give expression to a specific place and time. The giardino segreto of the third day is not just a delectable place but one where recreation (in the sense of recuperation, re-creation of the soul) is achieved along ritual lines and consolation is afforded. In the philosophical and rhetorical milieu dominating Renaissance culture the garden played a seminal role; in the sense that places were seen in terms of specific behaviour ('the sacred potency of space'), the pleasurable, enclosed garden was the appropriate locale for poetry, philosophy and love.

with the house and at times is even situated on a terrace above the cellar level. Thus in the Villa Rotonda the giardino segreto is an open space hewn from the woods, quite hidden from view and only accessible from the cellar. The Villa Medici in Florence has besides the opened-up hortus conclusus a giardino segreto on the west side of the house, invisible from the rest of the garden. In the first instance, the giardino segreto persists as a component of the ensemble, the intention being to bring out the landscape and the ensemble's position with regard to it.[11] The giardino segreto seeks out the central axis of the ensemble so that prospect and containment are directly confronted with one another.

In 1572 a rich merchant bought the Villa Capponi near Florence and had a garden laid out there. Next to the house is a wall topped with curling stone decorations and vases and grown with an alternation of pink ragged Robin, white balsam and dahlias. The sea of flowers is kept in check by geometric parterres of boxwood. The small contained garden is a 'sala scoverta' (a room with no ceiling) of a refined if opulent design and accessed from the house along an underground passage. (This entrance is now sealed up and replaced by an entry across the lawn.) On the north side a space has been separated from it that was originally used as a study.

PANORAMA. The spatial composition of the Late Renaissance villas consists usually of a principal axis slung off which are a number of autonomous interior and exterior spaces. Placing parts separately so that they cannot be taken in from one vantage point encourages movement on the part of the observer. As a result the route takes its place in the plan's organization as a structuring element. The polarities of the hortus conclusus return in an ambiguity active on various levels. Thus, wilderness and order are made to relate by bringing the wilderness (the barco, or bosco) within the garden boundaries.

11. The adjective segreto (secret) should therefore not be taken too literally; 'how many times will you hear that before you accept that it doesn't mean a mystery, that the plot it refers to isn't hidden or hard to find? True, it is usually small, sunken, and intense, but it may lie right below the house. ... Maybe segreto really means closed. Certainly Italians have no appetite for concealment. ... you can usually see every part at once, at the point of entry. ... Italian gardens are always frank about their purposes. ... you always know where you are.' Harbison 1991, 8.

Villa Capponi, Florence. Layout of gardens begun 1572. The giardino segreto.

Villa Lante

This villa was built around 1568 in an existing walled hunting ground, a barco. Here the wall surrounding the hortus conclusus is expanded to include the entire domain, so that the polarities and component parts of the hortus conclusus remain within the walls though are scattered. The wilderness once fearfully kept beyond the walls of the hortus conclusus is now invited into the grounds where it stitches the dispersed elements together.

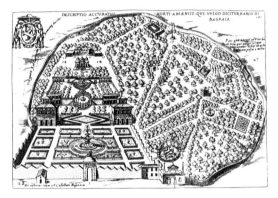

Vignola, Villa Lante, Bagnaia (begun 1568). Engraving. The walls of the hortus conclusus expand to contain the entire grounds.

An axis links this wilderness with the town of Bagnaia, confronting the town (culture) with the landscape (nature) and laying the groundwork for elaborating the various polarities. At the beginning of the axis at the top of the slope, a rill rises from a *grotto*, a dark earthy place surrounded by trees. Nature is cultivated in stages, the climax being the ordered parterre garden (a terrace of 75 metres square) at the foot of the slope. A pair of statues at the central point of the parterre form with their raised arms a circle sliced through by the sight line. By splitting the centre of the hortus contemplationis into two points – the beginning and end of the axis – time becomes an

additional dimension of the garden design. Source and reflecting pool stand for birth and death respectively.

Enclosure, endlessness and geometric order are extricated from the walls, the central point and the axial cross. The cosmogram is projected on to the parterre garden with a vertical alignment generated by the reflection of the sky in the pool. This is immediately put into perspective by the view across the barco on the west side. View and axis are set at right angles, thereby giving new meaning to the axial cross. The building is made subsidiary to the garden, being split into two *casinos* or ornamental pavilions that flank the axis and tie the lower garden to the hill. Unhitched from the hermetic cohesion of the hortus contemplationis, the axial cross is still the binding element in the composition. The sequence of water features ends here too; town and nature, villa and view are bound together.

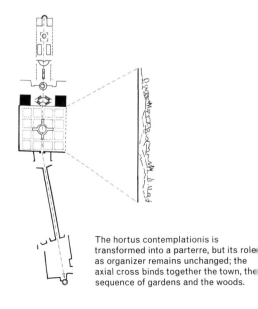

The hortus contemplationis is transformed into a parterre, but its role as organizer remains unchanged; the axial cross binds together the town, the sequence of gardens and the woods.

Villa Capponi

'Here parterre, lemon trees, bushes and pool are framed in by wall-tops so bubbling with fun that they chase away the cares of all who come.'

Shepherd and Jellicoe, 1966

In the villa, a game is played with the presence and absence of the horizon. The medieval enclosure contrasts starkly with the great expanse of the terrace as introduced in the Villa Medici.

A VILLA WITH A VIEW ACROSS FLORENCE. The villa sits on the southern slope of the Arno Valley, where olive groves cover the slope between two wooded ridges from the Pian dei Giullari to the river. The ensemble lies more or less parallel with the valley, on a promontory between the two ridges, so that the most prominent view spans the entire length of the valley, thus confronting the tiny villa with the greatest visible measure.

An avenue descends from the Pian dei Giullari towards Florence, ending opposite the Uffizi at a plaza on the Arno. It is a narrow and steep avenue hemmed in on either side by walls. The villa is discovered at the place where the road dives over the crest of the hill, with its gardens hidden behind a high wall.

In the central zone of the house is the hall and the *cortile* or courtyard, together linking street and garden; the living quarters lie on either side. This way, the entrance to the house is directly connected with the view over the estate from a balcony on the other side of the lawn. With the underground passage closed off, all gardens are accessed by stairs with a balcony at the upper end. These balconies briefly reveal the panorama before the garden walls once again hide it away.

THE SEQUENCE OF GARDENS. The central element is a lawn with a visual axis following the length of the Arno Valley. This axis begins in a garden enclosed on three sides and is framed by a gateway between garden and lawn. On the other side of the lawn are two giardini segreti that suddenly flip over the crest of the hill to

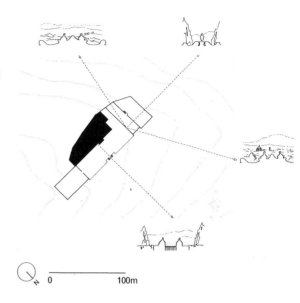

0   100m

above: The villa is built on a hilltop. The house stands along an elongated lawn which begins in the east in a giardino segreto and seems to end in the west in a precipice. An opulently decorated wall at the end of the lawn acts as foreground to the view. Only on reaching the wall does one get to see the two giardini segreti lower down the hillside and it is these that terminate the lawn. To the north of the lawn also there is a steep descent; a balcony gives one a view across the olive groves on this slope.

below: Villa Capponi on the southern slope of the Arno Valley, looking out across Florence.

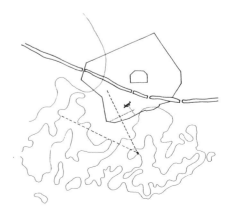

intensify the relief effect. The first garden is set five metres deeper than the lawn and the curlicues on the wall engage in a game with the panorama which is chopped into three by two clumps of trees, with the length of the valley in the centre, the wooded slope to the left and Florence to the right. At the corner of the lawn are two trees, a linden and a cypress, pivots between this lawn and the gardens on either side. The house stands to one side of the axis with the balcony on the other. From the house you can see across the lawn to the far side of the valley, from the balcony you look into the valley across the landed property.

GIARDINO SEGRETO. The axis of symmetry of this enclosed garden is at right angles to the main axis of the ensemble, ending on the north side in the study and on the south side in a window shrouded in boxwood looking out over the mountains opposite. Several metres lower is the following giardino segreto, added to the design in the nineteenth century (a third garden compartment with a swimming pool would be added later still). This garden is enfolded by hedgerows and is comprised of free-standing elements, each with hedges around it.

above: Plan configuration and geomorphology. The various segments of house and garden can be contained in a hypothetical system of rectangles. The south-eastern part of the design deviates from this system and follows the contours of the road.

below: The original route consisted of two distinct parts, the direct route from the street to the garden terminating abruptl at the head of the lawn, and a hidden route through a tunnel accessing the giardini segreti. These days the gardens are reached by stairs from the lawn. This route deviates gradually from the main axis, which is invisible from the enclosed gardens; from the second garden the house is invisible too.

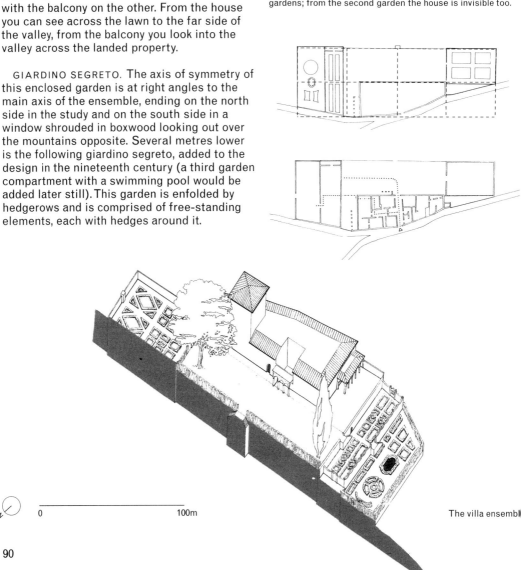

0   100m   The villa ensembl

Villa Giulia

Whereas the Renaissance garden had concentrated on developing the relationship with the horizon, the Villa Giulia, begun in 1550 resumed the vertical axis of the hortus conclusus. This was brought under control with the techniques of perspective acceleration, sequences of spaces and classical proportions that had proved their worth for the horizontal axis.

So in the villa we find a vertical as well as a horizontal axis. Both consist of telescoped spaces in which the route proceeds on either side of the axis. At the place where the two axes meet, is a balcony overlooking the length of the garden ensemble as well as the depth of the second garden. The vertical axis begins literally and figuratively in the earth, as the dark nymphaeum on the lowest level steps up to gradually engage with the vast expanse of the sky. The axis itself is left empty and is not for walking on, with the route circling round it.

The horizontal axis originates from the morphology of the landscape and consists of three spaces following the length of a north-west oriented side valley in the Tiber. The first and largest space is the forecourt whose form announces the beginning of the axis. In the last garden the panorama rises up above the walls; garden and landscape are stacked, the sense of containment being put into perspective by the external horizon.

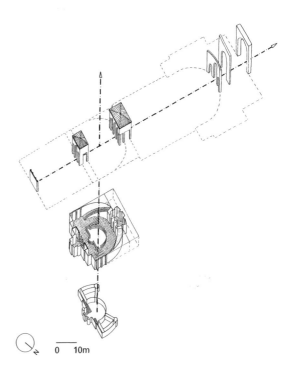

0   10m

Vasari, Michelangelo, Vignola and Ammanti, Villa Giulia, Rome (begun 1550). The horizontal and vertical axes are designed as two series of telescopically shifted spaces.

THE ENDLESS LABYRINTH. Enclosure and the materializing of endlessness, separated into the giardino segreto and the *panorama garden*, coincide once again in the labyrinth. In the widely diverse cultures of America, India and Western Europe the labyrinth has been a motif for more than twelve centuries. The *labyrinthine space* bears no relation to the motif. It represents the (pre-rational) consciousness of image-related experience, as opposed to intellectual awareness. In disregarding the laws of logic, the labyrinthine space is – for rationally-thinking man – shrouded in mystery. In it the dark, sensual and sacred are not that far apart.

It took the rational train of thought of the Renaissance to bind together the motif and spatial impact of the sacred mythical space into a maze distinct from the surrounding rational space. Only when rational space became rooted in geometric contexts and the idea of distance and interrelationships became common knowledge, was the labyrinth regarded as a separate spatial category.

Theseus and Ariadne in front of the Cretan Labyrinth. Woodcut by Pietro Sardi in *Corona Imperiale dell'Architettura militare*, 1618 (Munich, Bayerische Staatsbibliothek). The labyrinth as object in the landscape.

Villa Pisani

In a bend in the river Brenta in Northern Italy lies the Villa Pisani, with a maze in one of the wooded masses flanking the central axis. The formal space of the axis is diametrically opposed to the chaos of the haphazardly dispersed spaces, the spider's web of axes and sight lines and the monstrous sculptures populating the wood. Sandwiched between two avenues lies the maze, with a sight line through its centre. This central point is a double-height tower topped off with a sculpted female figure and accessible via two spiralling stairs around the tower. But because of the intricate network of paths bounded by hedges it is almost impossible to reach and this is its great attraction. The route is interminably long yet keeps within the bounds of the enclosed garden so that route and place, motion and stasis coincide. Climb the tower and you rise up above the maze to be rewarded with both an outlook and an insight. The view across the maze is of the central reflecting pool of the ensemble, with the confusing tangle of passages lying like a ground plan before the eyes of the successful venturer.

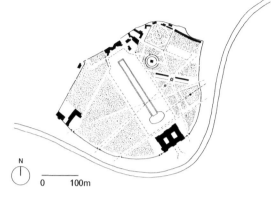

above: Frigimelica and Preta, Villa Pisani, Stra (begun 1735). Axes slicing through the woods link the maze with the central space of the villa ensemble. The irrational Bacchus garden calls into question the rationality of the Apollo garden.

centre: Plan of the maze.

left: The centripetal organization of the maze, offset by the centrifugality of the observation tower in the middle.

below: Maze and tower (etching).

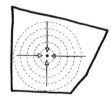

The static, hermetic space of the hortus conclusus is transformed into a materialized movement much like the frozen choreography of a dance.[12] The graphic labyrinth pattern coincides with the steps of the round dance, known to us from the Bronze Age, Cretan history, medieval liturgy and Greek tradition as it has reached us and even in our own time among the Basques. This follows a fixed pattern, a chain of dancers in whose ceaseless motion can be read the order of the cosmos. Likewise the maze is a depiction of the world and of life. It symbolizes the arduous path, the path to paradise, the path of life or indeed death, or, say, matters of the heart (love's labyrinth).

The endlessness of the panorama garden brings orientation and clarity, the enclosure of the hortus conclusus an overall view and insight. Whenever endlessness (not visible but felt) and containment are united in the maze, all they offer is disorientation and confusion.

Cabinet de verdure and vista: the Baroque garden

'Let [man] look upon that resplendent luminary set like an everlasting lamp to lighten the universe; let him remember that the earth is but a speck in comparison with the vast circuit which this star describes; and let him then consider with amazement that this circuit is itself no wider than a pinpoint beside that which is embraced by the stars that roll in the firmament. But if our sight stops here, let imagination pass beyond.'

Blaise Pascal, 1655[13]

Here Pascal is describing a new concept of space, an endless expanse where rational understanding can be ever extended with the help of mathematics and physics. Issues of logistics came to replace those of ethics and theology that occupied the thinkers of the Renaissance, and boundaries both scientific and geographic were pushed back. The world of ideas shifted from concrete to abstract, from incidental to universal.

Given the mastery of perspective and aided by treatises on gardening that describe proportions, geometry and symmetry, this spatial concept rooted in absolute values became translated into garden designs where all components are related to an absolute axis uniting garden, building and sometimes even the town in a single hierarchical order.

CABINET DE VERDURE. Hidden in seemingly solid *bosquets*, block-shaped clumps of trees, lie green passages, halls and rooms; *cabinets de verdure*, in analogy to the cabinet, a small room or closet in a house. These internal spaces of the Baroque garden are formally organized on plan, either axially or centripetally. The natural character of the wooded mass is

12. For an exhaustive explanation see Kern 198.
30-33.

13. Translation by Lovejoy 1936.

94

hidden behind the screen of hedges or trelliswork. Not just space, but time too is fixed and brought under control by trimming and shaping plants into architectural, immutable walls.

In 1661 Louis XIV, the Sun King, had his hunting lodge extended and embellished. André Le Nôtre was commissioned to design a garden that was bigger and more beautiful than any other. Basins and fountains figure uppermost in the bosquets of Versailles, which serve as permanent stage sets for the changing court spectacle. One of these was the Bosquet de l'Etoile, which owed its name to the five allées that converge in the middle. At the intersection was an opulent shell fountain, the 'Montagne d'eau'. (In the eighteenth century this fountain, like many others, was removed. This decorative side of Le Nôtre's design was not felt to fit with the noble lines of the ensemble.) The walls of the space were decorated with trelliswork grown with honeysuckle, porcelain vases full of flowers at the cornice and recesses with jets of waters. The bosquet was built up of three carapaces each with its own system of paths. Because the paths were set out of alignment there arose a labyrinthine access route which strengthened the autonomy of the cabinet de verdure. Here, behind the polished walls of the bosquet, lurks the sensuality of Bacchus.

De Montagne d'Eau (engraving by Pérelle). Central point of the Bosquet de l'Etoile.

THE VISTA GARDEN. According to the prevailing notion of those days the greatest pleasure to the eye was what one could take in at a glance (as in the hortus conclusus). At the same time the Baroque garden had to be impressively large and the mastery over the landscape clearly present. This resulted in the *vista garden*, the pinnacle in the development of the centralized perspectival axis. Here, the power the king had over France and the world is reflected in the absolute control over the landscape. In drawing the horizon into the garden, infinity is drawn in too. The vista garden has the dimensions of the landscape without denigrating the garden's architectural means. The garden is still the enclosed space from which the cultivated and natural landscapes were excluded.

The walls of the large spaces in the Baroque garden are shaped by the bosquets, with the cabinets de verdure hidden within them. Now the roles are reversed, from a striving after endlessness in the containment of the hortus conclusus to the creating of enclosed places in the 'endlessness' of the vista garden. The cabinets are exchangeable infills for the bosquets, depending on the place in the composition. A wedge had been driven between view and enclosure and it would be a long time before the two were back in confrontation.

Versailles

In this supremely grand spectacle, the castle is the central point of a cruciform plan. The urban horizon is brought in by way of the *patte d'oie* or goose-foot, the landscape's horizon by means of the garden's axis. The principal aspect is no longer the central point of the garden but the palace balcony. From this point one can take in the longitudinal axis ending as it does at the horizon. It is as if a field glass were bringing the horizon to the position of the observer. The enormous length of the Grand Canal (1500 metres) takes up the foreshortening caused by the great distance from the beginning of the canal to the castle (900 metres). The reflecting water remains in view as a shimmering surface between the avenues of trees of the Allée Royale. To emphasize this lighting effect still more, a semicircular slope has been added behind the canal to catch the light. Beyond that point the axis continues as a kilometres-long avenue to the horizon. The Grand Canal reflects the cosmic space and the axis as a whole suggests the path of the sun (as an allegory of the supremacy of the Sun King, in whose kingdom the sun never sets).

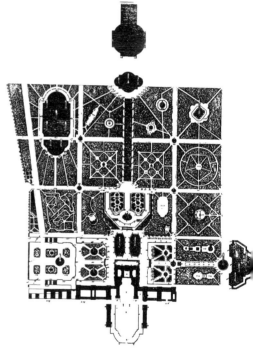

above: Louis XIV, Le Nôtre and Lebrun, Versailles, Yvelines (begun 1661). Drawing after Demortain, 1714. The Bosquet de l'Etoile (the pentagon within a circle) is one bosquet among many.

left: Transverse axis of Versailles (painting by G.B. Martin). At front, the Bassin de Neptune, at centre left the château. The cabinets de verdure are designed distinct from the axis.

Roman, Honselaersdijk country seat, The Hague, 1621 (engraving by Allard). Landscape 'rooms' contained by heavy trees and drainage ditches fit naturally into the grid of the Dutch agricultural landscape.

Here the axis mundi of the hortus conclusus that brings the earth and the sky into a vertical relationship, is transformed into an axis to the horizon. The line of the horizon forges the relationship between earth and sky, the axis at right angles to it is the link with the garden. The garden thus no longer represents the earth as linked to the sky, but rather orchestrates the encounter between earth and sky, which takes place elsewhere.

Whereas in the French formal tradition the axial system is aligned with the endless horizon, as well as enclosed spaces being created in the bosquets without this being visible in the plan as a whole, in the Dutch formal tradition that very containment is the primary component. There the system of axes is deployed to give shape to the enclosure, the view being of secondary importance. Because the land is predominantly flat, rhythm and variation in the axis have to be shaped in other ways. This is done using a sequence of landscape 'rooms'. Unlike the French example the Dutch parterres are surrounded by hefty allées of linden, oak or chestnut. This corresponds to the avenues framing the fields and meadows round the garden. The garden not so much organizes the surrounding landscape as forms part of the existing pattern of fields, like an architectural version of the Dutch landscape of rooms.[14]

14. In the sixteenth, seventeenth and eighteenth centuries the elite made their way from the city to the country. This was a quest for peace and quiet, relaxation and entertainment, but more than anything it was a status symbol. Just outside the towns, constellations sprang up of small leisure-oriented country seats with avenues and paths and dotted with taverns, pitches for games and menageries. Lining Dutch rivers like the Amstel and the Vecht like well-stuffed cabinets were richly decorated garden 'rooms' of *arbours*, pollarded trees, rare plants and birds, covered walks and sculptures.

15. The eighteenth-century poet Alexander Pope was one of the foremost theorists on the Romantic body of thought in England. In *An Epistle to Lord Burlington* he urges English gardeners to discover the underlying perfection of nature, 'the genius of the place'.

Kitchen garden and unlimited space: the landscape garden

'Consult the Genius of the Place in all:
That tells the Waters or to rise, or fall,
Or helps th'ambitious Hill the heav'n to scale,
Or scoops in circling theatres the Vale,
Calls in the Country, catches opening glades,
Joins willing woods, and varies shades from shades'

Alexander Pope, 1731[15]

In eighteenth-century England the world was no longer seen as a fathomable, ever constant entity and man no longer as an absolute power able to subjugate nature. Nature was now understood to be an independent, orderly system availed of intrinsic value and subject to the laws of a 'higher intelligence'.

Enlightened man was a creator and inventor who researched rationally and objectively the system of nature of which he himself was part. At the same time there emerged a romantic notion of nature as a living entity, as a source of all good. Quite the opposite, then, of nature in the foregoing period, described by Kant as a lifeless thing, a assemblage of phenomena that gains its coherence from the rules that reason ascribes to it. These two streams, Enlightenment and Romanticism, are seminal to eighteenth-century philosophy.

In the world of art, the open form of the fragment was set against the closed unity of the classical artwork. Analogue of this, the philosopher Edmund Burke made a distinction between two fundamentally different sensations, the Beautiful and the Sublime. While the Beautiful is linked to the bounded form, the Sublime is related to the formless, the boundless. Enlightenment and Romanticism, Beautiful and Sublime – these then are the bearers of the landscape garden.[16]

The 'genius of the place' or *genius loci*, the landscape as a source of inspiration for the garden, was the inducement to abandon the limits of the garden entirely and regard house, garden, and natural and cultivated landscapes as a single entity.

THE KITCHEN GARDEN. The aspect of seclusion remained present even in the wide expanse of the landscape garden. 'The love of seclusion and safety is not less natural to man than that of liberty.'[17] Within the garden the spaces were separated with an enclosure of their own. By far the most landscape gardens were laid out round an existing house and draped over the original garden sparing little of the old, generally Baroque layout. However the kitchen garden, which dates from before the Baroque, was usually retained for practical reasons. Besides being used for growing vegetables, this 'walled garden' was a social space that contrasted with the open character of the landscape garden. Walled and formally organized, the kitchen garden is an autonomous object within the artificial landscape of the garden, like the medieval hortus ludi which could be placed freely in the natural landscape.

On the east side of Rousham House is a sequence of walled gardens from which the landscape is excluded and a private world created with fruit trees, flowers, herbs and vegetables. A hidden gate opens on to the flower garden with its rectangular beds. A second garden with fruit trees, parterres and a lawn has a pigeon house marking its centre, and the largest garden consists of vegetable beds and a lawn, organized by an axial cross. A formal gateway links this garden in turn to the Bowling Green.

above: Sir William Amcotts Ingilby, Ripley Castle, Yorkshire, 19th century. The kitchen garden lies hidden in a plantation intersected by a star-shaped patterns of avenues. Within its walls are long rows of leeks, artichokes, carrots and cabbages, while carefully pruned trained fruit profits from the warmth of the walls. Functionality and beauty intertwined.

below: William Kent, Rousham House, Oxfordshire, 1738. The walled flower garden.

THE LANDSCAPE GARDEN. Not only is the surrounding landscape embraced by the garden, the nature inside its

16. Reh's terms for this is pictorial garden, which he defines as an composition in which the morphology of the natural landscape has taken over the integrating function of the architectural design matrix, determining the place of architectural objects in the space, and movement through it. (Reh 1996)

17. Loudon 1840 (1969), 107.

boundaries is simulated too. Just as in the hortus ludi the elements are placed together freely so as to create a spatial form that looked natural. The idea of an absolute truth such as was represented at Versailles by having the monarch's balcony as the centre of the composition, has ceded to that of a subjective truth, represented by the route as organizing element. Space is brought to the level of individual experience, with the panorama opening up a full 360 degrees. The formal axis as a fairly literal 'pointer' to the horizon is relegated to the imagination, being retained merely in the dynamic balance of the pictorial composition. The static hortus contemplationis based on the confluence of space and time now has a counterpart in the dynamic landscape garden, to be observed from a moving viewpoint.

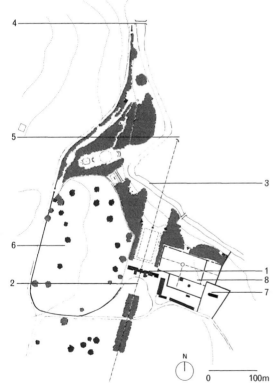

Rousham House stands on an axis of symmetry that is at the same time a dividing line in the garden. To the west of it the garden is landscaped with woods and meadowland, to the east it is an enclosed garden ensemble. 1. Rousham House / 2. Forecourt / 3. River Cherwell / 4. Heyford Bridge / 5. Eye Catcher / 6. Warren / 7. Church / 8. Walled garden

Rousham

In the eighteenth century William Kent (1685-1748) designed on the east side of Rousham House a number of garden spaces systematically premised on a view towards the valley of Cherwell across the river. The garden components are stitched together by the *perimeter walk*, a route taking in the garden boundaries that includes seats and viewing points. Various architectural objects outside the garden (Heyford Bridge over the Cherwell river, the Gothic Mill in the valley, the Eye-Catcher (a building in silhouette only) across the valley and Cow Tower on the edge of the Warren) make this panorama of 'borrowed scenery' part of the garden.

The perimeter walk has many alternative routes, but they all ultimately emerge at the three walled gardens there before Kent restructured the site, wedged between the house and the church and screened from the garden ensemble by thick woods. There are no broad paths hacked through these woods, such as in the wooded garden in the western part, so that the Pyramid House and the Classic Seat only loom into view at close quarters. This labyrinthine compaction serves to announce the walled gardens which contrast with the wide garden landscape on the west side.

Lancelot 'Capability' Brown (1716-1783) is the garden designer who most clearly illustrates ideas on integrating the garden and the landscape in the couple of hundred designs with which he enriched English eighteenth-century landscape gardening. Brown's park landscapes can be read as 'tableaux in which the beauty of the natural landscape, stripped of all "disruptive side issues", was displayed.'[18] Beauty is the sensation of reassurance and satisfaction, and is expressed in smoothness, gradual variation and refinement. These aspects accord well with the physical experience of speed and movement, the serenity and flow of line articulated by Brown's landscapes. Just as in the hortus conclusus, all unwanted elements are rejected (whole villages are moved, clumps of trees set before chimneys) generating an illusory context. The parks are built up of a foreground (a field of grass), a middle ground (most often water) and a background (the invariably wooded horizon). In Brown's classic spatial tableaux all details, references to the human dimension, visible boundaries and symbolic references are absent. In other words, every reference to the enclosed garden had been eradicated. The division between garden and landscape is engineered by the *ha-ha*, a sunk ditch. This extinguishing of the visual boundary signified the coup de grâce for the garden. Here natural and cultivated landscapes blend together in a *panoramic composition*, an open, unbounded spatial composition that in the mind's eye continues beyond the horizon.

18. Reh 1996, 47.

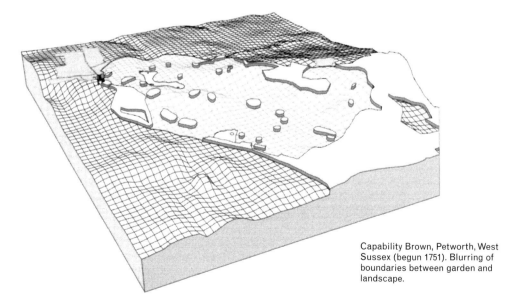

Capability Brown, Petworth, West Sussex (begun 1751). Blurring of boundaries between garden and landscape.

Petworth

Brown achieved the unprecedented sense of space evoked in the landscape park of Petworth by reducing the design to two lakes, encircled by grassy hillocks, clumps of trees and a lone folly. There are no fixed routes, movement is a matter of wandering at will. The landscape reaches up to the building so that cattle and deer can get as close as the window. Every reference to culture is erased and replaced by an unbounded artificial nature-landscape.

Hawkstone

Rising high above the rolling landscape of Shropshire are the tablelands of Hawkstone Park. The garden, the outcome of a clutch of interventions from 1699 to the mid nineteenth century, consists of little more than local additions to the landscape tied together by a route along an abyss, caves, steep precipices and viewing points.

'He that mounts the precipices at Hawkstone wonders how he came hither, and doubts how he shall return. His walk is an adventure, and his departure an escape. He has not the tranquillity, but the horror of solitude, a kind of turbulent pleasure between fright and admiration' (Dr. Johnson after a visit to Hawkstone, 1774).

Not the limited world of the garden but the landscape in all its facets has become a pleasure ground. By linking the garden to woods and through roads it has gained the dimensions and the spaciousness of landscape.

right: Sir Rowland Hill and Sir Richard Hill, Hawkstone Park, Shropshire, 1780-1795. The Cleft (illustration in *The Rodenhurst Guide to Hawkstone*, 1784, 2nd edition). Dramatizing the Sublime.

below: J.M.W. Turner, *Petworth Park, Tillington Church in the Distance*, c. 1830. Harmony of the Beautiful.

Dissolution

The twin strands of the garden's development would stay interwoven until well into the nineteenth century. The horizon-oriented garden and the enclosed garden were a complementary pair. But then the balance was lost. The horizon-garden evolved until garden and horizon coincided in a spatial abstraction. The enclosed garden was reduced to a category of function.

The Modern Movement and the demise of the enclosed garden

The colonizing of the world that had begun in the Renaissance is now complete. The democracy in the West is, at least in theory, a fact and the earth is at everyone's door. Space is limitless, stretching out to all sides, up to and even beyond the horizon. The image with which it all began, Petrarch on Mont Ventoux, has become reality. The new collective landscape needs stripping of enclosures that stand in the way of a harmonious coexistence with nature and encourage egotism and alienation. Has modernism succeeded in extinguishing the border between man and nature?

Karl Friedrich Schinkel, Observation Point, c. 1835. The image that began it a Petrarch on Mont Ventoux, is formalized in the design. It heralds the concept of space later wielded by the Modern Movement.

The relation of universal man to universal landscape is expressed in hovering, objective architecture, such as Le Corbusier's proposal for the Ville Radieuse or his buildings free-standing in the landscape. Landscape and space are no longer conceived in terms of differences but of absolute values. The landscape is a continuous, amorphous space, no more than 'a plane on which to project the object (the house), one that imposes no specific limitations on the order of space and architecture.'[19] It is, besides, a moral arena which while needing to be used socially, must be left unmanipulated. Nature is sacred and tampering with it is sacrilege and certainly improving on it is beyond us. 'Nature is beautiful', even though nature is no more than an abstraction.

Times were when the house and the landscape were spatial categories that could be compared and could therefore enter into a relationship. The landscape essentially is no different to the built environment, there is a 'between world' where the artificial and the natural meet. The garden plays a role in anchoring the house in the landscape, and represents this meeting. In the functional train of thought of the moderns the house is a machine and the landscape an image, a grand composition of sun, green, horizon and mountains. 'Modernism has been remarkably disinterested in collective space, valuing the landscape only as either picturesque pieces of the wilderness isolated within a monument, or, as in Le Corbusier's city of the future, a vast, untampered-with wilderness saved

19. Reh 1993, 52.

20. Schwartz 1992, 38.

through the heroics of high-rise living.'[20] The 'correct' landscape of romantic, unmanipulated nature and the manmade landscape are two different worlds that never meet. There can no longer be a relationship between two categories as different as these and with that the whole idea of a 'garden' evaporates.

In its most extreme form the functional garden is fully integrated in the 'machine à habiter', as the roof garden. Le Corbusier lifted his buildings high so that nature could continue undisturbed and unspoilt beneath them. Undemocratic individual activities can than be enacted in the roof garden, away from the gaze of passers-by. Because the ground plane is for everyone, the garden programme is unhitched from it and raised up to the roof garden or the balcony. Not so the reference to nature: 'real nature' stays where it is at ground level. Sunbathing, barbecuing, playing, conversing and the spatial game played between finite and infinite are brought into the building.

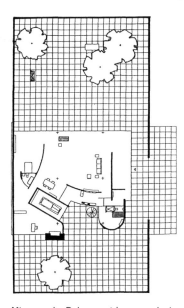

Mies van der Rohe, court-house project, 1934. The car is at the centre of the walled house. In the universal world of the moderns contemporary man is a cosmopolitan, the car his symbol. The car is the secure, mobile interior world (unbound space like the hortus conclusus) that brings the landscape into view.

Villa Savoye

The villa is a box held aloft, an autonomous object with a minimal encroachment on the landscape. In this respect we can compare it to the eighteenth-century landscape garden, Petworth for example, where the house stands baldly in the landscape and the deer come as far as the garden gate. In the Villa Savoye, designed by Le Corbusier in 1928, the house is as free-standing but the landscape is undesigned. Within the building's static framework, the polarities of open – closed, inside – outside, introvert – extravert, geometrical form – free form and the route provide the dynamics.

The relationship between house and landscape is immediate, without the intercession of a garden. There is a garden, to be sure, but on the roof, distinct from the rest of the building and far from the surrounding landscape. A *fenêtre en longueur* spanning all four facades links the internal space with the landscape, with the first-floor terrace acting as intermediary between the building and the landscape on equal footing with the remainder of the internal spaces. The roof garden is concealed behind a windshield anchored to the staircase, outwardly solid and assertively protective and inwardly tenuous and contained. A window punched in the shield terminates the 'promenade architecturale' by framing the view. The free form of the shield unhitches the roof garden from the building. Plant trays are the only references to nature, with the building as go-between in the visual relationship with the landscape. The roofscape provides a foreground for the panorama (in an earlier drawing by Le Corbusier pointed up with a balcony).

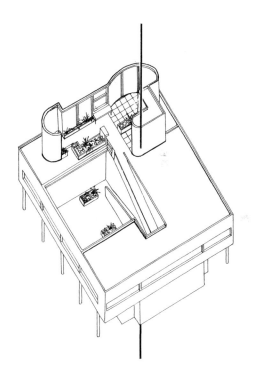

0   1m

The villa is composed round a vertical
axis: the stair, with the screen round the
roof garden attached to it like a pennant
to a flagpole. The terrace is incorporated
in the house.

Villa Noailles

Discovered in a bay in the South of France is a villa resembling a ship stranded on the slope. It is a stacking of rooms and gardens, terminating in a salon on whose roof is a walled lawn with orange trees and cypress. Four windows in the south wall of this garden give a view of the bay. Through two windows in the east wall you look down on the ship's 'prow', a triangular enclosed garden, wedged between the road and the steeply raked hill.

In 1927 Gabriel Guevrekian, ignoring the naturalistic tendencies of his contemporaries, designed this garden for the Villa Noailles as a visual feast: a tableaux-jardin. A chessboard pattern of tulips and mauve tiles are framed by a path of staggered planes in red, grey, yellow and blue. A reversal of the relief generates a grotesque perspective distortion. The garden ascends in terraces to the apex of the triangle so that, looking through the upper lights, you are confronted head-on with the garden plane. From the salon below, the garden presents an exaggerated centralized perspective with at the vanishing point a mechanically rotating sculpture. The dynamics of this accelerated perspective and the static chessboard pattern of the ground plane are two seemingly irreconcilable design layers that together exert an unexpected tensionality.

The stern geometry and the shrieking colours set the garden off as much from the villa as from the landscape. All attention is focused in almost complete isolation on the artificial element. Not that the landscape is shut out as a result: a third of the wall at the extremity is lowered so that the image of the tableaux-jardin and the landscape are brought into juxtaposition. The garden reflects the control of the mind over nature, a stylized ideal conception of nature pitted against nature as it really is.

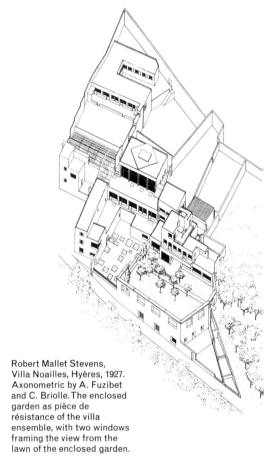

Robert Mallet Stevens, Villa Noailles, Hyères, 1927. Axonometric by A. Fuzibet and C. Briolle. The enclosed garden as pièce de résistance of the villa ensemble, with two windows framing the view from the lawn of the enclosed garden.

left: The enclosed garden, seen from the lawn as a tableaux-jardin. right: The same garden seen from the other side. A comparison between the two photos reveals the extreme manipulation of perspective.

LANDSCAPE ARCHITECTURE INTERNATIONAL STYLE AND THE GARDEN. If the idiom of the Modern Movement architects abandoned the garden, the tradition was kept alive in certain elements of landscape architecture.[21] For example, in the years before World War II and during the post-war period of reconstruction, the Dutch landscape architect Bijhouwer reinterpreted the Dutch landscape in gardens with 'a restricted number of large garden rooms of explicit form that constitute outdoor living quarters, articulated according to function.'[22]

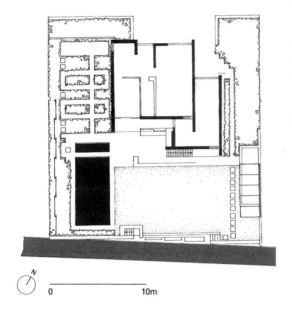

0   10m

Wim Boer and Cees de Bruin, house and garden of Professor W.C.J. Boer, Berkel en Rodenrijs, between 1961 and 1971. The garden as spatial ensemble. Timber screens, pergolas, thickets and low stone walls create a variety of garden spaces. An extension to the house, which was originally an almost square box, has generated an interweaving of house and garden, in that the projecting walls have the same spatial impact as the elements separating the gardens.

21. Whereas architecture is constantly launching new themes, landscape architecture refashions its traditions and brings them up to date, not being an autonomous discipline like architecture but dependent on its basis, the landscape itself.

22. Bijhouwer 1938, 213.

Urban transformations

'It is as if we had once again become aware that the open and communal urban space, after being swamped by monofunctional systems, is an essential component of urbanity (the void in proportion to the fullness of buildings), and that the urban condition can only develop and attain expression in this space (the urban scene). It is as though urban growth and the subsequent loss of contact with the rural landscape around impels the city to seek its own opposition within itself. This tendency, which is becoming more and more sharply pronounced these days, adds to our appreciation of urban public space as an open, free space and as a landscape.'

Sébastien Marot 1996

Garden and city

As we have seen, after the Middle Ages the garden in the
landscape, the enclosed garden of monasteries and castles,
opened up ever farther to the horizon to finally fully dissolve in
that landscape. But besides that, it was brought from the
landscape into the city where it transformed into an urban space,
taking the landscape with it. Thus the paradise gardens of the
desert became translated into the courtyards in Islamic cities
where they offer protection against the heat, the dust and the
noise of the city. The changeover from dark, winding alleys to the
openness, light and tranquillity of the garden is utterly
unexpected; the garden makes spatial reference more to the
landscape than to the city of which it is part. This landscape
reference would remain essential to the garden. An eloquent
example of this is the palace gardens of the Alhambra, a fortified
city with narrow streets once peopled with workers and soldiers.
In the palaces, the chaos of the Alhambra is excluded and the
mountain landscape beyond the walls brought into view. The
enclosed garden reveals the landscape as if through a field glass.

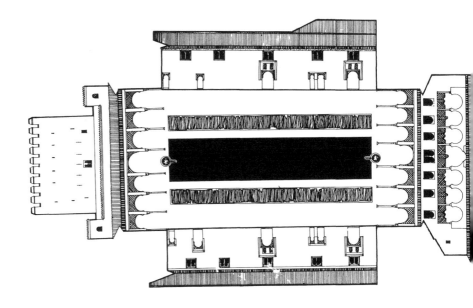

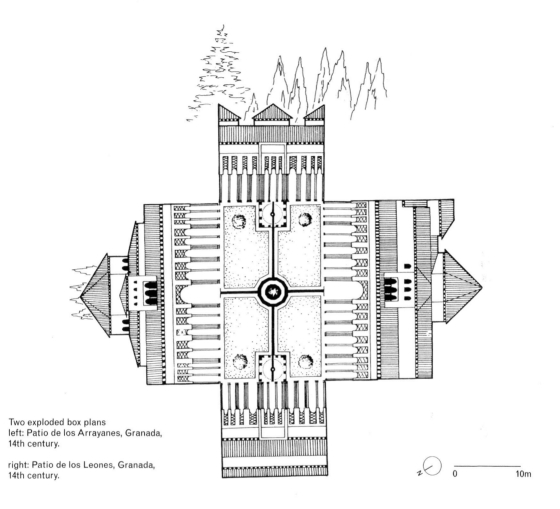

Two exploded box plans
left: Patio de los Arrayanes, Granada, 14th century.

right: Patio de los Leones, Granada, 14th century.

0   10m

Patio de los Arrayanes and Patio de los Leones

In the Alhambra, Islamic and classical traditions rub shoulders. Its core, the ensemble of palaces, is built around two courtyards or patios. The many fortifications, the gateways, the labyrinthine route and the solidity of walls contrast with the refinement and openness of the patios. These constitute the principal foci in the fort's spatial organization and its visual domination of the landscape.

THE LABYRINTHINE ALHAMBRA. Opposite the Generalife tucked into the hillside rises the Alhambra, a self-sufficient bastion at the tip of the Sabikah hill. From the thirteenth century on, the kings of the Nasrid, the Islamic rulers, transformed the fort which had stood here since the ninth century. From this fortress they ruled the town of Granada and the sultanate of that name. Set on an oval plateau with escarpments, the Alhambra was unassailable for centuries until the Christian conquest at the end of the fifteenth century. Granada lies in a semicircle at

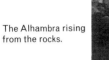

The Alhambra rising from the rocks.

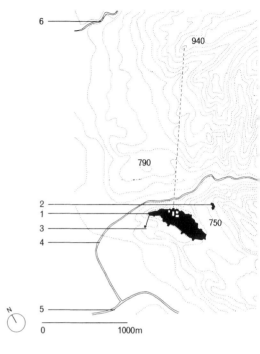

the foot of the hill, with the snow-capped peaks of the Sierra Nevada towering above the hilltop from the other side. Flowing in a deep gully at the bottom of the northern flank of the Sabikah is the river Darro, with the fertile plains of the river Genil on the south side.

On either side of the palaces are the Alcazaba and the citadel, together with houses for every social class, offices, mosques, workplaces, garrisons, baths, gardens and the royal burial chamber. The three parts are linked by two axes, the Calle Real and the Calle Real Baja, and are contained within the fortress walls with their twenty-three turrets. When the Catholic kings conquered the Alhambra, they spared the magnificent palaces. Even the over-proportioned Palacio Carlos V added in the sixteenth century was intended only as an imperial entrance to the palaces.

The Alhambra is so sited as to function as a link between plains and heights, town and landscape. Its red walls rising from the rocks are visible from a great distance. These days the bare red rock is covered with a dense wood that hampers what was once a supremely strategic view from the fortress. The Alhambra dominates the city from its position on the hilltop. At the foot of the hill, by contrast, it is all but swamped by the visually overpowering presence of the Sierra Nevada.

On both sides of the Alhambra there is a route running from Granada through the valley, past the Alhambra and then curving towards the entrance. The route presents a visible sequence: city – woods – grounds – palaces, with gateways marking the transitions between components. This indirect approach is allied to the movements inside the palaces. The routes through the valley are a scenographic succession of places and images separated by dense woods.

above: In the total ensemble of 720 by 220 metres the palaces take up a modest percentage of the surface area. Set against the outer wall, they gaze over the landscape. The two major palaces, the Palacio de Comares and the Palacio de los Leones, constitute the link between Alhambra and landscape. The Palacio de Comares punctures the outer wall and looks directly across to the farthest hilltop. The Palacio de los Leones, set more centrally in the ensemble, is rotated in deviation to the overall ensemble. 1. Alhambra / 2. Generalife 3. Torre Bermejas / 4. R. Darro / 5. R. Genil / 6. R. Beiro

above right: Plan configuration and geomorphology. The Alhambra occupies the tip of the Sabikah, the middle of the three spurs fanning out towards the plain. The surrounding wall stresses the natural escarpment of the plateau. The fan-shaped composition echoes the S-bend in the hill.

centre right: Plan of the ensemble.
Differences in height divide the plateau into three: the Alcazaba, the Nasrid Palaces and the Citadel, linked by a street, the Calle Real. This tripartition reflects the functional zoning of the city: workers' houses, palaces and fortification all have their own place, so that the king is protected on both sides and is also able to survey his soldiers and workers. 1. Alcazaba / 2. Nasrid Palaces / 3. Citadel

below right: The Alhambra is linked to Granada by a system walls, gates and routes. The two routes follow the valleys on either side of the hill, thereby making legible the geomorphology. The most important route from the Plaza Nuevo exhibits a scenegraphic succession of images. The numbers 1 to 12 refer to the illustrations on page 114.
A. Granada / B. Plaza Nuevo

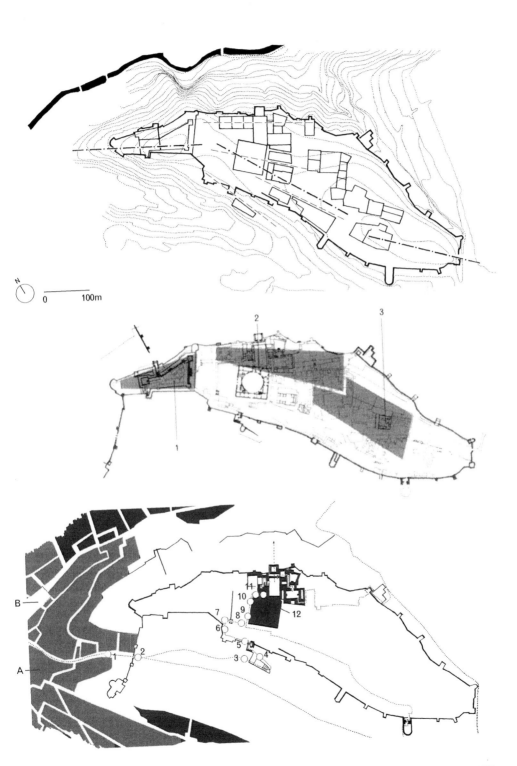

0   100m

Patio and landscape are visually linked in the Torre de Comares.

Succession of images: 1. Puerta de las Granadas / 2. Fork in the road / 3. Square with fountain announcing the Alhambra / 4. Puerta de la Justicia / 5. Narrow path to the Alcazaba / 6. Square between Alcazaba and the palaces / 7. Puerta del Vino, entrance to the palaces / 8. Palacio Carlos V / 9. Square fronting the Palacio Carlos V / 10. Ruins of the Palacio de Machuca, the original entrance palace / 11. Square fronting the Palacio de Comares / 12. Entrance to the Patio del Mexuar, the (current) entrance to the complex of palaces

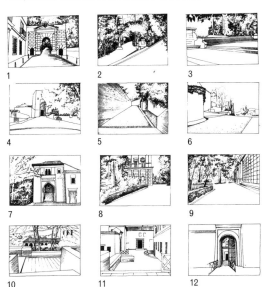

PALACIO DE COMARES. This palace continue the labyrinthine structure of the Alhambra. It consists of three parts, each organized round a patio configured about a central axis. The heart of the palace is the Patio de los Arrayanes (Court of the Myrtles), surrounded by a perimeter of spaces that is interrupted on the south side by the Palacio Carlos V. The central axis is terminated by a tower, the Torre de Comares.

The Patio de los Arrayanes is wedged between the Torre de Comares and the Palacio Carlos V, the other palaces being hidden from view by the side walls. Over the main axis there unfolds a sequence of spaces, from a large enclosed space (the patio) to a small space oriented to the prospect, the mirador in the Torr de Comares. This sequence occurs regularly in the Alhambra palaces. The patio can be viewed in its entirety from the gallery fronting the Palacio Carlos V. But the fullest visual comman of the surrounding space is to be had from the Torre de Comares, from whose roof and the recess at the end of the axis one can see both the patio and the landscape. The patio axis is aimed at the farthest hilltop so that the widest possible prospect is to be had from there.

To reach the patios means penetrating many layers. The routes are often indirect, such as the staggered junctions that pierce the walls lengthwise to reveal their extreme thickness. The entrances to the patio cannot be seen from the patio itself. This confirms the latter's autonomy and that of the route which does service in it as an ambulatory. The transition to the patio marks a turning point in the route. Disorientation, containment and uninterrupted movement here cede to openness, completeness and stasis.

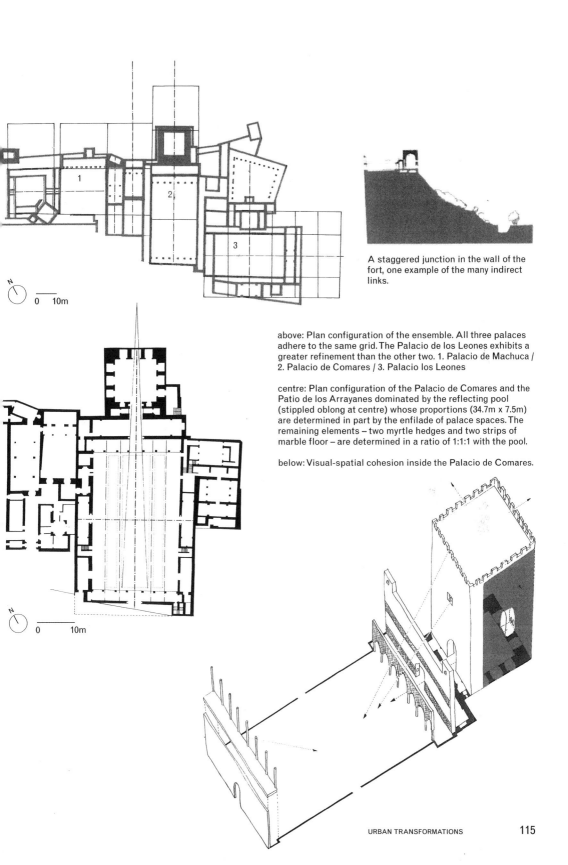

A staggered junction in the wall of the fort, one example of the many indirect links.

above: Plan configuration of the ensemble. All three palaces adhere to the same grid. The Palacio de los Leones exhibits a greater refinement than the other two. 1. Palacio de Machuca / 2. Palacio de Comares / 3. Palacio los Leones

centre: Plan configuration of the Palacio de Comares and the Patio de los Arrayanes dominated by the reflecting pool (stippled oblong at centre) whose proportions (34.7m x 7.5m) are determined in part by the enfilade of palace spaces. The remaining elements – two myrtle hedges and two strips of marble floor – are determined in a ratio of 1:1:1 with the pool.

below: Visual-spatial cohesion inside the Palacio de Comares.

PATIO DE LOS ARRAYANES. In this, the largest space of the palace complex, some components attain more than human proportions. The galleries, for example, are 7.4 metres tall with 5.2 metre high arcades and walls ninety centimetres thick. Elements like windows, doors and planting are sufficient to forge a relationship with the human scale. The patio is parallel to an axis of symmetry zoned in two marble strips, two broad hedges and an oblong pool. At the head end are galleries with six columns, placed there independently of this zoning. The pool acts as the axis in the axial composition and as the centre of the centralized composition. Because of the fan-shaped configuration of the ensemble, the Palacio Carlos V and the Patio de los Arrayanes meet at an angle. This angle of rotation is taken up by the gallery.

Here, sky and horizon are polarized. The great expanse captured in the reflecting pool is in opposition to the true distance of the horizon. The alignment with the horizon is rendered not only in the lengthwise direction of the plan, but also in the difference between the massive side

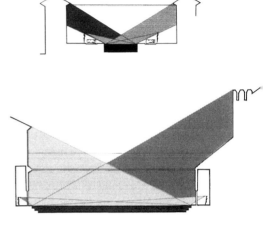

Perspective control of space. The reflection of the heads in the water dictates the length of the pool, the height of the heads and the position of the galleries. The width of the pool, the height of the side walls and the position of the hedges are attuned to one another.

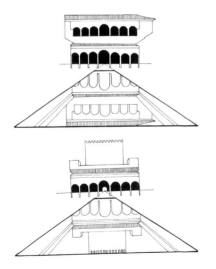

Mirroring of the heads. The transparency of the galleries makes visible the enfilade of spaces on the north side, something that the south side lacks but is suggested by the stacking of two arcades.

walls and the articulated galleries. Against this is set the binding role of the continuous eaves and the mirrored galleries. Seen from the galleries, the buildings as a whole are reflected in the pool where they register the dimensions of the garden, thereby bringing the perspective of the space under control.

Abstraction and tangibility enter into an exchange on every scale. The heavily decorated internal spaces are confronted with the emptiness of the patio. The vertical tower, the transparent gallery, the flat walls and the simplicity of the ground plane contrast with the horizontal walls, the solidity of the tower, the rich texture of the gallery and the myrtle hedge of the garden. Even the wall decorations have a layered structure of a geometric and an organic pattern. A series of polarities are elaborated: refinement and abstraction, central point and view, unadorned low side walls and layered heads. This together with a strong chiaroscuro effect imparts enormous variety to the image.

This variety interacts with the unity of the symmetrical plan configuration, the continuous walls and the large reflecting surfaces. Lengthwise the pool points almost literally to the horizon, and is at the same time a channel, symbol of mastery of the landscape.

Water, marble and myrtle are articulations of the organic and mineral aspects of nature. The abstraction and clipped evergreens evoke an artificial sense of timelessness that brings out the natural rhythms. There is a duality in gallery and garden that accords with the programmatic duality of social space and emblem.

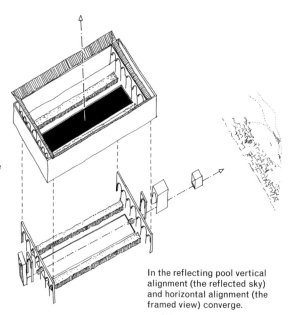

In the reflecting pool vertical alignment (the reflected sky) and horizontal alignment (the framed view) converge.

PALACIO DE LOS LEONES. If the Palacio de Comares makes connections, the Palacio de los Leones (Palace of the Lions) extricates itself from the others by being organized round a central point, and moreover rotated ninety degrees away from the principal direction. An axial cross of channels organizes the palace which consists of the patio and four main spaces, encircled by a shield of smaller spaces. The Patio de Lindaraja and the Rauda (the royal burial chamber) link the Patio de los Leones with the surrounding palaces, a relationship expressed by their errant plan configuration.

As the palace is right in the middle of the complex the confrontation with the view is less direct. The mirador as observation point is dissected into the Mirador de Lindaraja and the Torre del Pleinador, and the lower-lying Patio de Lindaraja enlisted as intermediary. From the uppermost room of the mirador you can see the Patio de los Leones, the Patio de Lindaraja and the landscape beyond. The room below gives a view of only the Patio de Lindaraja, as a moment of repose after the complexity and intensity of the Patio de los Leones. The labyrinthine structure of the complex continues on into the enclosed garden. Diaphanous walls and an enfilade of spaces suggest a horizontal expansiveness underlined by horizontal planes and lines such as edges, plinths and elaborately ornamented ceilings. Subtle differences in the floor levels add an element of diversity to the open and continuous space. On the longitudinal axis, the main space is tucked into the patio as a pavilion. This reversal of the customary

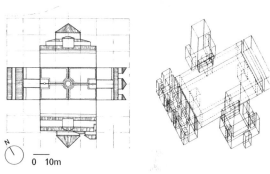

0   10m

left: The proportions of the plan and the walls adhese to square grid.

right: Spatial transparency.

below: Patio de los Leones. 19th-century etching.

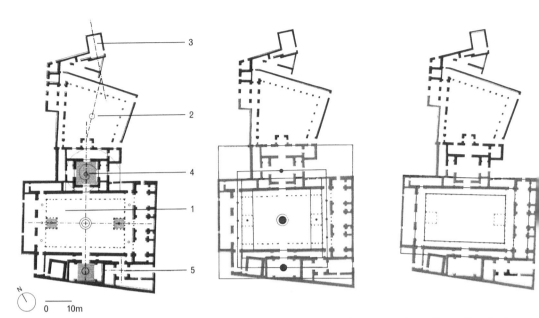

3
2
4
1
5

N

0   10m

left: In the Palacio de los Leones the static notion of the axial cross is subjected to a series of dynamic transformations.
1. Patio de los Leones / 2. Patio de Lindaraja / 3. Mirador de Lindaraja / 4. Torre del Pleinador / 5. Rauda

centre and right: The dimensions of the spaces are determined by superimposing squares and (right) rectangles on to the scheme.

below: Interior and exterior worlds.

sequence of spaces – from the patio via the gallery and an elongated hall to a small square space – makes for a differentiation between the main axes.

Spaces, walls, windows, columns, decorations, light and shadow all meld into a single image in which the details are as resolutely present as the total entity.

PATIO DE LOS LEONES. Here the plan configuration is a mathematical game played with squares and rectangles. The axial cross spans a square and the basic form of the patio is a rectangle, reduced by the pavilions and orange bushes back to a square. On the longitudinal axis the building continues into the garden as the pavilions, on the transverse axis channels prolong the garden inside the building. The axial cross welds the sundry spaces and geometric layers together.

The many columns (150 in all) serve to interweave inside and outside as well as articulate the field of vision. This gives rise to a great effect of depth, though without penetrating the space beyond the garden. This suggestion of horizontal expansiveness pits a strong dynamic against the static qualities of the plan organized as it is around a central point, and the containment of the space. The patio has at its head ends two identical spaces that generate both a longitudinal axis and a central point, the centralized axial composition also found in the Patio de los Arrayanes. This concept of two identical heads is 'fractalized' up to and including the recesses in the passageways between the spaces.

The forest of stems with the lacelike plasterwork above call to mind the clearing, an effect strengthened by the diffuse play of light and shadow. The focal point of the garden both spatially and iconographically is the fountain, borne aloft by twelve lions. This pivotal status is further confirmed by the sound of water overridingly present in the garden. The symbolism of the Patio de los Leones is more complex and more specific than in the Patio de los Arrayanes. The axial cross is as much a representation of the cosmos as an agricultural model, in which the irrigation system symbolizes the prosperity of the land and the control of nature. The lions under the fountain represent the victory in whose honour the patio was built, and the fountain (originally built up of several dishes) shows the technical ingenuity of its makers.

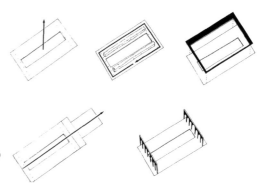

above: Materiality and infinity: the reflecting pool, the gallery with continuous roof overhang, the visual axis to the horizon and the mirrored heads.

below: The axial cross is deployed to underpin the intertwinement of inside and outside by means of channels and a graduated sequence of spaces.

SYNTHESIS. The patio is both the sublimation of the cultivated landscape and the place from which to survey the domain. The landscape is present in the patio both as prospect and emblem. Geometry, spatial form, detailing and meaning are intertwined in a balanced composition in which inside and outside (building and patio, patio and landscape) are visible simultaneously. The Patio de los Leones suggests an interweaving with its context, in that the many columns blur the boundary between interior and exterior. The visual relationship between inside and out, by way of the mirador, is merely an isolated incident in the composition as a whole. The seemingly autonomous Patio de los Arrayanes by contrast derives its entire composition from the visual axis to the outside world. Whereas the spatial ambivalence of the Patio de los Leones conflicts with the unity of the image, the Patio de los Arrayanes is spatially unambiguous but has a more complex visual composition. Both patios have a basic enough arrangement, yet one's attention is constantly being distracted by a glimpse of some new detail or a subsequent deviation from the pattern. The endlessness of the landscape is gathered into the urban fabric by attending to the horizontal and vertical components separately in the patios. Boundlessness vertically is made manifest in the large reflecting pool in the Patio de los Arrayanes, and horizontally in the forest of columns in the Patio de los Leones.

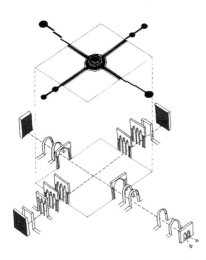

Introducing the great expanse of the landscape into the condensed tissue of the city-like Alhambra places these patios at the onset of the garden's development in the city. Paralleling the history of the garden in the landscape, the peaks in this development shifted steadily over the years further north, successively in Italy, France and England. This linear evolution was however continually interrupted by isolated periods of prosperity, such as the Golden Age in the Netherlands. With trade (barter) as one of the most important raisons d'être, the city became part of a national and international network. The landscape, on the other hand, whose greatest changes came from developments in agriculture, was determined most importantly by the geography. This relationship between the site-bound landscape and the universal city can likewise play a part in designing the cityscape of today.

In the town as it evolved after the Middle Ages and particularly after the Industrial Revolution, the landscape was too far removed for the garden to engage with it in a direct relationship and so the garden turned increasingly to the town itself. To what extent, though, was the garden able to assimilate urbanity without losing its landscape qualities? As the distance between town and landscape widened, so the relationship between enclosed garden as architectural space and as landscape reference fell apart. Interwoven with urban types such as the square, the enclosed garden was stripped of its landscape attributes. Deprived too of its clear definition of space, all that was left was a stereotyped landscape image, such as one sees in front gardens and public urban greenspace. Ultimately parks, parkways and swimming pool complexes would take over the role of the garden as a landscape reference.

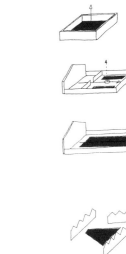

Garden

In the development of the designed public space in the city, we can distinguish three principal lines, pertaining to the square, the park and the town garden. All three have been influenced to a greater or lesser degree by the enclosed garden. Projected on to the square, the enclosed garden was used to organize the urban fabric. The cruciform plan configuration and the direct relationship between ground plane and urban elevations permitted a hierarchical relationship between the square and the buildings around. In the development of the landscape park, as discussed in the previous chapter, the relationship between house, garden and landscape remained intact at all stages. But when the landscape park transformed into a public town park, the relationship between house and garden was extinguished and the city took the place of the landscape. Once again, the direct relationship with the urban elevation was the means used to integrate the park in the city. The open park reverted to an enclosed garden, the garden of the town. The park retained its rural attributes (grass, trees) and now had the city as its horizon.

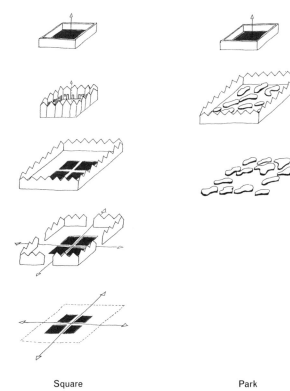

Evolution of garden, square and park as transformations of the hortus conclusus.

Square   Park

In addition, the enclosed garden transmuted into a private town garden, forfeiting its autonomy as a result. The town garden became an inseparable component of the built ensemble or urban composition.

In this development, the garden's kit of tools was deployed to relate it to the city (see Places des Vosges and Birkenhead Park later in this chapter), but at the end of the day the spatial concept of the garden proved untenable in the park and the square, and so city and landscape were once again unhitched. The spatial disintegration of the square is best illustrated by the French *place* that evolved from space organizer of the urban mass into a square like Place de la Concorde in Paris, where the lack of spatial definition is complete. Place de la Concorde is a 'non-place', a traffic interchange that illustrates the absence of space instead of creating it; an inversion of the enclosed garden into the very opposite. The park, too, grew beyond its spatial limits and so relinquished its architectural relation to the city. Thus, for example, the Amsterdamse Bos came to lie alongside the city rather than in it.

Implantation

In the eleventh century the phenomenon 'city' made its reentry. Unlike the Greek *polis* or the Roman *urbs* it was not conceived as a geometric, visual and social umbrella concept but as an organically evolved complex. Only one city was presented as a unity with a symbolic meaning; the heavenly Jerusalem, an imaginary concept bearing no relationship to reality. The irregular and compact medieval town consisted primarily of narrow streets and alleyways with little open space. In this context the hortus conclusus was deployed as an isolated incident, to fill in some unbuilt space or organize a *hofje* (of which more later).

Monastery garden and hofje: the medieval town

A clear rise in the population, an increase in agricultural produce, an increasingly stabilized politics and an increase in the significance of money together engineered a shift towards non-agricultural professions such as trades and crafts. By being granted a franchise the town was extricated from the surrounding area where 'land rights' obtained. This franchise needed to be defendable and access to the town monitored. Which is why walls, turrets and battlements are so typical of the medieval town which, like the hortus conclusus, was an exclusive domain from which the rest of the world was shut out.

The sense of space then was still a long way from what it is today, as we can see from the churches and cathedrals which still presenced as isolated objects in the city surrounded by an unprogrammed void. It would be much later, in the sixteenth century, that these churches would gain a forecourt. Open space appeared where there was a need for them: a widening of the main road or crossroads to receive a market place, in front of the city gates to take up the traffic there, in front of the church where the congregation gathered before and after the service. Villages that burgeoned into towns sometimes retained the gathering place in the centre of the village, the anger or village green, which shared the duties of orchard, bleaching field and watering place.[1]

Vrijthof, Maastricht, in the Middle Ages (17th-century print). The square is as yet little more than an open field, a landscape fragment enclosed by the town.

THE MONASTERY GARDEN. Towards the end of the twelfth century trade and commerce steadily won over geographic restriction, and developments beyond the province of the Church rapidly gathered momentum. The Church, recognizing the shift from country to town, accordingly saw its place of work there too. The monastery garden became the cathedral garden, such as the garden of the Cathedral of Santa Eulalia in Barcelona.

1. It was only in the Late Middle Ages that towns got designed as a whole on the basis of a grid scheme in which the marketplace took a central position.

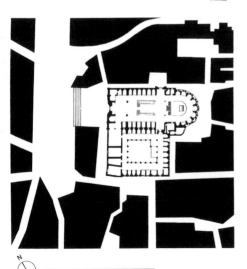

Cathedral of Santa Eulalia

On a plain bordering the Mediterranean, hemmed in by mountain ridges, lies the city of Barcelona, which originated on a low-lying hill in the plain, the Mons Taber. Nowadays the plain of Barcelona is characterized by Cerdà's grid of perimeter blocks. The narrow winding streets of the Barrio Gòtico on the Mons Taber present quite a different world, of which the cathedral and the garden are part. Standing out against the pattern of streets can still be seen the original Roman fortified town with its axial cross – the basis of the street pattern – set square to the coastline. In 1298 work began on the construction, atop the foundations of three successive churches, of the Cathedral of Santa Eulalia. The cathedral is linked to the axial cross and therefore deviates from the universal east-west orientation; the actual city prevails over abstraction.

A small informal square at the front of the cathedral links it to the Avenida de la Catedral, a high-powered 'urban' axis. Broad steps separating the square from the Avenida double as a prefatory space or stair head for the cathedral. Between the cathedral and the square lies the 'Archbishop's House', so that

above: The cathedral fully absorbed in the urban fabric.

centre: The garden of the Cathedral of Santa Eulalia in its urban context.

below: Plan configuration and geomorphology. The universal templum of the original Roman fortified town confronted with the topography. The siting of the cathedral is a variation on this given.

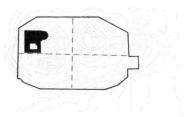

0   100m

above: Town and garden

below: Transformation of the type.
• The underlying principle is the hortus contemplationis, surrounded by a gallery and a series of cells.
• Being related to the Roman axial cross, the cathedral is rotated away from the east-west orientation. The dimensions and position of the garden are determined by the church and the existing chapel of Santa Lucia, which is assimilated in the western wall of cells.
• Openings punched in the walls of the cells link the garden with the urban spaces beyond.

only the front facade of the church can be seen between the other buildings, and the adjoining garden walls are hidden from view. The densely packed neighbouring buildings draw the cathedral into the tissue of the Gothic district. There on the exterior, the cathedral resembles a city of spires and fortifications, as if referring to the heavenly Jerusalem.

Locus and topos, the autonomy of the hortus contemplationis and the location in the city, are here played off against one another. On the one hand, there is the garden, a closed system. Here the autonomy of the planting and the centripetal plan configuration of the hortus contemplationis is borne out by the hefty enclosure of arcade wall, gallery, side chapels and the twelve-metre-high wall with grotesque gargoyles and window only at the top. The garden itself is prohibited to entry and is separated from the gallery by a tall fence. Against this autonomy is set the accessibility of the gallery from the street. The openings and the corresponding open spaces in the surrounding buildings serve to embed the garden in the public domain. At the front, the garden wall is assimilated with the church and the chapel in an unbroken urban elevation. The side chapels here are enlarged into a row of chambers stitching together the church and the chapel of Santa Lucia, with the garden tucked in-between the pre-existing Romanesque chapel and the cathedral.

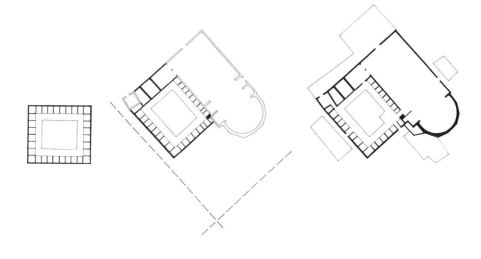

THE HOFJE. This type *(hofje* literally means 'small court') bridges the gap between the isolation of the hortus conclusus and the openness of urban space. As the Middle Ages drew to a close, Netherlandish cities were among those to gain importance on both the spiritual and economic fronts, and a type emerged that forged an unambiguous link between garden and town. A hofje is a cluster of almshouses around a communal courtyard off which are all entrances. It was accessed through a gate which in those days at least was locked at night to create a truly enclosed space.[2] The first hofjes in the twelfth century were béguinages where béguines, unmarried women, lived together like nuns though without the binding conditions. Later too the new inhabitants, the aged poor, lived as a community, often bound by strict rules. In both cases the whole cohered around the communal court. The hofje contained elements for which there was no longer a place in the town proper yet which were important in daily life. These elements derived from the castle garden or farm, such as a pump, a bleaching field or an orchard. The yard of castle and farm had moved to the town. In the hofje it blended with the hortus contemplationis, which can be recognized in the ambulatory, the centripetal organization of the plan and the physical containment. The hofje hides its face from the town, being related to the perimeter block alone by way of an unprepossessing locking gate.

Through the years the accent came to lie more on this entryway. The Teylershofje in Haarlem (1785) sports a monumental gateway between the hofje and the street that elevates the former to spatial intermediary between the individual dwellings and the town. As the public realm swelled, the hofje lost its yard functions and went representational. The pump became a fountain, the bleaching field and the orchard became parterres and paving.

above: Teylershof, Haarlem, 1785.
The gate is the most important element of the garden court and at the same time a representative facade to the street.

centre: Eva van Hoogeveenshofje, Leiden, 1650. Detail of an engraved map of Leiden by Christiaan Hagen, 1670 (Leiden, Gemeentearchief).
The hofje slots into an existing block and plays no part in the urban structure. The gateway is little different from the other doors on the street.

left: The centre of Leiden. The urban structure is built up of canals, streets and blocks and the Oude Rijn, the river which forks at the Burcht or medieval keep. The thirty-five hofjes play no part in the urban structure and are hidden away in the blocks.

2. Van Erp-Houtepen, 1986, 6.

St. Salvator's hofje

In a busy street in Leiden, a small gateway
opens on to a seventeenth-century hofje. A
narrow passageway leads from the sounds of
the street to a courtyard with sixteen houses
around it. Marking the centre of the square
courtyard is a brick plinth with a 'gallery' of
twelve plane trees in a strip of planting, and a
paved path along the houses. The housing is not
continuous but has open corners so that the
framing walk has a dynamic pinwheel
configuration. The row of trees and the raised
ground plan keep the central courtyard space
static. The rhythm of the gallery reverberates in
the composition of the facade, with brickwork
arcades crowning the doors and windows.
White-rendered walls, red-tiled roofs and the
square courtyard unite visually in a single entity
which stitches together the functionally
discrete dwelling units framing the courtyard.

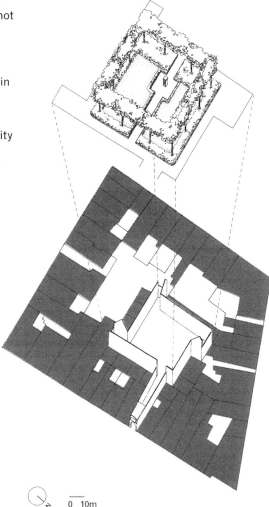

0 10m

St. Salvator's Hofje, Leiden, 17th century. A hofje with a
'gallery' of twelve trained linden trees.

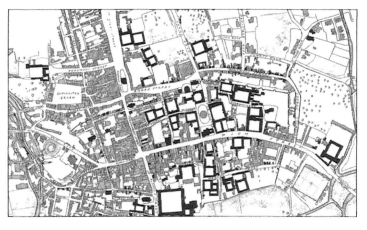

Oxford, 16th century. The enclosed garden as urban building block.

THE ENCLOSED GARDEN AS URBAN BUILDING-BLOCK. In towns like Oxford, Salamanca and Cracow we can witness the occasionally deployed hortus conclusus and the practically applied urban square joining forces. It is remarkable to see the enclosed garden, a space geared to seclusion, and the square, the public urban space par excellence, converging in a single type. Here in these university towns was the first organized education outside of the monasteries. As the powerful symbolic form of the hortus conclusus was an encouragement to study, meditation and discussion it became the principal building block of these towns. 'It [the hortus contemplationis] was so self-centred that its general adoption at Oxford and Cambridge created two cities whose independent quadrangulated colleges jostled one another indiscriminately for position. Oxford was compact; Cambridge followed the graceful curve of the river'.[3] From an infill, then, the introverted garden evolved into an organizer of urban texture. It absorbed the city, a role it would continue to play in the Renaissance, Classicism and the Enlightenment, to finally be overwhelmed by the city.

3. Jellicoe 1975, 153.

Evolution

In the Renaissance, cities, buildings and enclosed outdoor spaces would all receive a more theoretical response. This produced time and again a compelling confrontation between the universal model and local conditions. In Italy the new design methods were tested out primarily in courtyards and gardens. Examples include the perspective manipulations of the Cortile del Belvedere and of the *Hortus Botanicus* in Padua, where clipped box marked out an ideal city plan. The open spaces – the squares of Greek and Roman tradition, the cortiles and gardens – became the means of organizing the city and to this end the open space itself became the object of study and experiment.

When the Renaissance reached Holland a century later the garden played a structuring role in the urban layout, becoming part of a composition involving both house and street. During th period of French Classicism the experiments were reversed and the hortus contemplationis made its entrance in the city. With the *place*, there once again came into prominence a phenomenon that was symptomatic of the development of the enclosed garden. It underpinned the urban fabric with a material order that would ultimately replace the symbolic order of the hortus contemplationis entirely, as in the Place de la Concorde. With the horizon reached and the city ordered, the enclosed garden was no longer needed. But there was also a complementary development in evidence, one that led back to the archetype of the garden.

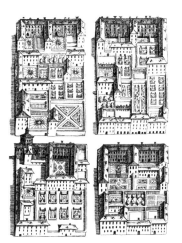

Turin, 17th century. In 1565 the town was devastated by a major fire. When it was rebuilt the plan remained unchanged but the perimeter blocks were filled with courtyards. The medieval stone-built town ceded to a composition in which open space has a structuring function.

Cortile, hortus botanicus and town garden: the Renaissance town

In medieval thinking on the city, there was in fact only the isolated and enclosed space of, say, the monastery garden, all other urban outdoor space being indefinable or at least not recognized as being space. In the Renaissance, by contrast, the town was regarded as a coherent geometrical system that could expressly be designed as such.[4] In the first half of the sixteenth century, gardens were designed that combined Renaissance theories with the notion of the hortus contemplationis. These experiments added to the two-dimensional ideal schemas a spatial dimension that would ultimately determine how the town planning theories would be implemented. The volume of the buildings holds the open space in balance, mass-form versus spatial form. Open space now presenced as form in its own righ as against medieval open spaces which were often fortuitous gaps between buildings.

Squares continuing the Mediteranean tradition of the Greek agora and the Roman forum would come to dominate the look of the city. For the time being, each enclosed garden would relate t an individual building: the cortile as one of its components, the botanical garden alongside it and the town garden assimilated i a building plot.

4. For an exhaustive treatment of the Renaissance town and the theories pertaining to it, see Zücher 1959, 99-142.

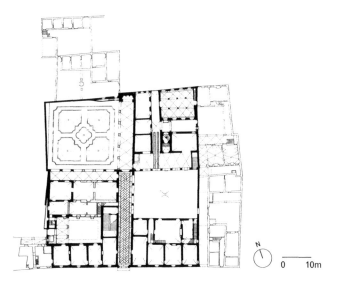

THE CORTILE. Even as it burgeoned into a refined and strongly organized garden, the enclosed garden was also represented by archetypes that had changed little over the centuries. One of these, the Roman peristyle, can be identified in the forecourt of the Château de Bury and in the cortile of the Villa Capponi. And as early as the Roman domus we see the cortile making the move unmodified from the villa to the urban house.

In Italy the surviving Roman towns were elaborated upon further so that already in the Middle Ages an urban culture existed. In the densely built-up towns, which were increasingly dominated socially, economically and spatially by merchants, a type evolved that was dwelling, warehouse and office in one: the urban palace or *palazzo*, its basic rectangular plan organized by a cortile. The cortile provided the dwelling with light and air, and with its paved surface was able to collect rainwater. A cistern in the centre meant that sieges lasting many days could be borne. On the street side the palaces exhibited a heavily strengthened frontage to withstand the many outbursts of violence in the towns.

The cortile was initially a cavity in a building that would transform, as would the hofje in later years, into an urban space. If the Cortile del Belvedere was still related to the Pope's residence, the Cortile del Uffizi in Florence played a key role in shaping the architectural relationship between city and river. Like the patios of the Alhambra it revealed the landscape through an aperture. The city of Florence had become so large as to render invisible the landscape beyond its walls, and so the river, explicit element of landscape, was enlisted as an intermediary between landscape and city.

above: Piazza della Santissima Annunziata, Florence, 16th century. The first tentative influences of the hortus conclusus on the square become apparent. The originally formless piazza has been formally framed by adding loggias to the buildings. The central point is marked by a statue, with fountains as urban furniture.

below: Giorgio Vasari, Portico degli Uffizi, Florence, 1560. The Cortile degli Uffizi is a 180-metre-long 'office street' linking the Piazza della Signoria to the river Arno, thereby forging a relationship with the landscape beyond the town.

left: Palazzo Avogadro, Brescia, 17th century. The cortile brings light, air and space to a densely built-up town.

Cortile del Belvedere

At the beginning of the sixteenth century, the Villa Belvedere was built close by the Vatican, with the Cortile del Belvedere between the villa and the palace. Perspective manipulations brought the horizon within the bounds of this mega-hortus contemplationis. Because the horizon now appeared as if shifted back, the space when seen from the balcony of the palace looked deeper that it really was; this we call perspective acceleration. The space could not be surveyed in one glance but was revealed gradually by way of an axial movement through the plan. Just as with the statue of David in the garden of the Château de Bury, man was manifested at the central point of the world image, in this case the Pope on his balcony around which the cortile was composed.

Donato Bramante, Cortile de Belvedere, Rome, 1505 (engraving c. 1560). The cortile consists of three levels, terminated at the upper court by an exedra, a semicircular recess of raised seats. The space is flanked by arcades, decreasing from three levels to one, with smaller openings between them at the uppermost court, so that this seems farther away. The coulisse effect of the towers halfway along and the exedra, the rising floor plane, the differences in level and the stacking of tiers of seating, stairs and nymphaeum make it easy to misjudge the actual dimensions of 100m x 300m.

THE HORTUS BOTANICUS. The formal concepts in this testing ground for design theories were a reworking of existing medieval types. In the botanic garden the hortus contemplationis and the hortus catalogi were blended together and processed. By having all its components related in a geometric context it was possible for the first time to put the medieval ideal of the completeness of God's creation into practice. 'The value of a Botanic garden was that it conveyed a direct knowledge of God. Since each plant was a created thing, and God had revealed a part of himself in each thing He created, a complete collection of all things created by God must reveal God completely.'[5] But when the geometric plan is related to the optical space, which we see happening in the Cortile del Belvedere, this completeness is put back into perspective. The medieval idea of the divine could hold its own so long as attempts to make it tangible failed, but fell flat as soon as the Renaissance provided the means to materialize it.

The study and classification of nature is an essential component of the Renaissance. Contact with Ottoman sultans and explorers precipitated an explosive growth in the knowledge of plant species from all over the world, and these were collected in the botanic garden. This garden represented a map of the world, a square field divided into the four points of the compass and into the continents of Europe, Asia, Africa and America, a scientific rendering of the medieval idea of the divine order as expressed in the hortus medicus. Only now the plant collection had another purpose, namely that the medicinal plants earned a place in the garden through their aesthetic value.

5. Prest 1981

Clusiustuin

In 1590, the University of Leiden founded in that town a walled garden, the Clusiustuin, at an open space between the Academy building and the former moat, the Vestgracht. (Later the garden would be reconstructed at another location in Leiden in a smaller version though with the same proportions.) The garden consists of four parts adhering to the classical harmonic proportions with a length-breadth ratio of 4:3. The central point is accentuated by a pavilion and the garden further subdivided into eight parts on either side of an axis of symmetry.

Each of the quarters consists of sixteen compartments of plants themselves divided into many segments with one plant in each. This ordered system offers the possibility of dividing up the plant collection in a scientifically methodical way, according to their properties. The inventory of 1594 reports 1070 plant names in the beds and along the walls. A further 171 species were planted in pots and at other places. Besides the traditional curative, poisonous and other useful plants such as hemp and madder from which to make rope and paint, there were a large number of ornamental species.

The gallery set on the south side before the building presented a monumental elevation with a blind rear side and a windowed wall facing the garden. The axial cross was differentiated into, on the one hand, the north-south axis which ran parallel to the canals and in the garden ended at the gallery, and on the other, the east-west axis which was pointed at the centre of the town, puncturing the walls to relate to the urban context. This latter axis drew the garden into the following series: Academy building – orchard – garden – avenue – canal.

Here in this garden, nature, art and science joined forces. In the gallery, objects were put on show for the public's edification, for the same reason that plants were exhibited in the garden. The garden was a so-called hortus publicus, accessible to a wider public and consequently embedded in urban life.

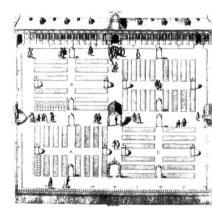

above: Clusiustuin, Leiden, 1601. Ground plan from P. Pauw, *Hortus Publicus Academiae Lugduno-Batavae*, 1601. The garden is designed for education and admiration alike. Above the entrance are words to the following effect: 'Ente this court and learn what the arts keep hidden'.

below: Clusiustuin in urban context, city plan o' 1657. These days the garden is 200m farther south, reduced to scale to fit into the new site.

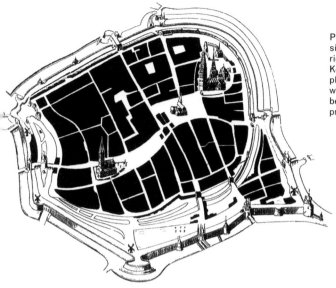

Prinsenhof as one of a series of spaces of urban significance. From bottom left to top right: Vismarkt (fish market), Grote Markt, Kerkhof (churchyard), Prinsenhof. Adaptation of a plan from 1594, when Prinsenhof, laid out in 1626, was still the courtyard of a monastery, with beyond it the town walls which were levelled just prior to laying out Prinsenhof.

Prinsenhof

At the beginning of the seventeenth century Prince Maurits had the Prinsenhof built in Groningen. This marks the metamorphosis of the garden from an isolated incident with a universal character to one element in a series: the town garden. For this garden is an incident as well as part of a larger concept, being the last in a sequence of urban spaces (fish market – main market (Grote Markt) – churchyard – Prinsenhof) and set at the divide between town and country. This transition is visible in the wall on the canal side and the buildings on the town side.

The subdued exterior conceals a festive interior where the severity of the buildings is offset by the flowers, variously clipped hedges and arbours. Six beds form a sequence of an ever greater architectural control. On the west side, the garden is a yard, then come two fenced orchards, two parterres and the climax, two circles enclosed by berceaux that are autonomous both geometrically and spatially. Here the church tower is the only visible reference to the town. The motif of two barely touching circles is a rendition of the world as shown in seventeenth-century maps.

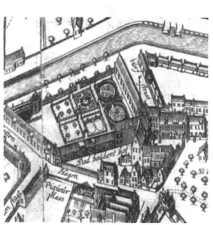

G. Peters (Town Architect to Groningen), Prinsenhof, 1626. Detail of an aerial perspective by Haubois, c. 1645. The design is done in the manner of Willem Janszoon Blaeu's map of the world, which shows the two hemispheres of the globe side by side in an azimuthal projection.

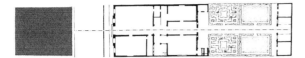

THE DUTCH TOWN GARDEN. In Leiden, the hortus botanicus was implanted as an isolated incident in the existing medieval urban fabric, which otherwise stayed the way it was. The private town garden, however, was to become one of the permanent ingredients of urban organization. Particularly in the Renaissance towns of Holland, the enclosed garden was applied on a large scale as an urban building block.

In the sixteenth and seventeenth centuries Holland underwent a strong economic and demographic growth, with rapid urbanization following in its wake. The urban expansions were necessary for military and economic reasons, and towns could not permit themselves the luxury of squares and marketplaces. Indeed, the explosive urbanization succeeded in pushing up land prices enormously. So dividing up the land for maximum efficiency was a prerequisite for the success of such expansions.

The 1613 expansion plan for Amsterdam was typified by a hierarchy of canals and a mathematical relationship between canals, quaysides and premises. 'As opposed to all medieval extensions, the expansion plan opted for a system of waters, roads and blocks of properties considered separate from the existing structure of the site and whose rectilinearity and system of measures are essentially distinguishable from the urban pattern of the old town.'[6] One component of the town expansion was the concentric ring of canals, exclusively the preserve of wealthy merchants. The unambiguous parti of the expansion plan with the canals acting as supports made it possible to deploy the closed architectural system of the country seat in the town. Next to the water was the quayside planted with trees, then the pavement, the facade and stair, then the corridor, the rooms looking down on the yard, and finally the garden with its parterres.[7]

The house borders directly on a yard or 'erf' with beyond that the garden proper, separated from the yard by a wall, a hedge or a berceau such as in the hortus ludi.[8] This division into two and an axial land plan continuing the plan of the house gave the garden its basic components. Whenever the garden has had to support a wide range of functions, this architectural order is absent. The presence of a yard, a parterre, kitchen gardens, a stable for the horse and suchlike made it impossible to extend the main axis into the garden.

above left: Philip Vingboons, Belin de la Garde House on Herengracht, Amsterdam, 1664. The plans of the garden and the house are contained in single organizing scheme, with an axis extending from the canal to the back of the garden.

above: Pieter de Hooch, *Woman and Maid in a Courtyard*, c. 1660 (London, National Gallery). An axis running from the canal to the rear of the garden links a functional yard with a representation hortus. The housewife and the maid in the courtyard and the gentleman in the hortus represent the bipartition into negotium and otium, work and leisure.

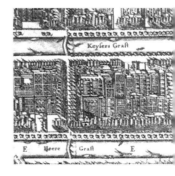

The canalside courtyard in its urban context (detail from a map of Amsterdam by Balthazar Florisz, 1652 (Amsterdam, Gemeentearchief).

6. Taverne 1978, 152-154.

7. The rows of trees that divide the flat landscape of Holland into 'rooms' were transferred to the city, not to articulate the space but as a reference to nature.

8. Such courtyards or backyards presumably derive from farmyards and contain pumps, basins, bleaching fields and orchards.

Jardin d'hôtel, place and square: the Neo-classical city

From the second half of the sixteenth century, the development of the European city was determined by two artistic strands, Baroque and Classicism. Against the dramatizing of spatial awareness that the Baroque stood for, Neo-classical architects and planners strove after a reduction in physical and visual tension. They sought to achieve a spatial balance by way of a sharp contrast between the space and its three-dimensional borders, and an elementary geometrical plan configuration with a dominant axis. Clarity and simplicity replaced the excesses of the Baroque.

Baroque and Neo-classical form principles each had their own role to play in the organizing of cities. While the French rulers resorted to the Baroque arsenal for their residences outside the city to manipulate and dramatize the natural space, Neo-classical means were deployed to organize the city and its populace along with it. The manipulating of perspective as applied in the Baroque gardens was admittedly transposed to the city but only in private gardens, where there was no call to organize large crowds and the only important thing was the individual relationship between the observer and the space.

Informing the dynamic composition of the Baroque garden was an interaction between garden and horizon, between the observer and the vanishing point of the perspective. The question is, how was this perspective construct rendered in the town garden, where the horizon could scarcely be the point of departure.

THE JARDIN D'HÔTEL. It was in the seventeenth century that 'hôtels', houses for well-to-do citizens, made their first appearance in Paris. Here, just as in the townhouses of wealthy Renaissance citizens, the architectural system of the country seat was reapplied in the city, compressed within a small and often irregular plot. Most characteristic of a hôtel is that it has no direct contact with the street. A relatively small gateway leads to a forecourt, the 'cour d'honneur', where the front facade of the house is presented in all its splendour, often with a monumental stair to dramatize the entry. All available means are applied to preserve the symmetry and enclosure of the forecourt. This latter was often joined in the larger hôtels by a second court, the 'basse cour' around which were the stables and coach houses. The central portion of the house is wedged between the cour d'honneur and the garden. The classical proportions make the buildings and exterior spaces seem larger, and are continued inside the building to tie together inside and outside.

The division into two characterizing the Renaissance town garden was abandoned. The yard disappeared, so that the entire space could be treated as a single entity and gain stronger relations with the house. The Baroque town garden was predicated upon the principle of 'de faire du grand dans du petit'.[9] Limited to a single motif, the small town garden was able to take on something of the grandeur of the Baroque garden outside the town.

Ideally, the jardin de hôtel was a rectangular space. Irregularities in the perimeters of large gardens were obscured by bosquets containing cabinets de verdure. The greatest lengthwise measure of the domain was made visible by an axis of symmetry, generating an explicitly horizontal alignment. At the end of the garden this transformed into a vertical alignment, given shape in an *exedra*, sometimes with a trompe-l'oeil to reinforce the perspective effect. The exedra or 'echo' shifts the perspective horizon forward so that the space seems deeper.

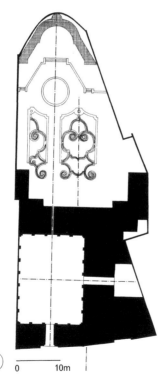

Hotel de Saint-Agnan, Paris, 1640-1650. Reconstruction of the probable site plan. The symmetrical ideal scheme is achieved by variously manipulating the asymmetrical ground plan.

Hôtel de Saint-Agnan

In the Rue de Temple in Paris, we find a system of symmetrical exterior spaces composed upon an irregular plot. Here the autonomy of the adjacent buildings has been sacrificed to achieve this. The entire organization is aimed at giving the monumental cour d'honneur (31 by 21 metres) and the garden the fullest amount of space, thereby suggesting that the ensemble is many times larger than it is. The basse cour is small with a narrow passageway to the larger court, and the living spaces around it are grouped together in the awkward northern corners of the plot. A mock facade is deployed to get the cour d'honneur symmetrical. The central wing is shallow, but the two facades with monumental Corinthian pillars along the square and the garden suggest a far larger building.

As with the front, the axis of symmetry of the rear facade is unhitched from the exterior spaces as a result of the plot's asymmetrical shape. This is rendered in the garden as two axes in dialogue. The exedra with the pool is made to relate to the cour d'honneur, and the parterre to the facade. Staggered axes imbue the sequence of street – cour d'honneur – house – garden with a dynamic that compensates for the lack of tension in the relationship between garden and horizon.

THE PLACE. The axiality and integration of regularly shaped spaces typifying the French formal garden are best represented in city planning by the *place*. Reflecting the absolute power of the kings who ordered their construction, these *places* are a component of larger urban gestures subjecting the entire city to a severe order. The enclosed spaces are removed from the urban bustle with a mathematical plan configuration, uniform walls and an accentuated central point. Here the relationship between buildings and urban internal space is reversed, from a built mass with a hollow scooped from it to space with a built backdrop. The *place* is so organized not just to gather up the surrounding buildings but to reach to the outer limits of the district.[10]

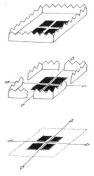

9. Dezallier d'Argenville 1760, 57.

10. In his book *Collage City* Colin Rowe describes such spaces as 'stabilizers', points 'which essentially exhibit a coherent geometry' (Rowe 1978).

Palais Royal

An old Parisian garden is framed by later
buildings and transformed into an urban space.
At the end of the eighteenth century a 'grand
ensemble' was erected round the garden of the
Palais Royal, of sixty dwellings with shops and
'galeries' on the ground floor. The gallery and
the grand étage are held in a giant order of
pilasters welding the facade into a single entity,
with a balustrade at the attic level serving as
frieze. Until the nineteenth century this garden
was the locus for social life, first in the shops
and restaurants, later in the cafés, gambling
dens and brothels. The palace garden had
become public domain.

Place des Vosges

In a subsequent move this public domain was
actually designed as such and made to
harmonize with its context. Place des Vosges
was another to be built on existing gardens. Bu
these gardens were little more than marshy
tracts, orchards and vacant land, and at the
beginning of the seventeenth century Henry IV
decided to use them to realize his ideals of
organized urban development. The first step wa
Place des Vosges, which was built in its entiret
and then sold to private individuals, a clause in
the contract stating that the uniformity had to l
preserved. This *place* constitutes the centre of
the district of Le Marais, where Parisians could
retreat to from the pressures of the city. It was
also the locus of court processions, festivals
and was even used for duels.

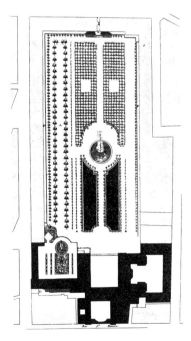

François Blondel, Palais Royal, Paris, 1754. The garden is a
miniature representation of the world, as much socially as
spatially and in its symbolic-geometrical aspect. The cortile
at bottom left again is a miniature representation of the
garden, an interior world where the garden and not the city
is the world outside. Enclosed garden, cortile and *place* are
united in a single design.

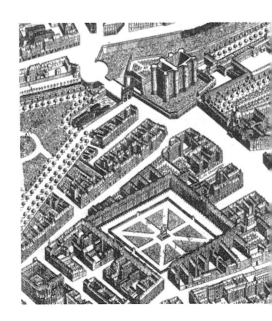

138

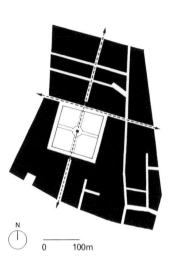

N

0   100m

Jacques-Ange Gabriël, Place de la Concorde, Paris, 1753.

above: Place des Vosges adopts the organization of Palais Royal, with the axial cross linking garden, building and city. The axial cross of the place, with an equestrian statue at the intersection, imposes a formal order on the organically evolved, introverted district and makes the connection with the major roads around. The main route (the north-south axis) runs under the Pavillon du Roi.

left: Place des Vosges, Paris, early 17th century. Detail of Turgot's plan of Paris of 1739. The place (140m x 140m) is contained by abutting walls. Behind this square of frontage are 36 houses with ground-floor shops, the whole stitched together by a gallery. The pavilions of the King and Queen facing each other across the place rise above the otherwise uniform roofscape.

Place de la Concorde

In a steadily intensifying integration with the urban landscape, the *place* as a discrete entity ultimately made way for the *place* as the centre of a *centrifugal* space.

With the expansion of Paris the fortifications west of the Tuileries lost their significance and were transformed by Louis XIV into boulevards 36 metres wide. Also, the arterial roads were straightened into spatial axes that tied city and region together. A node between one such boulevard and axis is the Place de la Concorde. Along the short north side of the square is a symmetrical wall, designed with a view through to the Madeleine church. On the south side the *place* is open to the Seine; the east and west sides have no walls either, and are framed by canals. The statue in the centre is the only feature that still recalls the closed system of the hortus contemplationis.

The transformation of Bloomsbury, 18th century. The landed property is assimilated into the urban fabric and the gardens condensed into squares. The Baroque parti of the urban plan is perpetuated in the squares primarily as lawns and parterres. After two centuries, with annexation of the landed property complete, the squares have taken on an expressive form of their own.

11. In Bath crescents and circuses were laid out in the eighteenth century as a formal variant on the square. The elevation – already unhitched from the four straight sides in the circus – is curved open in the crescent to enfold, as it were, the landscape.

THE SQUARE. At that time an almost antithetical development was taking place in England, which saw the *square* becoming more and more like a garden. The second half of the seventeenth century witnessed the emergence in England of the bourgeoisie, merchants and company owners who had ceased practising their craft but unlike the nobility could not rest on the financial laurels of earlier generations. They sought a mode of dwelling appropriate to and representative of their new status, an expression of their lifestyle which can be described as one of elegance and stylishness: gracious living, if you like. The *place* type offered the ambience they wanted and, transformed into a communal garden, the comfort and privacy too. These citizens took an ever greater part in city life and the city structure but did not have the wherewithal the nobility possessed and so they collaborated. They set up home in what were then the country estates of noble families, who leased their land in single lots. Th first form in which the square occurs is not surprisingly an extension to the forecourt of the noble house which itself features prominently in the composition.

Bloomsbury Square was laid out in 1667 by the Earl of Southampton on the axis of Bedford House, his city residence in Bloomsbury. The forecourt was kept intact and acted as an intermediary between the house and the square. Behind the house stretched the gardens of the estate. Where Bloomsbury Square was assimilated in the formal system of Bedford House, century later Bedford Square was laid out isolated from its surroundings. The oval enclosed space is loosely hugged by four identical frontages, each crowned at the centre with a tympanun Here a hierarchic build-up brought unity to the facades, rather than by making walls into an arcade as in the Parisian *places*. The third and decisive stage in the evolution of Bloomsbury was the demolition of Bedford House and the gardens behind it. In its place there came Russell Square and Bedford Place, the first in the heart of the gardens and the second linking Bloomsbury and Russell Square. Also, the formal parterres and lawns of the existing squares were replaced by plane-trees. Both interventions placed the isolated squares in a larger context without negatively affecting their private character. The immens masses of trees are strung together in a picturesque staging, with a route stitching the squares together visually.

Thus we have the monumentality, connecting axes and close relations with the urban structure of the *places* set against the privacy and seclusion in the squares.[11] Whereas the formal organization of the Parisian *places* ultimately led to the dismantling of the enclosed garden, here the cohesion of components derives from the gardens' very containment.

The public park: the industrial city

At the dawn of the nineteenth century the garden, which had evolved outside the towns into a park, returned in a new guise, namely as saviour of the condensed and polluted city. The public park introduced to the cities a compact and illusory world of nature to compensate for the landscape which had got out of reach. For example, between 1820 and 1914 the radius of the urbanized area of London had grown from five to fifteen kilometres. The park retreated from an unpleasant outside world as an enclosed garden, yet paradoxically taking as its model the most outgoing of all garden types, the English landscape garden. This was, so to speak, turned inside out and tied to the urban morphology.

Thus we see New York's Central Park (1877) despite its 320 hectares still closely linked with the city. A thickly planted outer ring acts as a leafy horizon for the central portion, bringing about a diametrical contrast between the idyllic image of nature and the surrounding brick mass of the city.

Joseph Paxton, Birkenhead Park, Liverpool, 1843. Engraving by Alphand in *Les promenades de Paris*, 1867. The wilderness is shut in by the 'garden', whose walls are formed by the town.

Birkenhead Park

In 1844 Joseph Paxton designed Birkenhead Park as an integral component of a working-class area of Liverpool. An undulating perimeter of woods and buildings blurs the confrontation between the park and the urban tissue, giving the impression that the open expanse of grass goes on for ever. The pinnacles of the composition are found here, 'secret' islands of nature hemmed in by hills. Rocky outcrops surround the entrances to stress the containment and the illusion of being natural.

At Birkenhead the enclosed garden is blown up into a public park, with the urban built development acting as garden wall. The aspect of containment however is unhitched from the garden and given a place of its own in the islands of nature in the expanse of the park. If the wilderness represented infinity to medieval man, here it is rendered as enclosure, with the park now expressing the endlessness around it.

Disassembly

The year 1917 saw the publication of the book *Une Cité industrielle. Etude pour la construction des villes*. Written by Tony Garnier, it proffered the design for a city of fifteen thousand inhabitants up to and including the construction of the buildings: this was the 'Cité Industrielle'. Apart from the progressive architecture and the use of reinforced concrete, his plan made the most impact through its separate zoning of functions: work, dwelling, leisure and transportation. This functional division would influence thinking on the city from then on. The Cité Industrielle signified the break with the unbroken typological series from hortus conclusus to square, persistently informed as this was by a closed spatial system. The spatial unit, no matter how contradictory this sounds, had ceased determining the way space was given shape.

Not just the Cité Industrielle but also the nineteenth-century urban experiments that preceded it, contributed to the dismantling of the enclosed garden which in the functional city, where the two ideas converged, ultimately disappeared altogether. In the public park, the relationship with buildings would end, in the garden city the garden forfeited its exclusive character and, together with the 'collective lawn' of the American suburbs, lost out to the expansiveness of natural space.

Both the collective lawn and the public urban park would gain a sequel in the twentieth century. Boundless space, inviting a walk to the horizon, figured prominently in the thinking of the Modern Movement. With human activities divided into the functional categories of sleeping, working and travelling, a new programme made its appearance: recreation. There was as yet no form for this and so the public park and private garden were transformed into People's Parks (Volksparken) and functional gardens.

Serial garden and collective lawn: the garden city

In the garden city, town and country were interwoven in low-density development between expansive collective and private green space. This ended at a stroke the dialectic between city and landscape, between inside and outside. The term 'garden city' can be construed in two ways: the city as garden, or a city full of gardens. As an ensemble, the garden city is an autonomous unit, bounded by a 'green belt'. Inside it, the paradise of old is fractured into twenty to thirty hedge-bound private paradises per hectare. With such repetition, the exclusive status of the garden is seriously debilitated.

THE COLLECTIVE LAWN. Almost concurrently with the emergence of the garden city, the first planned suburbs were built

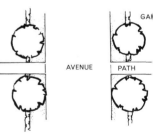

Raymond Unwin, Hampstead Garden Suburb, London, 1907. The picturesque plan is based on strict rules, such as the prohibiting of walls as property boundaries. The houses are set lengthwise with tree-lined avenues, ea with a front and back garden surrounde by a uniform hedge.

in the United States, free-standing houses in the unbounded space of a democratic and fraternal society. These American-style garden cities fostered the same ideal of an intertwining of city and landscape as did their European counterparts, but the form it took on here was almost the polar opposite. The contained character of the European version was regarded with loathing. In 1868 Frederick Law Olmsted was commissioned to design the suburb of Riverside. He invented for it the collective lawn, which flowed imperceptibly from one plot to the next, with the houses set back ten metres from the road in the centre of the plot. Walls and hedges are taboo in Riverside.

Some years later the landscape architect Frank Scott described the lawn thus: 'A smooth, closely-shaven surface of grass is by far the most essential element of beauty on the grounds of a suburban house.'[12] Those who failed to look after their lawns were regarded as selfish and undemocratic. Facilitated by the recently discovered mobility offered by the automobile, the *suburbs* rapidly spread all over the continent and the green carpet went along for the ride: '[The lawn] tumbles down a hill and leaps across a one-lane road into my neighbor's yard. From there it skips over some wooded patches and stone walls before finding its way across a dozen other unfenced properties that lead down into the Housatonic Valley, there to begin its march south towards the metropolitan area. Once below Danbury, the lawn ... races up and down the suburban lanes, heedless of property lines. [Across the continent where] neither obdurate soil nor climate will impede the lawn's march to the Pacific: it vaults the Rockies and, abetted by a monumental irrigation network, proceeds to green great stretches of western desert.'[13]

Free-standing houses along the streets of suburban Maryland (US) surrounded by uniform lawns.

Ornamental garden and functional garden: the modernist city

The cities of Garnier and Le Corbusier are open for everyone. In a democratic society there is no place for particularizing and certainly not for spatially defined if functionally multi-interpretable places. The ground plane here is merely a passive support for object buildings. Here the garden is relegated to ornament or leisure facility.

The ornamental garden has all expressive and spatial aspects stripped away. In 1898, for example, the landscape architect Fritz Encke made a design for a public garden in the Viktoria-Luise-Platz in Berlin. Flowerbeds, lawns and thickets act as decoration. The brief asked only that pedestrians be taken into account, so that nothing should be in their way.

'Our masses don't want their own tree and shrub museum in the park; they rightly desire to use the contents actively and not

12. Scott 1870.

13. Pollan 1991, 65-66.

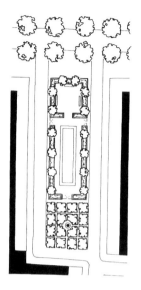

just look at them. So today's community garden will once again become a functional structure, made to accommodate the highly specific activities of most people. The populace will use it as much during the week as at the weekend – we have no need of Sunday gardens! The entire country must be able to frolic in the People's Park.'[14] The illusion of grandeur and vast expanses embraced by the Romantics, illegibility (lakes that look like rivers, clumps of trees as a screen), mythological references and the moralizing, elevating charge linked to it – all these were rejected by the moderns.[15] The functional garden had to be immediately legible and look as though it had sprung purely from being used, without the intervention of a designer, without referring to a larger whole. Illusion, ornament and manipulating measures were regarded as hindrances to orientation and an understanding of space. The home environment had to be an environment for living.

Semiotics took the place of symbols. Function admittedly was conceived more broadly than just physical material and contains what van Doesburg called 'spiritual functions' but the aspects of meaning this embodies speak only of immediately verifiable matters: the height of the water table, the worn-down circulation route, the organization of the house.[16]

In modernist thinking, the ideal garden was public and satisfied the functional needs of the majority of the population. The garden was intended for sports and games and so an 'architectural' (read 'functional') form was considered the most serviceable. 'After all, children can't play on deliciously rolling slopes, wavy lines are no use at all to joggers, and for walks you need at least a grassy expanse that is more or less flat', as Leberecht Migge – architect, urban designer and landscape architect – defines modernist ideas on gardening. The functional garden, then, had a moral and therapeutic meaning but offered no aesthetic pleasure.

left: Fritz Encke, Viktoria-Luise-Platz, Berlin, 1898. The garden reduced to a representational element.

centre: Finkenplatz, Cologne, 1910. The garden reduced to a functional element. At this time Encke designed a series of small recreation grounds in the city. These are functionally divided narrow strips of green 'within pram-pushing distance'. Finkenplatz divides into an intimate playground, a flower garden surrounded by a hedge, and a plaza (with a fountain and plane trees providing a roof) as a neighbourhood meeting place, with a formal idiom fairly directly derived from the enclosed garden. The functional subdivision used here was elaborated upon further in the German 'Volksparken' of a few years later, and still later in sports parks, amusement parks and other monofunctional green facilities.

right: The buildings are free-standing in the undifferentiated landscape. Sketch by Le Corbusier in Maison des Hommes, 1942.

144

That was something everyone could find in equal measure in nature. The functional and expressive layering was reduced to unambiguous categories, effectively doing away with the garden's paradoxical quality. The garden as a spatial and expressive unit simply ceased to exist.

THE WORLD A GARDEN. The garden was now seen as a blinkered world in which nature was manipulated. The garden wall was demolished, or with a grand gesture it invited in the whole world. Whereas the enclosed garden once represented the world, now the whole world had become a garden. The garden did not in fact belong in the modernist world – neither as a paradise in a world that is itself ideal, nor as an introverted and secluded place in a dynamic world made accessible by the car, nor as a particularized space in a world where the everyday and ordinary have become the highest good, nor, finally, as a defined and compact space in the modernist open city of light, air and space.

Designing external space shifted to the level of the city. At that time the post-war surge of urbanization was the subject of heated discussion. Urban designers debated on the correct tactics needed to get this unforeseen phenomenon under control, and how to define the city in relationship to the landscape. The scale and complexity of this set of problems was such that spatial tools were shoved aside and replaced by functional categories. Was the city to be organized using 'green wedges' or was the meshing of 'green' and 'red' the best solution? In this reduction of three-dimensional reality, the garden had become 'green' – space had become surface.

Cornelis van Eesteren and Jacoba Mulder, Amsterdamse Bos, Amsterdam, 1930. The 900 hectare 'Amsterdam wood' is not a park, and certainly not a garden. It is a landscape created on the principle of one third water, one third woods and one third grass. It is a continuous space, a texture, with broad paths and spacious lawns. All visual contact with the city is extinguished, and with it the relationship between culture and nature.

Revival

Each development in the sequence of urban transformations has seen one more aspect of the hortus conclusus demolished: the unambiguous relationship with the surrounding buildings, the reference to nature, the space-defining quality. Yet like a chameleon, the garden in its Ur-form has survived the changes. The landscape-architectural theme of the hortus conclusus has always been latently present and it is this that gives it renewed strength.

In 1835 Karl Friedrich Schinkel designed a viewing platform in a spiral shape, consisting of a terrace and a bench (see illustration on page 102). A large oak in the centre draws the two elements together with its crown. The intimate and secluded nature of the bench is transformed in the terrace into a sweeping gesture that relates the landscape to the finite centre. Here the hortus conclusus is turned inside out; the inversion from centripetal to centrifugal space is complete. In the villas of Gerrit Rietveld and

16. 'The forms deriving from the purpose of the artefacts are merely the expression of their physical-material function. But there are also counter-physical or rather spiritual functions and it is these that are most important to us.' Van Doesburg 1929, 630.

14. Migge 1909.

15. Paul Westheim speaks in 1914 of 'gardening going socialist'.

the Prairie Houses of Frank Lloyd Wright we see the dialectics between the finite centre and infinity metamorphose into a composition round a finite central point, embedding the house in infinite space. 'The openness is found where the nature in Loosdrecht requires it, and yet the plasticity of the brick fireplace wall ties us into the natural expanse and prevents us from getting lost in all that nature.'[17] 'Outside was pulled into the very core of the house, and the fireplace chimney, occupying the space as an independent and free-standing element, took on more and more the character of a central point round which the floor plan exfoliated.'[18] Even at the nadir of the garden's development during the modernizing mania in the early years of the twentieth century, the hortus conclusus was not allowed to disappear entirely but was reanimated from an unexpected quarter. For though outlawed by the moderns as a spatially independent category, the garden was brought into the building as an internal component by the selfsame architects. And it was from that vantage-point that the garden could once again figure in both the city and the landscape.

17. Regarding the experiencing of space in Rietveld's house 'De Braamakkers' in Loosdrecht, see Bakema 1941, 106-107.

18. Polak 1989, 58.

Plan configuration and side elevations of the German Pavilion in Barcelona.
1. Patio / 2. Gallery / 3. Internal space / 4. Terrace / 5. Entrance / 6. Palacio de Alfonso XIII

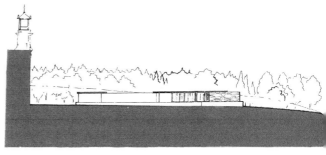

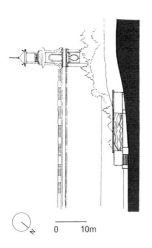

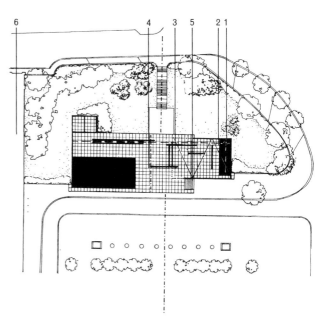

0   10m

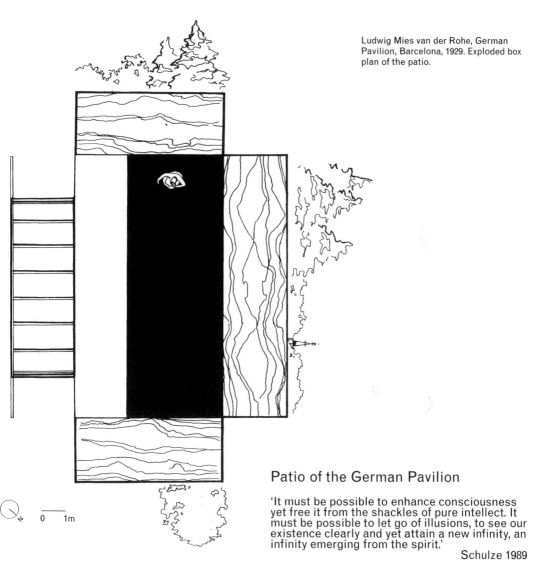

Ludwig Mies van der Rohe, German Pavilion, Barcelona, 1929. Exploded box plan of the patio.

0 1m

Patio of the German Pavilion

'It must be possible to enhance consciousness yet free it from the shackles of pure intellect. It must be possible to let go of illusions, to see our existence clearly and yet attain a new infinity, an infinity emerging from the spirit.'

Schulze 1989

Even as the finite, closed space seemed to be dissolving in infinity, it proved to have a part to play in free and continuous spatial compositions. In the German State Pavilion in Barcelona, for example, we see once again an enclosed garden, not as a go-between but – like the fireplaces of Wright and Rietveld – as a means of anchoring a centrifugal composition.

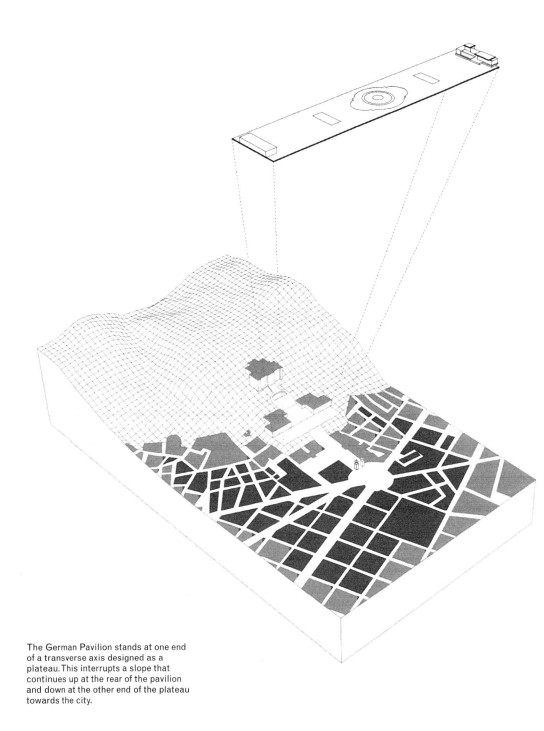

The German Pavilion stands at one end
of a transverse axis designed as a
plateau. This interrupts a slope that
continues up at the rear of the pavilion
and down at the other end of the plateau
towards the city.

PAVILION IN THE CITY: DISPERSAL OF THE FORMAL COMPOSITION. Where Cerdà's urban grid touches the foot of Montjuic it is sliced off at a diagonal. Here on this hillside, we can find the system of formal axes of the World Exhibition of 1929. The slope is abstracted to a terraced north-south axis, where the differences in height in an east-west direction are taken up on either side of the terraces. The pavilion designed by Mies van der Rohe occupies a decentralized position in the overall composition, set square to the transverse axis and terminating one end. This siting is pointed up by the plateau on which the pavilion stands.

Partly buried, this plateau frees the pavilion from its surroundings and brings into view the slope following on from the transverse axis. These aspects are further strengthened by the contrast between the transparent pavilion and the chunky Palacio de Alfonso XIII looming above it. Informing the pavilion is a spatial compression diametrically opposed to the shelter – view duality of the setting. The large, open terrace lies sheltered beneath the tall, blind palace wall towards the mountain; the small, bounded patio faces the open valley. A second duality is that between the open front and the closed rear, corresponding to the east-west slope.

The smooth surfaces, the light colours of glass, steel and cut stone and the pavilion's horizontality, all act to hold the coherent image of the building clear of the solidity, the textures, the opulent ornamentation and the earthy hues of the overgrown mountainside and the Neo-baroque palace.

The design for the German Pavilion belongs to the modernist conception of an ideal city of light, air and space, as in the proposal by GATCPAC, the Catalan branch of CIAM, to replace the Cerdà grid with an object-by-object, free-standing infill. Regarded in such an urban context, the pavilion is a resumption of the continuity of the urban space. In that respect the patio is a closed box in an open urban fabric.

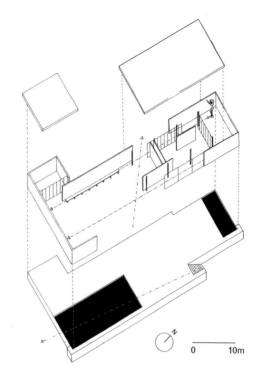

The plateau, the vertical elements and the ceilings. Two sight lines show the full length of the pavilion while the openings in the walls give sidelong views of the landscape. The view of the palace is formalized in the stair.

PAVILION: A FILTER BETWEEN CITY AND PATIO. All elements of the pavilion are related to a horizontal plane with an orthogonal grid. The walls are freely placed in a centrifugal composition. Within this plan configuration we can identify three units: the terrace, the internal space and the patio. The space condenses steadily with the enclosed patio at the end as the only elementary space in the composition.

Inside and outside are intertwined in a spatial continuum sparked by the free placement of the walls. These are anchored by eight regularly placed columns and the pavilion's four closed corners. Because the walls slide by and mirror one another, it is difficult to gauge the size and bounds of the space. The sequences from open to closed and from 'outside to inside to outside' are engineered by two sight lines. Patio and pavilion are linked by a 'gallery' where the columns, floor and ceiling of the pavilion all terminate.

By reducing the design to horizontal and vertical lines and planes, smooth materials in cool colours (water, glass, steel and stone) and constructing a resolute horizontality without differences in height or vertical highlights, Mies subjects the image to a far-reaching abstraction. This abstract image is put into perspective by the images of the city that ooze in through openings between the wall planes. The palace rises above the large pool of the pavilion, the trees and church tower can be seen through a hole in the rear wall and the exhibition area at the open front. Only in the patio are the surroundings almost entirely shut out.

On entering the patio you are made aware of two abrupt transitions. A formal entry in urban landscape mode over the axis changes inside the pavilion into a movement across a free space. This changeover occurs at a broad stair in the plateau. The stair runs parallel with the pavilion, so that the gaze is directed towards the monumental palace wall beyond. A second visual fragment is the planted slope seen through an opening in the rear wall. After that there are no further views out. The next transition is effected by entering the patio, where the ability to move freely is abruptly restricted to the narrow strip of the gallery.

THE PATIO: LE MOMENT SUPREME. The patio, a closed rectangular box composed of three all but blank walls and the gallery, is a static frame confirmed by a female statue placed off centre in the pool.

The boundless space is given shape as an abstract void that transcends the limitations of the rectangle. Two lines of sight from the open corners of the patio and the containment of the four walls generate a tug-of-war between endlessness and enclosure. The static plan configuration vies with the dynamic of the statue, which seems to be rotating upwards, motion and motionlessness locked together. Shielding her eyes from the sun, her feet in the water, Georg Kolbe's bronze female nude makes a link between patio and sky that is also metaphorical. She draws the attention to the sky above and its reflection below. In its

Transformation of the type:
• The underlying principle is a square hortus contemplationis surrounded by a gallery and with a fixed centre.
• The gallery is reduced to the south side of the patio, where the built portion is.
• The patio is stretched to articulate its non-central position in the pavilion.
• The centre of gravity is shifted to the west side.
• The wall between the gallery and the internal space is made transparent.

The pavilion with the Palacio de Alfonso XIII at the rear.

abstraction of form and material the patio is motionless and timeless, the screening walls serving to keep the wind out and the water unruffled. The difference between the walls expresses the position of the patio with respect to the pavilion and the surroundings. Visible above the opaque walls are the tops of trees in the world outside, while the interior of the pavilion showing through the glazed gallery plane adds a fourth wall to the view inside the patio. The water and the marble walls refer to nature, to the sea and the mountains.

The German Pavilion is a public space for collective use, though it was designed within the typology of the traditional pavilion: a garden shelter for the individual to temporarily retire from the world. The geometric parti and an abstraction taken to extremes attest to a striving after universality. If the carpeting and furniture give the pavilion the feel of a living room, the emphasis on light and air and the abstraction of the space into horizontal and vertical coordinates impart a cosmic orientation.

SYNTHESIS. Inside the patio, enclosure and endlessness are exchangeable commodities. The limited space seems limitless in the reflecting pool, and if the walls seem distant because of their smooth reflecting surfaces, the capricious lines on their surfaces leave them earthbound and close by.

Typifying the sequence of landscape – pavilion – patio is a constant reversal between absence and presence of context, inside and outside, spatial flow and centric configuration, open and closed, motion and stasis. The series is accompanied by marked changes in the route. In the court there is a reduction in the complexity of the plan configuration, spatial form and appearance. Because of this abstraction, but also because the polarities of the entire pavilion converge here, the court presences as a unit in itself, a microcosm. Yet paradoxically, the patio is also an inseparable component of the *free plan configuration*, the spatial subdivision and the overall image of the pavilion.

So here we see a double inversion of the

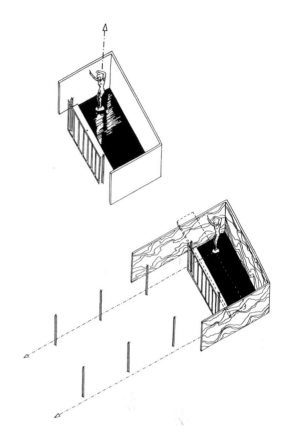

Vertical and horizontal alignment.

hortus conclusus. The internal space of the pavilion is broken open into a centrifugal, endless space, the exterior space condensed into a enclosed patio. In the pavilion, endlessness is materialized as a centrifugal space with a horizontal expansiveness. In the patio, it is expressed as an introverted space with a vertical alignment. The curious aspect here is that these two diametrically opposed forms are not mutually exclusive but happily coexist.

Current Transformations

'I have had the idea for some time now that we should start thinking about the park altogether differently. "Seeing and being seen" and strolling have shifted to the shopping malls. Shouldn't we be returning to "gardens" in the city? To dazzling, delightful places where you can enjoy the sky? To courts that belong to a building, to courts you can discover in the bend in your street, perhaps with a fence round it, perhaps with something of an orangery in it? Flowering places but also places without green.'

Hans Warnau, 1990

Urban landscape and enclosed garden

The landscape is no longer the unambiguous natural or rural counterform of the city, but is getting more and more woven with the city itself and is being absorbed in a diffuse urban landscape. This new relationship between city and landscape is able to find expression in the enclosed garden. The garden can be as much an Arcadian counterpart as a representation of the city, but it can also possess one of the much more complicated intermediate forms. Thus we see the Jardin des Bambous creating in the centre of Paris an idealized image of a fairytale bamboo landscape, withdrawn from the city by being sunk several metres below street level. But in that same garden a number of crossing sewage pipes and a concrete wall make the city manifest.

Brewery in Haarlem and the country seat of Velserend. Pen drawing, 1627 (Haarlem, Frans Hals Museum). The enclosed garden in the urban landscape.

Gardens are likewise an expression of the image we today have of nature. In the medieval concept of nature the notion prevailed of a delectable paradise and a terrifying wilderness distinct from one another, but these could also proceed in concert in an ambivalent image of nature. In our society this paradox has vanished, its once contradictory qualities fused into the idea of nature in an unspoilt state. In a world that is becoming more urbanized by the day, the wilderness has come to represent paradise. In Berlin Daniel Libeskind has proclaimed a thicket of Robinia a paradise garden. A tenuous forest of birch trunks or bamboo stems – images of 'unspoilt nature' in Russia or China – become paradises in the hands of Desvigne and Dalnoky, and Alexandre Chemetoff respectively. The idea has, moreover, arisen of the city as a wilderness; an incomprehensible, ineluctable force that powers our cities, the machinery of production and consumption, motorways, railways computer networks, sewerage, electricity and water pipes. This is a world created by people that has swelled to the extent that has long surpassed the understanding of the individual and is quite as threatening and as real as the medieval wilderness. Los Angeles, for example, may be considered the urban landscape par excellence and it is this city more than any other that is in thrall to gates, walls and fences. The need for boundaries is a need for clarity and safety. Walled or gated communities, closed-circuit video, sheltered and patrolled shopping malls and gated holiday parks bring us back to the old theme of exclusion and the creating of safe internal worlds.

So, the classic concept of nature as the counterpart of culture or cultivation, and as an all-embracing force beyond man's comprehension, has split into two complementary notions: the unsullied if fragile nature of paradise – nature beyond the sphere of influence of the city – and the unstoppable power of the urban machine.

In the sixties, Roel van Duijn, the founder of the anti-establishment Provo movement, drove round with a garden on the roof of his Volkswagen.[1] This was his way of arguing for more 'nature' in the city. But besides being a nature-island this motorized garden is inextricably linked with the city itself, an emblem for this new and ambivalent angle on nature.

Nature in the city as expressed by the so-called Provo movement.

The distinction between city and landscape continued up to the nineteenth century, until the modern notion of spatial continuity called into question the dividing line between city and landscape. The meshing of city and landscape that is now becoming more and more evident has added a new term to the existing pair: urban landscape. Its qualities will be researched here using the typology of the enclosed garden, premised as this is on the cross-resonance between town and country. It is also assumed that each reworking of this exchange requires a new mode of perception. It is, after all, an analytic or more associative interpretation of city and country in which some aspects are featured and others omitted. The enclosed garden has accordingly become, as it were, a tool enabling us to critically view the city, the landscape and the urban landscape. The types we shall introduce here show an analogy with instruments that make possible such specific ways of looking: the telescope, the kaleidoscope, the field glass and the magnifying glass. Each type gives a reading of the landscape, the urban landscape or the city. These reworkings can be arranged in a series informed by an increasing degree of palpability.

In this chapter we will be using four design experiments to examine these types and place them in a contemporary urban context.

1. Anarchist and critical of society, the Provo movement in the Netherlands campaigned in the sixties for, amongst other things, better living conditions in the major cities.

The enclosed garden as telescope

A telescope gives us the opportunity to break free from earthly matters and turn to the reaches of the cosmos, where givens such as unity, void and spatiality, ever scarcer commodities in an urbanizing landscape, are immutably present. Space as a quality can be concretized by compressing it between four walls. In the garden we see not nature represented but natural processes – rain, snow, sunlight, dusk, the moon, the stars – processes over which we have no control. Only the form, the container of space, is given expression by the arrangement of the walls and the ground plane.

Dom Hans van der Laan, convent garden, Mariavall, 1994. The enclosed garden as telescope.

The enclosed garden as kaleidoscope

In a kaleidoscope, a fragment of reality is captured and reflected in a fantastic play of colours and shapes. In this garden, then, the existing context is erased and replaced by an illusion of nature, isolated from and elevated above the real thing. As in the hortus catalogi, a selection is made from nature to represent the complete arsenal. A suggestion of completeness is evoked by presenting the selected species in vast quantities – simplification and abundance in one. This abundance suggests a landscape of far greater dimensions than that of the garden and thus transcends the limits of the space. The containment is no longer created just by the walls but also by the density of the planted species.

Carlo Scarpa, Brion cemetery garden, San Vito d'Altivole, 1969-1978. The enclosed garden as kaleidoscope.

The enclosed garden as field glass

This garden faces outwards like a field glass, capturing expansive prospects which might lend coherence to an area in the throes of urbanizing. Both the stable givens (the genius loci) and the changes are registered and made to relate. The means deployed to do this is the window on the (urban) landscape. This window can be enlarged to such an extent that the landscape penetrates the garden. Enclosure and openness are placed in opposition. Because the horizon is visually brought into the garden, the vertical orientation (of the archetypical enclosed garden) becomes less absolute. The illusion of the garden and the reality of the landscape are impossible to distinguish between. Landscape has become illusion.

Knud Friis, Elmar Moltke and Sven Hansen, Entrepenørskolen, Ebeltoft, 1968. The enclosed garden as field glass.

The enclosed garden as magnifying glass

This garden activates dynamics, diversity and networks by showing a detail, as would a magnifying glass, and shutting out all other aspects. It can respond to (urban) landscapes that are so complex that the organizing components are difficult to identify. Organizing the urban landscape is an infrastructure of roads, railways and tubeways, but also of computer networks and sewerage. By putting frames (walls) round points where the urban dynamic is strongest (nodes or interchanges) components can be disentangled, magnified and thus particularized as parts of a complex totality. By being framed, a garden is loosed from its surroundings, so that the real image is replaced by an ideal image. A tension is thrown up between the autonomy of this ideal image and the strong ties with the surrounding structures and/or infrastructures. The deviant position adopted by the garden with respect to the objects around can be expressed by

OMA, Pattou & Pattou, Espace Piranésien, Lille, 1994. The enclosed garden as magnifying glass.

having the garden raised above or sunk below ground level. This not only articulates the vertical orientation inside the garden but also expresses it in the spatial relationship between garden and surroundings.

From the analysed examples we will see that a type is often coupled to a specific situation. A complex urban situation can best be observed through a magnifying glass, and a landscape situation through a field glass. The type can also depend on a certain theme from urban – rural dialectics. The garden aimed like a telescope at the sky is closely bound to the ever scarcer empty space of the landscape, and the kaleidoscopic distortion of reality evokes the image of a nature that is truly paradisiacal. Though these links cannot be claimed to be actual qualities of the types, they do contribute to providing insight into the problematics of urbanization. Each of the following sections accordingly devotes a brief description to these themes.

Condensed emptiness

'The place in which he found himself was absolutely flat. In the human world we seldom see flatness, for the trees, and houses and hedges give a serrated edge to the landscape. Even the grass sticks up with its myriad blades. But here, in the belly of the night, the illimitable, flat, wet mud was as featureless as a dark junket. ... In this enormous flatness, there lived one element – the wind. ... This wind came from nowhere. It was going through the flatness of nowhere, to no place. Horizontal, soundless except for a peculiar boom, tangible, infinite, the astounding dimensional weight of it streamed across the mud. ... The Wart, facing into this wind, felt that he was uncreated. Except for the wet solidity under his webbed feet, he was living in nothing – a solid nothing, like chaos. His were the feelings of a point in geometry, existing mysteriously on the shortest distance between two points: or of a line, drawn on a plane surface which had length, breadth but no magnitude. No magnitude! It was the very self of magnitude. It was power, current, force, direction, a pulseless world-stream steady in limbo.'

Terry White, 1958

The expansiveness of the landscape is a quality that seems destined to become lost in spatial developments hell-bent on densifying and urbanizing. There is admittedly concern for nature development and scaling-up as a counterpart to urbanization, yet the spatial (oceanic) dimensions of the landscape are absent. Nature development is deployed to counter the urbanizing process (take the reafforestation of the Dutch polders); scaling-up emerges of its own accord through the demands of the infrastructure, or is carried on site with the design task (transferia, high speed rail). To get a grasp on the spatial condition, it can be made measurable and tangible in small spaces.

In 1995 Christian de Portzamparc drew up a scheme for Masséna, an inner-city area of Paris, in which he combined the compactness, diversity and measures of the old city with a metropolitan ambience. To do this he used the 'îlot ouvert', free-standing masses held together by the building lines of a city block, with a mix of internal and exterior spaces. The streets are narrow and are bounded in part by high- and low-rise development and low walls. The larger and smaller volumes are sited independently of one another yet adhere to the building lines of the street. A park in the centre of the district has been divided by Portzamparc into four 'gardens'.

In the first of our design experiments the four garden areas are further condensed with buildings and walled gardens. By these means, a pair of strips thirty metres wide, one an open expanse, the other a thickly wooded area, are defined that introduce a horizontal alignment to the scheme. The point where the strips intersect is marked by a garden which takes the openness of the first strip and concentrates and frames it. Hidden on the edge of the wooded strip is the entrance to the garden through a narrow passage where wooden slats cast striped shadows on the floor, as if a filter between the woods and the garden. A row of poplars ties the two strokes together and ends in the garden, where the trunks present a natural gallery. Framed by blocks of black basalt, the empty space of the garden can be observed from a turfed seat behind the poplars.

Design experiment in Masséna, Paris. The design is an adaptation of the competition design Christian de Portzamparc made for the district in 1996. The public space is divided into a wooded and a grass strip that together organize the free-standing built masses, with the garden at their intersection.

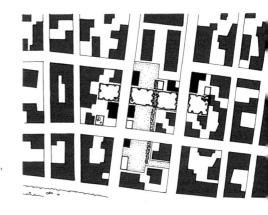

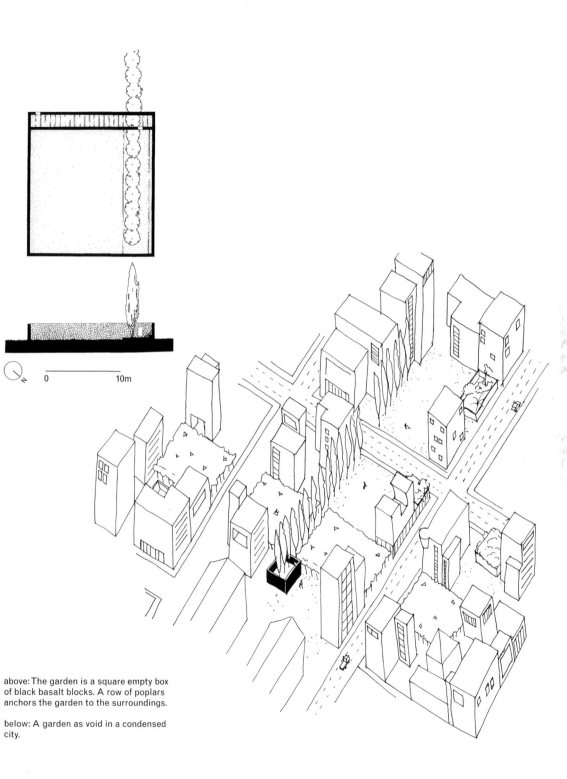

0   10m

above: The garden is a square empty box
of black basalt blocks. A row of poplars
anchors the garden to the surroundings.

below: A garden as void in a condensed
city.

Mariavall convent garden

This garden is a void bounded by bare grey columns. The landscape is eliminated, the garden reduced to an expanse of grass. Can landscape architecture be more rarefied than this?

A CONVENT IN THE WOODS. Tucked away in a dense forest in the south of Sweden lies the Benedictine convent of Mariavall. Its construction in 1994 was a sudden intervention in a forest that had remained unchanged for centuries. The province of Skåne in the south of Sweden lies along the border between the coniferous forests of northern Sweden and the broad-leaved woods in the south. Around the convent in close proximity are a wood of pines and spruces and another of beeches.

The design for the convent is based on a system of proportions consisting of seven successive measures, developed by the convent's designer, the Benedictine monk Dom Hans van der Laan, as a universally applicable system. This system of 'the plastic number' is based on generally obtaining concepts pertaining to our powers of perception. According to van der Laan, we are only capable of perceiving infinite space by chopping it up into measurable finite portions. The plastic number represents the dimensions recognizable to human perception. The seven ratios deriving from this proportional system were determined from experiments done with perception: 5:7 is the smallest difference we are able to perceive, 1:7 the largest in which the parts are individually recognizable. All other proportions fall between these two.

A rectangular ideal scheme of east-west orientation is the result, at least on paper. The qualities of the landscape – relief, infrastructure, water table – are rendered in a second rectangle superimposed over the first. The result is a polygonal topological shape borne out by a double row of trees twice interrupted by buildings. The encounter between universal model and genius loci is given expression in the periphery of the site.

The ensemble consists of a number of layers or skins: the woods surrounding the grounds, next the double row of trees and finally the convent buildings themselves hugging two garden courts. The double row of trees not only brings into view the encounter between the two geometric basic forms, it marks the transition from dense forest to open space, from nature to architecture. A like transparent transition obtains in the building where it faces on to the exterior space. Each of the galleries, *porticoes* and loggia has a thick internal wall and a perforated external one.

The convent is quite invisible in the dense woods. Only the car park, a clearing in the trees divulges that somewhere here there must be a building. Whereupon the road ducks back into the woods to skirt the next open space. A low wall and an avenue of trees form a screen between the road and this second clearing. Through an opening in the wall you can see across the forecourt straight into the front porch of the convent.

In the sequence of spaces, nature and culture are made to relate. This sequence runs from a high degree of abstraction in the nuns' garden court by way of the open field, where the natural relief and the grasses and herbs have free rein to a small hillock between the trees, pointed up by an exedra. This is the convent's burial ground, where the series takes on a second meaning: the life cycle from birth (the secure space of the garden) to death.

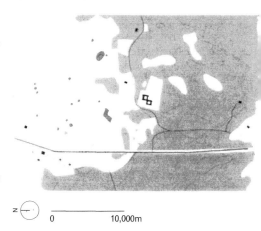

z 0 10,000m

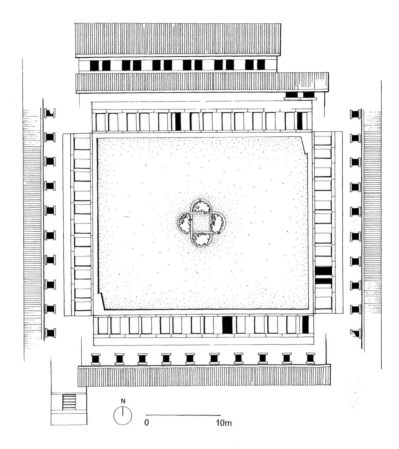

above: Exploded box plan of the garden
court at Mariavall.

left: Plan configuration and
geomorphology. To the occasional
clearings in the forests the convent adds
a designed open space.

right: In the original design the open
space is a crisp lawn, whereas now the
building sits in a rough open field
mediating between architecture and
nature. Stone walls in the beech woods
are relics of a medieval landscape of
fields and meads.

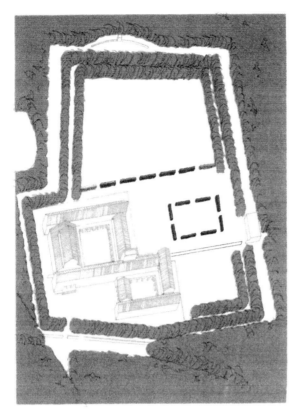

left: Spatial organization. Differentiation into open, half-open and closed spaces and into open, transparent and opaque walls. Taken from outside to inside there is a sequence of spaces of decreasing size, from the unformed natural space of the forest to the most condensed space of the nuns' garden court. Trees lining the basic space of the field present a snear-continuous tunnel-shaped space. Each of the six subspaces of the foremost part has its own variant on the row of trees.

0 10m

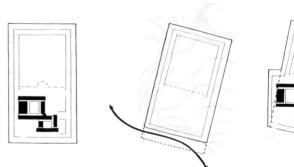

above: Plan configuration and geomorphology. The ideal plan for the convent consists of a rectangular domain divided into smaller rectangles in which the same proportions can be identified. The ideal scheme is oriented exactly east-west with the church pointed to Jerusalem. A second rectangle is a geometrical version of the topography: the boundaries formed by the road, two marshy areas and a hill.

This rectangle meets the ideal scheme at an angle of twelve degrees. Superimposing the two rectangles gives us the plan in reality. The various directions converge at the forecourt. The entrance (north-west edge of complex – see uppermost illustration) likewise reflects both layers. Aligned to the entrance to the convent, it simultaneously continues the row of trees behind it.

THE CONVENT: THE INSIDE IS BIGGER THAN THE OUTSIDE. The convent buildings consist of two quadrangles linked by a diagonal, a doubling of the monastic building type. Seven autonomous wings slip out of alignment to enfold two cloister garths. Each wing has the same linear structure, with a colonnade separating a corridor from a string of cells. In the church and the loggia we see this principle mirrored round an axis of symmetry, generating a central open space.

The geometric composition is spatially elaborated by siting the bell tower at the pivot point and transforming one of the volumes into a church. The dialogue between church and bell tower is enacted in the void between the two, in the nuns' garden court. The two quadrangles are a composition of rooms, galleries and cells in two layers. In Dom van der Laan's terminology the cells are 'blocks', strung together in the gallery into 'bars' and joined yet again in the rooms and gardens into 'slabs'. In this way all volumes can be read from the dimensions of the bounding planes and the lines defining those planes. The seven volumes

are held clear of one another, joined only by a timber-clad bridging piece, so that they can be individually distinguished from the outside. Only in the garden courts does the gallery give rise to a stratification, and lends the emphasis on the sky an unbounded verticality. Thus, the limited true dimensions are transcended and a spatiality suggested that is not legible on the exterior.

Soberness, purity and tranquillity are conditions necessary for Benedictine nuns and monks to be able to concentrate wholly on the liturgy. 'The life-ideal expressed in the Rule of Saint Benedict sets high demands for architecture. These concern not only the great variety of spaces needed to support the complete development of monastic life, but above all the spiritual quality of the building. The rule does not demand the use of any particular religious symbolism, but rather the mutual attuning of, on one hand, the building as external framework of the inner life, and on the other, the inner life of the monks that inhabit the building. The interior and the exterior, spiritual life and material framework for life, are not

Transformation of the type:
• The underlying principle is a square hortus contemplationis with four volumes built around it, with the east-west wings wedged between the north-south wings.
• Two units are linked as opposing quarters of a square.
• One portion is expanded by two gallery widths, and the other contracted to the same extent whereby one side of the gallery is dispensed with. The longitudinal axes of both garden courts cross at the forecourt, with the point of intersection marked by a clump of trees.
• The wing on the north side of the nun's garden court is

transformed into a church by doubling it. Similarly, doubling the gallery on the north side of the smaller visitors' court transforms it into a loggia. The wing on this side disappears, while the transformation is a way of reinstating the disposed-of gallery side.
• A tower marks the intersection of the quarters and is so sited that all four are determined by it. The southernmost volume is extended to terminate the central volume.

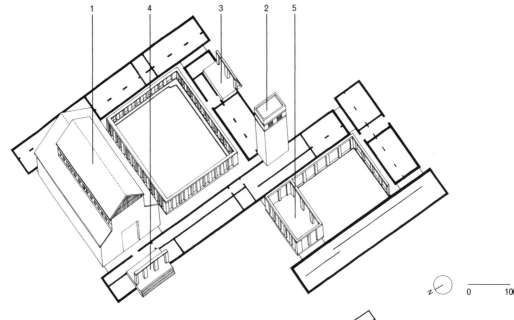

1   4   3   2   5

z   0   10

separate domains, but closely bound to each other. The balance, this harmony, lies at the core of the Benedictine life-ideal.' (Father A.E. Van Hooff OSB) Seven key words describe the convent's contemplative character and these are expressed in the architecture: quiet, simplicity, peace, prayer, labour, study and seclusion. To this end the design is reduced to an orthogonal system of lines, planes and volumes. The only colours used are the grey of the floors and walls, the green of the grass and the red of the roofing tiles. Through the absence of colour and ornament, the building is no more and no less that the visible spatial form. The architectural space is so obvious and legible that all attention can be devoted to contemplation.

THE TAPIS VERT OF THE NUN'S GARDEN COURT. In the composition of blocks, bars and slabs, the garden court is a slab based on our largely horizontal field of vision. The vertical orientation is concentrated into a single point on the edge of the court, the bell tower. The separated volumes are joined again by the gallery round the garden. This has a rhythm of narrow and broad columns that is interrupted at the corners. The gallery accesses various building portions on the ground floor, making it

z   0   10

above: Spatial organization. Like the grounds, the building is composed of open, half-open and closed spaces. The nuns' garden court is closed in entirely and is surrounded by an ambulatory. The church and the bell tower set on opposite sides balance each other out. The porches accessing the private portion are only open to the outside. The loggia mediating between the forecourt and the small garden court of the visitors' wing is open on both sides in deference to the more public nature of the visitors' sector. 1. Church / 2. Bell tower / 3,4. Porch / 5. Loggia

below: Plan configuration. Each wing is built up of a series of cells and a passage. An ambulatory mirroring the passage intercedes between wing and garden court, a construct that reverses at the pivot point between the two quarters. The tower is incorporated into the wings' system of lines. The wall around the garden courts is accompanied both inside and outside by a colonnade, thereby effecting a gradual transition between court and building.

164

the main artery for circulation flows in the building. Door and window openings punched in the rear wall of the gallery bring three-dimensional form to a flat surface. The columns and lintels of the colonnade as well as the openings between, or intercolumnia, are legible as forms in their own right, so that mass and space are in equilibrium.

The gallery sets a rhythmic and spatial layering against the two-dimensionality of the walls and the ground plane. The soberness and uniformity of the materials make every nuance important, the green tints of the herbs amidst the grass, the blue and grey tints of the sky and, depending on the light, the suggestion of blue, green and pink in the concrete. White roses symbolizing the Virgin Mary are contained in a bed shaped by two (infinite) lines that together tie a (finite) knot. The centre of the knot is left empty.

The nuns' garden court. The ground plane is a rectangle, bordered by fourteen intercolumnia on the long sides and eleven on the short, in a ratio of 7:9 or thereabouts. This is a form that the eye is just able to distinguish from a square.

'The main quadrangle of the convent [the part reserved exclusively for the monastic family] is an aid to deepening awareness and attentiveness to God. The garden court – closed off on all sides but open to the sky – is an expression of this.'

The Benedictine nuns of the convent of Jesu Moder Maria, 1993

PROGRAMME AND MEANING. The cell, the basic space, is small to best facilitate daily activities such as cooking, cleaning and praying. The 'bar' of linked cells has a limited width based on walking, the physical link between one space and another. The 'slab' of linked bars is derived from looking, the horizontal field of vision with its far greater reach than the physically accessible. The distinction between the two garden courts is indicative of the different intentions. Whereas the guests' garden court is open on one side, demonstrating its worldly alignment, the nuns' private garden is a space shut off from the world and open to the sky only.

The garden court is static and unchanging. Here the natural processes seem to have no grip at all. Only the colour and the intensity of the light falling on the almost pure white concrete change during the course of the day and with the seasons. All events in the garden court are erased, so that nothing remains other than a white screen on which are projected the formless rhythms of time.

SYNTHESIS. Garden court and building together form a unit based on the same orthogonal pattern, with the same proportions, material, balance between mass and space, and reduction to horizontal and vertical planes. If the plan configuration and the appearance are unambiguous, spatially the ensemble is layered. In the garden court, earth and sky are two planes in opposition with the horizontal play of lines of the building in-between. The complete suppression of landscape influences, together with the balanced play of space and mass in the convent and the void of the garden court – all help to make this hortus contemplationis a cosmic space.

The enclosed garden as telescope

In the condensed city, emptiness can make a welcome change It presents a silent reduction against screaming advertisements and rampant consumerism, openness against fullness, an unprogrammed space against programmatic urban congestion, the possibility of seclusion against the publicity of the street.

The excesses of the city áre here replaced by absence: 'less is more'. At Mariavall the emptiness of the convent garden accentuates the endlessness of the sky, given form in the abstract composition of horizontal and vertical planes. By contrast, in the flat expanse around the building the void presences through an absence of form, through the irregular relief with its tangled growth and desolate character. In the German Pavilion, the emptiness in the patio is designed in a lik manner. There, too, it engages the void of the surroundings in th boundlessness of the space between the freely placed planes o the pavilion.

The void has no expressive layer. The void offers no illusion, it reveals implacably. The void has a temporal dimension other than that of the city, in that it is unchanging and emphasizes aspects like the rhythms of day and night, the motion of the heavenly bodies and the changes throughout the seasons, temperature, precipitation, light. These natural phenomena have a slower speed than the artificial time of clocks and diaries, an their rhythms are apparently unchanging.[2] The chronology of past, present and future (linear time) is swept away so that infinity and the moment seem to coincide in a cyclic temporal experience. Here nature is represented not by natural processe as is usual, but by natural rhythms.

But emptiness without end is oppressive and terrifying. 'Ther is no freedom in the desert ...'[3] We want freedom, but not withou some sort of footing. The endless expanse of the sky is regarde through the lens of the telescope, for contemplation (literally, studying an area of the sky) needs to be done with both feet squarely on the ground. In the garden courts of Mariavall and th German Pavilion space is defined by the enclosure. The enclosure is the most important material component of the garden, whose purpose is to bring into view the prime immaterial component, the void. This way the void is defined, bu not the programme. There the possibilities are endless, and this is what keeps the imagination fired.

2. For the theoretical work of the French historian Fernand Braudel, who distinguished different 'time frames' in human history, see Braudel 1969.

3. Translated from Komrij 1987, 9.

Wilmkebreek Polder

In Amsterdam-North, wedged between a canal, a motorway, garden villages, sports fields and the remains of the peat landscape, lies Wilmkebreek Polder, a relic of the cultivated landscape now grazed by sheep and an evocative pointer to the flat pastures beyond the city.

Originally, Wilmkebreek was a large stretch of water, left there by a breached dyke along the IJ. In 1633 the lake was dyked and drained. The system of drainage ditches was laid lengthwise in the polder so as to leave a minimum of useless residual lots. The instruments used to organize the polder are the same as those employed for the enclosed garden, namely the axial cross and the enclosure. The main axis running from north-west to south-east and the transverse axis aligned to the water mill, make manifest the length and the breadth of the ovoid polder. Lying three and a half metres lower than its surroundings, the polder is bounded by dykes that define the space particularly on the long sides. At the head ends, clusters of built development form an opaque zone between the enclosure and the space. Like an oversized enclosed garden, the vanishing emptiness of the landscape is dyked in. The landscape has been captured.

Wilmkebreek Polder, Amsterdam. A landscape 'room' of 17.5 ha.

The captured landscape

'One of the pleasures of travelling this fractured coast was such a vista. The irregularity of the English coast offered unusually long views, and these heights helped. A vantage point like The Gribbin made this part of Cornwall look like a topographical map with raised features in bright colours – the best views were always like dazzling maps. And in contrast to the sea, there were the reassuring pastures; on one side the cows and bees and sheep, and slate walls and the smell of manure, and on the other side the gulls and cormorants and whiff of salt spray; and these mingled. The gulls crossed into the pastures, the cows strutted on the sand, and the smells of muck and salt mingled, too. I walked on.'

Paul Theroux, 198

In the northern periphery of Rotterdam lies a nameless polder sandwiched between the railway line and the motorway on one side and the river Rotte on the other. Along the motorway stands a broad noise baffle with a few scattered openings punched in it

In our second design experiment, we have isolated a fragment of this landscape. One of the openings looks out on to the little church and the windmill in the old village centre of Terbregge, the ground is a carpet of rare herbs of every kind and exotic fungi. In the design the motorway, the vista across the Rotte and the intervening polder are made to relate. Three concrete walls each have their own role to play here. The front wall shields the garden from the road and makes a place for cycle stands, the rear wall gathers the panorama (framed on one side by a dense screen of personal allotments) in an elongated window, with a balcony to mediate between the polder and the garden. The third wall is shoved into the soil at an angle, exposing the underlying ground. The resulting incision is aimed at the windmill, visible through the gap between the rear wall and the dyke. From the road, you can look through a hole in the front wall along the incision to the windmill. In the dyke embankment are a number of manhole covers, square horizontal planes in the slope reached from the gardens by flights of steps. Both garden and dyke sport chairs and tables, thereby linking the panorama from the dyke with the garden.

So a fragment of landscape is fixed in an urban periphery in the throes of change. There the last remaining relics of the cultivated landscape will be swallowed up by the city in the not too distant future, if not already. In the experiment, the fragment has been made an enclosed garden, a 'field-glass garden' with the view of the landscape as borrowed scenery.

The defined space is like a temenos, a vacuum impervious to developments around and in which the qualities of the landscape are placed on a pedestal. The landscape is made an object of wonder.

The many facets of the landscape unravelled by Paul Theroux during a four-month hike along the English coastline express the beauty of the edge of an island, the edge of a civilization. Four months to expose the landscape in all its glory, or to travel to the coast to discover the natural boundaries that the urban sprawl cannot overstep, is more than the average city-dweller can permit. Might we not capture the landscape in compact units of time and space?

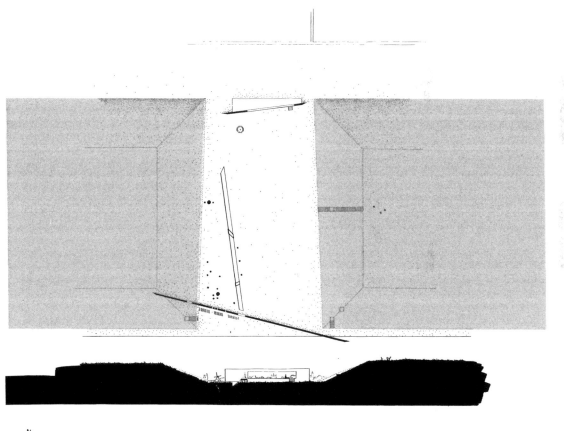

N

0   10m

Design experiment on the Rotte, Rotterdam. The existing dyke embankments become the walls of the garden. Two concrete shields are so placed that the space is closed off while continuing to form part of the landscape. Benches, a fountain and a chess table are sited both in and out of the garden, thereby downplaying the border between garden and landscape. Toadstools and other plants give a suggestion of a natural habitat and an incision in the ground plane reveals a lower (artificial) stratum. See also page 242.

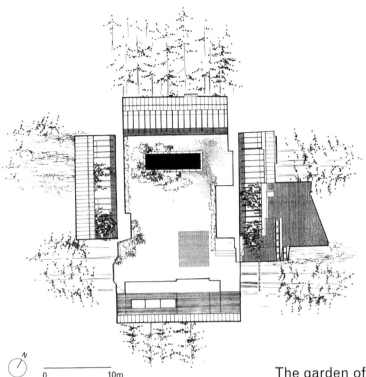

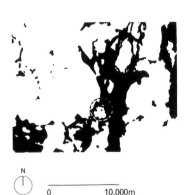

Alvar Aalto, the garden of Säynätsalo
Town Hall, 1950. Exploded box plan.

Säynätsalo is one of the islands in a
landscape where land and water are
equals.

The garden of Säynätsalo Town Hall

In one of the inland seas of South Finland can
be found the island of Säynätsalo. There
between the pines stands a brick building
hugging a raised courtyard.

TOWN HALL ON AN ISLAND: A CENTRE
ADRIFT. On a plain by the water stand the larg
premises of the timber industry providing work
for the local community, whose members live i
timber houses in the woods. In 1950 the
architect Alvar Aalto made a design for the
centre of this community; it features a wedge-
shaped clearing that was to draw wooded hill
and industrial plain together. The town hall wa
the only component of the scheme to be built.
This analysis looks back to the original,
complete plan because in it the island, the
village centre, the town hall and the courtyard
gel in a close-knit composition. The town hall i
sited along an open space, at the point where
relatively steep incline flattens out somewhat.
   Overlooking the endless mesh of lakes is the
plain, a natural balcony terminated on one sid
by the edge of the wood. In a fold of the hilltop
sits the town hall. The climax in this sequence
of spaces is the one in the building reserved fo

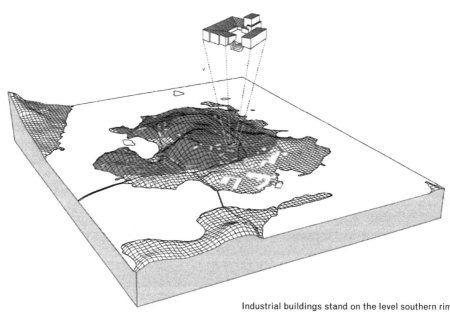

Industrial buildings stand on the level southern rim of the six kilometre wide island, with in the woods small timber houses about a village hall. The latter marks the transition from a steep to a gentle slope and looks out over the open space that was to have been the village centre. The road across the island is a branch of the through route stitching the many islands together.

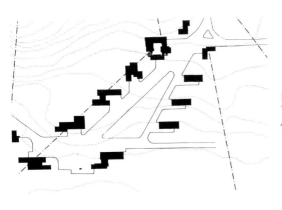

The original design for the village centre. A fork in one of the ridges generates a wedge-shaped open space, with the village hall standing at the narrow end of the wedge.

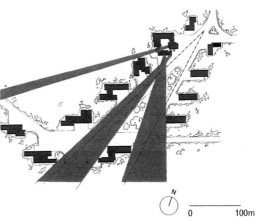

The form of the spaces derives from the cone of vision.

above: A fan-shaped stair of timber and grass accesses the garden from the woods.

below: A granite stair is the formal entry from the village and gives a view of the tree-studded lawn.

Transformation of the type:
• The underlying principle is the square hortus contemplationis enclosed by four volumes.
• The south wing is held clear to generate two openings.
• This wing is reversed with the open side to sun and view.
• The gallery is transmuted into three parts: a broad head as a component of the council chamber tower, a central part along the garden court and a tail as central corridor of the apartment zone.

Transformation of the Karelian farmhouse type:
• The basic premise is a main building to which elements are added producing a head-tail configuration.
• The elements are differentiated and placed in succession.

Cloister type and farmhouse type unite.

the courtyard. Taking its cue from the topographical features, the building unfolds into a U-shaped volume and a free-standing slab. The parts facing the hill have a wall that is blank outside and transparent inside. The portion looking out across the tree-studded lawn has its open side facing outwards.

Inspiration for the materials and colours of the town hall (copper; brick, timber) came from the natural surroundings of the inland sea and the pine and birch forests. The spread of the built masses recalls ruins and transience, which the tangle of ivy only serves to accentuate. The materiality of the steps symbolizes the relationships the town hall enjoys with the landscape and the village. A formal granite stair leading to the central space expresses the cultural side of the facility. Nature is likewise expressed by the contoured steps that fan out to draw the landscape into the building in a generous gesture. There is no mistaking the reference to the Palladian grass bridge and thus to the ideal Arcadian landscape of the locus amoenus, a Finnish Arcadia of grass and pines.

The combination of the Finnish landscape of water and land and Aalto's response to it results in a clear-cut division into four scales: inland sea, island, village centre and town hall. Interestingly the village, rather than being treated as a distinct unit, is absorbed by the woods. At each scale the same relationship between route and object obtains: the road, in approaching an object (island, village centre, town hall, courtyard) never does so directly but skirts round it. The main road runs across the island, the ring road along the tree-studded lawn and the path past the town hall. When one route finally seems likely to enter the town hall it continues past the entrance, through the garden and off into the woods. The front facade of the public library included in the complex, and more especially the council chamber tower are further advantaged by this oblique approach. (One of the original design drawings includes a small building in the wedge-shaped void, so that the view of the town hall is then framed on both sides.) A terrace along the route through the internal court marks the entries to the town hall and the library.

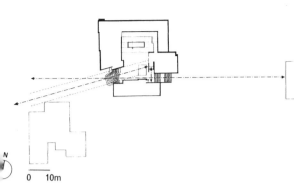

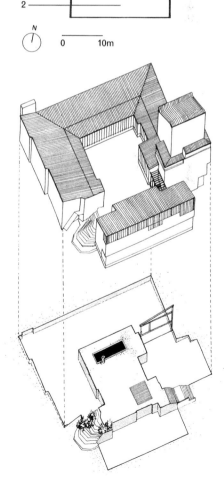

N
0 10m

above: Plan configuration of the garden.

right: Plan of the town hall. The gallery is rendered as a corridor inside the building. 1. Tower-like council chamber / 2. Public library / 3. Apartments / 4. Offices / 5. Hall / 6. Gallery / 7. Stairhead / 8. Garden / 9. Terrace / 10. Pool

below: The various volumes tucked into the slope, with the garden as an elevated plane.

N
0   10m

TOWN HALL AND COURTYARD: BRICK AND PINE. Two plan types seem to have been fused in the built ensemble: the monastery and the Karelian farmhouse. The Karelian farmsteads of East Finland expand like clusters of biological cells from a main building in one direction creating a head-and-tail configuration. In the town hall this is then wrapped round the courtyard, just as the monastery buildings enfold the hortus contemplationis. The raised court represents nature within the building. The relationship between building and landscape is further developed only in the openings between the wings. Each of the three sets of steps materializes another facet of this relationship. The openings, placed opposite each other, create a lifeline between the woods and the village in the building's orthogonal schema. This is formalized in the granite stair. The western opening is modified generating a diagonal between the woods and the tower of the council chamber that takes on visual form as the contoured timber stair. A third line – the entry at the tower pointed up by the pergola – links together the town hall portion and the public library. In the courtyard, there is a division into two caused by indentations in the massing. The lines to the landscape influence only the front portion of the courtyard, the introverted part at the rear being organized to an orthogonal grid.

The pines are an extra enclosure for the garden,
a continuation of the vertical lines of the gallery.

There are two central areas, the reflecting pool
in the rear section and the terrace between the
openings. Despite the courtyard's central
placing in the composition, all components of
the town hall are related to the council chamber
tower. Its counterpoint, the pool, forms the
centre from which the building spirals outward,
with the terrace subsequently tying the tail to
the head. The sculpture next to the pool, like the
tower, is shifted off-centre in the overall
scheme of things.

The court is raised above ground level as the
piano nobile of the building, where views of the
village and the landscape come together. From
this raised plaza, the trees register as a second
horizon above the gallery and the building,
marking the town hall's position in the woods:
dense forest on the side towards the mountain,
and the crowns of individual trees on the lawn
on the village side. The gallery takes the form of
a long internal hall, a Southern European type
exported to the cold Finnish climate. Building,
court and gallery slide by each other in
independence. The relationship between the
components of building and courtyard is
heterotopic, without an oversailing schema.
Thus we see the granite stair and the indented
library wall related, while the elongated pool
has the same proportions (1:3) as the horizontal
glazed wall behind it.

The route inside the building is the backbone
of the plan's organization. A landing atop the
granite stair, the gallery and a transparent wall
lead the visitor in, bridging the difference
between inside and outside in stages. Although
the stairs linking the central courtyard to the

landscape are invisible from the courtyard, the
landscape itself is manifestly present in the
courtyard as a backcloth. The exact opposite
holds for the route to the courtyard: here it is
the courtyard that is out of view, the only visible
reference to it being the resolutely present
stairs.

The town hall has three difference
countenances to show: the tall defensive brick
outer wall, the tall, transparent formal front
facade of the library, and the low transparent,
informal side overlooking the courtyard. The
copper roof, the trees and greenery, the vertical
wooden slats and the tiled plinth together
create a differentiated courtyard, whereas the
outward-facing elevations are uniform. The
garden enfolded by the town hall registers as
an island in an ocean of trees. Inside it the
island metaphor is reversed. Here it is the water
that is enclosed by vegetation and the building

PROGRAMME AND MEANING. A great many
components are concentrated in the town hall,
in a programme that ties in with the head-and-
tail configuration and the vertical
differentiation. The head – the council chamber
– is the locus from which all other components
of the programme exfoliate in equal measure.
The shops and the public library are downstairs
and relate to the island, the housing and
administrative and executive areas upstairs are
related to the courtyard. Raising the courtyard
gives literal expression to this more elevated
function, 'set free of the vulgar influence of the
business premises', as Aalto himself puts it.
Towering above it is the council chamber. The
library is held clear of the rest of the building
parts and being the most shared feature of the
facility, faces outwards.

Besides conveying the 'exalted' executive
purpose of the town hall, the courtyard
expresses the identity of the landscape and
Finnish culture. The natural contours are
deliberately accentuated by their close
proximity to the artificial plane of the raised
courtyard. Materials and colours refer to the
natural surroundings and the local formal idiom
(the stone plinth also used in the traditional
timber houses, the Karelian plan configuration

allude to local cultural history. The informal plan configuration seems to derive from the amorphous texture of inland seas and islands.

SYNTHESIS. Itself an urban symbol, this town hall enfolds part of the landscape. Whereas landscape and village are impossible to distinguish between on the island, in the town hall they register as two separate, complementary elements of the building.

The courtyard spins out a network of relationships which are independent of one another though of equal stature. Each with its own logic (of the heterotopic variety), these relationships desist from mutual reinforcement so that vertical alignment is almost entirely absent. The courtyard, as much a microcosm as a fragment, is particularized by being enclosed by several cutaneous layers: the inland seas, the island, the woods and finally the building. This distinction is emphasized by the courtyard's position above ground level but is at the same time weakened by the penetrating presence there of the woods. The courtyard is made part of the landscape. Its wall planes are fragmented, low-lying and tenuous so that they scarcely define the space they contain.

Entrepenørskolen at Ebeltoft

On the east coast of Denmark lies the peninsula of Ebeltoft, largely covered with coniferous forests and dune grass, with the small town of that name nestling in the bay. Hidden away in the dunes is a concrete building concealing a world full of surprises.

A SCHOOL IN THE DUNES. In the centre of the peninsula, high above the bay and the town, stands a school for contractors, the Entrepenørskolen. Its autonomous quadrangular parti has a distinct front and rear, in response to its position just below the summit of a ridge of dunes. The rear barely rises above the hills, while the front has a striking double-height glass facade anchored in its grass setting by a screen of piers placed at right angles to it. Four wings sunk into the

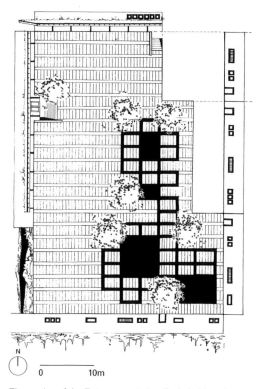

The garden of the Entrepenørskolen. Exploded box plan.

hillside have outward sloping roofs with a large overhang, so that the wall plane seems to dissolve and the rooms seen from inside appear tucked into the slope. A large opening in the wall draws the dune landscape into the building to be abstracted into a courtyard. The tops of the pines rising above the roof give the impression that the landscape continues unhindered inside the building.

Dominating the landscape is the vast blue emptiness of the bay, the undulating expanse of dunes and the forests of spruce. The school accords with this image through its sober garb – concrete walls and grass roofs – and horizontal volume, and outward sloping roofs corresponding to the slope of the dunes.

The main routes on Ebeltoft are the north-south lines paralleling the principal alignment of the island. The access road to the school branches out from one of the main routes at an almost perfect right angle. Its last few metres are across a grassy bank penetrating the front facade, so that the difference in height is visible on approaching the school but the courtyard

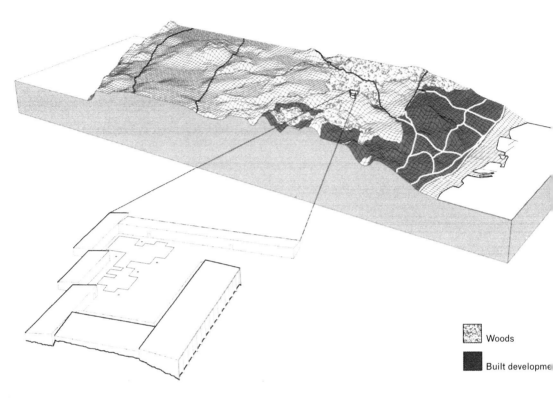

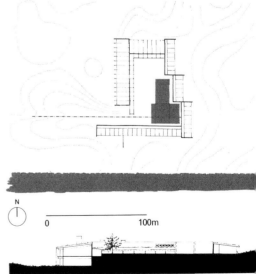

Woods

Built developme

above: The elongated peninsula of Ebeltoft has a steep east coast and makes a gentle descent to the bay in the west. The roads and the built development in general follow the length of the peninsula. The town nestles between the bay and the dunes, whose highest peaks in the centre of the peninsula are wooded. Overlooking the town and the bay, with the woods as a wall behind it, is the school.

above right: Plan configuration and geomorphology.

below right: Tucked into the slope, the school expresses the difference in height in its sequence of classrooms, gallery and garden.

N

0   100m

Transformation of the type (here East is at the top):
• The underlying principle is the square hortus contemplationis framed by four volumes.
• The south wing is shifted outward creating a garden courtyard parallel to the length of the peninsula. The opening left in the process is accentuated by extending that wing. The gallery is reduced to the north and west wings of the building.
• The east wing, transmuted into an exedra, terminates the line linking the building to the bay (both access road and view).

remains hidden. It is only at the last moment, with the courtyard at eye level, that the internal world looms into view.

TWO FACES. The sole components of the school are the courtyard, a gallery and four bar-shaped volumes of outward-facing rooms. Each volume is so shaped as to express the various segments of the programme and the geomorphology. A public section is reached from the gallery. In the individual and more introverted part of the building the gallery metamorphoses into an internal corridor.

The courtyard is lifted clear of the natural contours which continue all the way up to the building. The gallery by contrast is sunken, cutting the courtyard loose, so to speak, from the building. The latter has two faces: one layered and changing, turned to the busy contours of the dunelands, the other flat and looking towards the abstracted courtyard through windows with broad white-painted frames set in an abstract composition.

THE COURTYARD: GEOMETRY AND A LOW PROFILE. The ground plane of the courtyard divides into a flat concrete expanse and a sheet of water with stepping stones. The concrete connects by way of the gallery with the public portion of the building, and the far less accessible water adjoins the private rooms, separated from them by a smooth concrete wall. In the L-shaped pool we see united the two principal directions of the courtyard: the orientation to the view and the longitudinal direction of the space. The land-water division is based on the module size of the concrete floor slabs: 60 by 180 centimetres with a mortar joint of three centimetres.

top to bottom:
Duneland, school, facade, entrance, garden. The school is barely discernible amid the rolling dunes of Ebeltoft. Only the wing facing west towards the bay has a prominent facade resembling the prongs of a rake. It is only on reaching the school that the opening comes fully into view. The garden is raised up to eye-level when seen from the gallery.

In plan, the composition is framed by the horizontal lines of the facade in the low roof, the frieze of windows and the gallery. Vertical elements – Scots Pines, concrete cylinders and lighting elements – gather the space around them without modulating it. Behind the long south facade can be seen the treetops of the spruce forest, relating the internal space to that outside.

Concrete panels, concrete walls, a smooth reflecting sheet of water, white pebbles, Scots Pines, white concrete cylinders for seats and oxidized copper lamps create a serene ambience in the courtyard. This is countered by a view of the bay and the setting sun, a stage set for the courtyard. The latter also has two faces. Here the Danish landscape avails itself of a Japanese vision of nature, giving the reference to the local landscape a universal twist. In this microcosm, land and water, mineral and organic, horizontal and vertical are in equipoise.

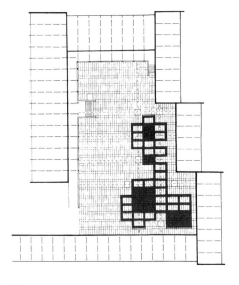

above: At the side overlooking the bay are the communal functions, with the individual rooms on the side tucked into the dunes. This dichotomy returns in the material of the garden, with concrete slabs set before the public part and water before the private. 1. Gallery / 2. Foyer / 3. Reception and offices / 4. Communal rooms downstairs with classrooms above / 5. Kitchens and services / 6. Staff rooms / 7. Guest rooms

right: The plan configuration of the garden is comprised of three interrelated grids. The division into land and water is dictated by the module size of the concrete floor slabs (60cm x 180cm). Against this is set a grid of 7.5m x 7.5m indicating the positioning of the trees. The columns of the gallery adhere to the building's system of measures. Just how severe this modular system is can be judged from the top left-hand corner of the gallery where two columns all at once have very little distance between them.

N

0   10m

PROGRAMME AND MEANING. Located off the beaten track, the building is a centre of learning for contractors in the building industry and includes accommodation. Like a monastery, it is one building designed to accept a complete daily rhythm of working, eating, sleeping and leisure. Differences in geometries and spaces coincide with the zoning according to function. The side facing the panorama contains the classrooms with their large glass partitions, the bedrooms are stashed away among the dunes and the remaining wing comprises the kitchens, wedged as these are between the shared and private zones. All accommodation is situated on the exterior with the views and circulation space on the courtyard side. The communal portion of the building is reached from the sunken gallery, at which point the garden is visible at eye level. Stepping stones in the water give access to the other side of the building. There, four doors lead through to the bedrooms, whose air of isolation is increased by the fact that you can only enter them from the inner court; there is no internal access. The courtyard unites two quite disparate functions: it is both a reception area and a place of rest, a duality expressed in the division into land and water.

SYNTHESIS. Together, the school and the courtyard are a unit, spatially, visually and functionally. The low-lying spacious building and the rolling dunelands which seem to continue into the garden, lend both school and courtyard a powerful horizontality and forge strong links with the landscape. The alignment with the horizon is expressed by the panorama across the bay. Against this is set the illusion of nature in the raised courtyard. Loosed from its context, it becomes autonomous, universal: the garden as kaleidoscope. A duality of inside and outside arises through the combinations of layered outer wall and flat internal wall, flowing forms of the landscape and geometry of the courtyard, and the reduction to horizontal and vertical lines in the building. The courtyard's autonomy and its ties with the landscape meld in a single composition.

Japanese simplicity in a Danish landscape. The concrete floor slabs and the sculptural Scots Pines allude to tatami and bonsai.

The enclosed garden as field glass

It takes a frame to turn a fragment of landscape into a garden distinct from its surroundings. This frame is made manifest not in the garden itself but in the transition between landscape and fragment. Whereas the enclosed garden as telescope is characterized by a tensionality between earth and sky (cosmic orientation), here we see garden and landscape (inside and outside) as the paradox of an enclosed space informed by territorial orientation.

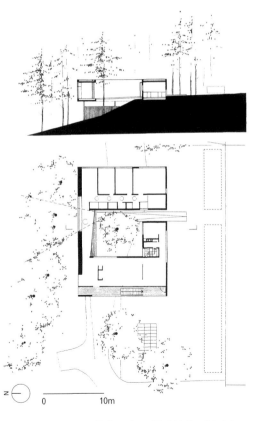

Stéphane Beel, House P., Rotselaer (B) 1994. A solid slab at the front, the house is suspended like a tree-hut at the rear. I n the middle of the square design is a gaping hole.

House P.

On the edge of a wood in the village of Rotselaer in Belgium there stands a flattened grey box with a hole at its centre. Seen from the front it is a contained volume, from the rear it is lifted high above the hillside. Having the building and landscape mesh together – seemingly without mutual influence – has generated a 'bottomless' garden. It is in the gaping void at the centre of the house that complete integration takes place: the woods penetrate the building, the building surrounds the woods. Through the combination of raised box and open core, the woods are present everywhere in the building: inside and out, above it and below it. We can see it in the large deep-set windows, in the round glass holes in the floor, in the footbridge slicing through the front facade and leading across the garden to a large wall of glass in the hall. The autonomous element is not the garden but the house, the garden being merely a fragment of the surrounding landscape. Here microcosm and fragment are set side by side.

The courtyard of the Entrepenørskolen in Ebeltoft has an opening so large – twenty metres is a third of the wall – that the open landscape pours into the courtyard, putting the putative containment into perspective. Then again, the town hall in Säynätsalo has a pair of openings (one of four metres, the other of six) set in opposite walls so that the landscape 'flows' through the courtyard. In both spaces the openings are so positioned as to bring about a subdivision into a more and a less contained part. There is a turning point when a reinforcing of the containment gives way to its dissolution. Openings between the ends of walls call the primacy of the space into question, in that the walls become autonomous. Once these have greater emphasis than the space, the containment ceases to exist.

The act of framing allows us to deploy the fragment of landscape as an 'urban' element without negatively affecting, or being negatively affected by, the urban fabric. They even strengthen each other through the contrast. The pastures of Wilmkebreek Polder and the tower blocks of Amsterdam-North are made manifest by being in close proximity. The relationship between inside and outside, as expressed in Ebeltoft and Säynätsalo, is the first field of tension. A second field is enacted between the landscape represented in the garden as an immutable given, and the changing (urban) context.
'My father is a very old man. A while back we were driving up the Bitterroot Valley of Montana, and he was gazing away to the mountains. "They'll never see it the way we did," he said, and I wonder what he saw.'[4] This urge to somehow fix the landscape seems an expression of nostalgia, an attempt to hang on to a past seen through the eyes of an old man. Yet this moment, captured in the lens of the field glass, is not just simply a question of holding on to a landscape that will soon be history; it is the act of registering changes against the backdrop of a changing context. To expose the layered condition of the landscape, we need only take one layer, the landscape as it is today, and distil from it a fragment. This allows us to visualize the process of change in the landscape as a whole.

4. Kittredge 1987, 62.

Artificial nature

'It seemed to him that he had stepped through a high window
that looked on a vanished world. A light was upon it for which his
language had no name. All that he saw was shapely, but the
shapes seemed at once clear cut, and if they had been first
conceived and drawn at the uncovering of his eyes, and ancient
as if they had endured forever. He saw no colour but those he
knew, gold and white and blue and green, but they were fresh and
poignant, as if he had at that moment first perceived them and
made for them names new and wonderful. In winter here no heart
could mourn for summer or for spring. No blemish or sickness o
deformity could be seen in anything that grew upon the earth.
On the land of Lorien there was no stain.'

J.R.R. Tolkien, 195

Let us return to the northern periphery of Rotterdam where
the issues of urbanization are clearly etched. The experiment
with the fragment of landscape was enacted in a small-scale
undefined environment. A little further to the east we find a
patchwork quilt of such large-scale functions as 'brain parks'
and water purification plants. In 1996 the Office for Metropolitan
Architecture designed for this area a *transferium*, an 'empty'
asphalt expanse seven metres above ground level. A mound in
the otherwise level surface shows where the rapid tram burrows
below ground. Holes punched in the asphalt give access to an
underground world of parking garages, a rapid-bus terminal, a
sports centre, a drive-in restaurant, a shopping centre and
auditoria for congresses. This subterranean city is pitted against
the uplifted void – two real worlds of an illusive size and
dramatic potential.

By way of experiment, our third, we shall define within this
encounter area a tangible if unreal world, a shady island in an
endless sea of cars. An impenetrable concrete wall leaves just
the tops of trees in sight, the suggestion of an Arcadian world
beyond. A stair next to the wall descends to the parking garage
below the asphalt expanse, and a ramp ascends to the garden
which is lifted into space and away from the bustle on the
asphalt. The door to the garden opens onto a gallery held clear
of the wall and encircling the garden in its entirety. The broad
edge of the gallery provides comfortable places to sit with
openings to the flower-filled meadow at irregular distances. The
ground of the garden is supremely rugged – in ascending and
descending you feel the layer of turf beneath your feet and the
act of walking. Lilies of the valley, wood hyacinths, anemones,
wild strawberries and winter roses make for a flowery mead; you
can smell the ramblers and honeysuckle around the columns of
the gallery. Wall fruit in recesses against the south wall and
star-apples invite fruit-picking in summer. A pool in a clearing
mirrors the sky. Between it and the edge of the gallery is a gully
where the water pours over the edge to disappear in the depths

Design experiment at the Kralingen
transferium. A metre-thick concrete wall
enfolds an Arcadian landscape of
undulating flowery mead, birches, fruit
trees and reflecting pool. The route,
which is perfectly circular with neither
beginning nor end, leaves the square
envelope briefly for a view of the hectic
reality of the transferium.
See also page 240.

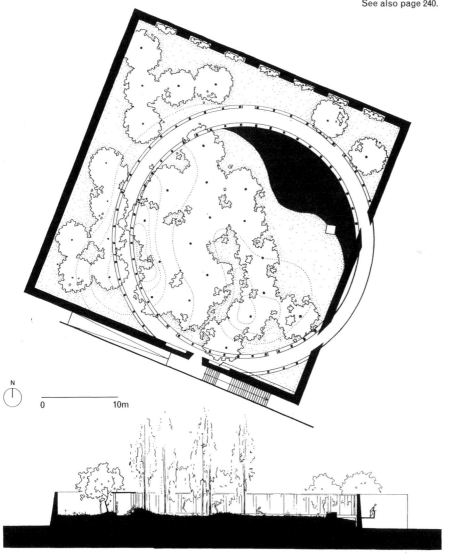

N

0   10m

The gallery drills through the wall to become a balcony giving the broadest view out across the ocean of cars and the motorway, with the double bridge (Van Brienenoordbrug) in the background.

Isn't it an escapist act to make a Utopia in such unpretentious surroundings? In the kaleidoscope garden, Utopia, the paradisiacal image of nature, is invariably confronted with a version of the local landscape or simply coincides with it. This is using Utopia as a means of perceiving local features from a new perspective, in the way that Frodo's perception of the land of Lorien gives a fresh look to the colours he knew from his own world. The Entrepenørskolen in Ebeltoft lends a Japanese-tinted perspective on the ideal landscape. Elements are enlisted from the local landscape – Scots Pines, land and water – to give shape to this perspective: a marriage between Utopia and a reworking of the local landscape. The block hewn from the centre of House P. in Rotselaer reveals the existing woods, an image of nature as an accepted part of our daily living environment. The thicket of Robinia in the Paradiesgarten of Libeskind's Berlin Museum sprang spontaneously from the detritus of war. It is a metaphor for nature, which can heal even the deep wounds of conflict, and transcend the banality of a pile of rubble.

Nature is something we confine in national parks, or a thing we have to save by using the car less and producing less waste. From a condition for life it has evolved into a problem, a delicate abstract thing we are concerned about, but which these days has little to do with reality. In the Entrepenørskolen nature is conceived as a simple, tangible given, a harmony of water and trees. The current vision on nature strives after authenticity, a reconstruction of a time when man had no noticeable role to play. Yet the nature we see is a nature affected by thousands of years of human habitation. Is it a feasible proposition to exclude man from an image he has invented and guided? Which is more real: the abstraction of a historicist primeval nature, or an illusion of nature that we can touch? The unspoilt nature shown on television, or the sensation of a mist machine and jungle noises in quadrophonic sound, such as in the Parc de la Villette?

Parc André-Citroen

Fragrant blue flowers, splashing water surrounded by green foliage, fiery orange tints of autumn and rich textures, red fruit, a silver stream and diffuse sunlight through a roof of Robinia leaves, give an ideal image of nature. In six enclosed gardens, the senses are successively tantalized, the last being the sixth sense, the suggestion that nature can only be grasped intuitively.

This series of gardens forms part of the Parc André-Citroen. In the tradition of the great formal gardens on the banks of the Seine, this one orders the districts around it with an axis of symmetry square to the river. The axis runs over an expansive tapis vert, flanked by follies on the south side and behind these the six gardens. The great size of the tapis vert mediates between the dimensions of the Seine and those of the garden 'rooms', its openness engaging with the containment of the gardens. In the gardens the theme of enclosure is thrashed out in a game of exclusion, visibility and accessibility. The individual relationship between man and space alters with each garden. Thus, for example, the silver garden is viewed from a balcony, the orange garden accompanies a route and the green garden is a self-contained space seen from inside.

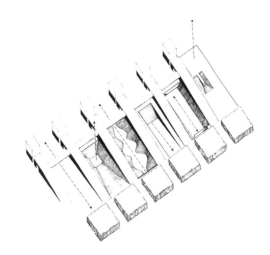

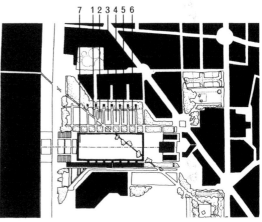

0   100m

above: Gilles Clément and Alain Provost, Parc André-Citröen, Paris, 1992. Hidden behind blocks of trees are the 'jardins sériels', a sequence of themed gardens held apart by cascades. Raised solar courts behind these gardens indirectly link them with the tapis vert on the other side. The six gardens adhere to a system of measures that ties park and city blocks together. A regular rectangle with a ratio of 1:2 is distorted in various ways to construct in each case a different relationship with the tapis vert, the edge of the park and the sky. Thus, for instance, the 'golden garden' is lengthened to 1:3 so as to terminate an axis running behind the gardens.

below: The park lies on the bank of the Seine and connects to one of the 19th-century boulevards. 1. Blue garden / 2. Green garden / 3. Orange garden / 4. Red garden / 5. Silver garden / 6. Golden garden / 7. Tapis vert

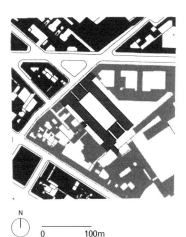

N
0   100m

above: Renzo Piano, Christine Dalnoky and Michel Desvigne,
Square des Bouleaux, Paris, 1992. The Parisian district
containing the housing block consists of a dense texture cut
through by an irregular street pattern.

middle: The garden entrance on the street.

right: The garden of Square de Bouleaux serves as an access
to the houses, as the intermediary zone between house, and as
a fragment of an ideal nature at a great remove from the city.

Square des Bouleaux

Hidden behind an introverted elevation in a
narrow street stands this clump of birches on a
carpet of honeysuckle. A subtle game is being
played here, between the self-sufficiency of the
garden and its integration with the apartment
building and the landscape morphology.

The facade of the building conforms to the
surrounding development but behind it a perfec
square has broken free from the piecemeal
context. This state of freedom can be seen at
the rear where the chinks that appeared have
been filled with birches and honeysuckle.

The building's design is based on the concep
of the 'residential path'. This slices through the
blocks and accesses the apartments from the
inside. The garden constitutes the entrance, the
lobby of the building. This functional
relationship between building and garden can
be read in the garden design, a grid of red
terracotta tiles with the slender birch trunks in-
between continuing the wall with its pattern of
white concrete strips over a surface of
terracotta tiles. The wall is spatially layered
with an alternation of vertical window openings
and horizontal slats, an alternation echoed in
the fine pattern of stripes in the tree bark.

The apartment building stands at the foot of
hill, in an orthogonal grid of planes, slopes and
stairs. A ramp on one side emerges with the
stairs at a plane composed of three tilted
surfaces, putting into perspective the symmetr
of the garden. (The original design was fully

186

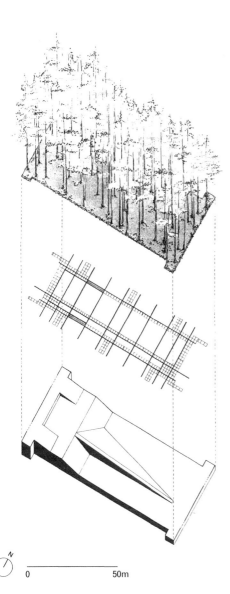

symmetrical and boasted two ramps.)

A carpet of wintergreen honeysuckle and a transparent forest of birches, their crowns growing together, present an abstract image of nature, one that differs little in summer and winter. The lack of light in the garden and the great density keep the trees looking long and spindly. The image is motionless and timeless, making the visitor feel like an interloper.

The garden can only be entered through a gate and a narrow passage that shut out the sounds and images of the street. Rather than following a straight line from the entrances, the route is staggered so that the two openings disappear from sight. This strategy slows one up and heightens the feeling of containment. The perimeter walk is shifted in from the sides so as to be absorbed by the garden.

SYNTHESIS. The birch trunks, though echoing the white lines of the windows and slats, seek to negate even this relationship with the building. Through a suggestion of horizontal expansiveness and the sense of reaching for the farthest corners of the sky they manage to shake free of the restrictions of the garden space. Autonomy, derived from the forceful rendition of nature and from the elementary space, and a sense of attachment through the plan configuration and the materiality, are here set side by side. Quotidian reality and alienation inform the way the garden is used. If the route is functional, the representation of nature is awe-inspiring.

N
0   50m

above: Geomorphology, plan configuration, spatial form and appearance. The natural relief gets a geometric treatment, with over that a grid of paving and a carpet of planting (8500 honeysuckle plants and 120 birches).

right: An autonomous unit in a fragmented urban context. Only at those places where the honeysuckle and birches fill up the residual spaces outside the garden is an indirect relationship forged between the box and the context.
The walk around the enclosed garden is held clear of the built development and the entrances.

Garden of the Jewish Museum

When extending the Berlin Museum with a new Jewish department Daniel Libeskind designed a fragmented park containing two paradise boxes. The ensemble materializes the invisibility and emptiness that Libeskind feels typify the deadly past of German-Jewish cultural relationships. References to the Jewish faith and key moments in recent Jewish history endow both the museum and the gardens with a symbolic charge.

THE URBAN FIELD. Emptiness and invisibility as the downside of history are deployed here as a negative print of the historical context by rendering each component as a vacuole. The splintered urban context consists of new-build development and a sixties estate. Pinning the 0.8 hectare museum grounds and the surrounding housing areas together are fragments of seemingly endless lines and planes. The empty spaces by contrast represent complete and finite worlds. The long lines mesh in an autonomous layer that is in opposition to the free-ranging volumes. One such line is the Jewish department which stands as a twisted screen between the old Baroque garden of the museum and the new public space. A straight if broken line drills a tunnel through the screen. With these lines, objects and planes superimposed on the existing context, the whole looks supremely haphazard. Clarity of

above: Spatial form and appearance of the E.T.A. Hoffmanngarten. The three layers – pit, ground plane and grid of columns – are tilted away from one another.

right: Daniel Libeskind, Jewish Museum, Berlin, 1998. The two gardens are set at seemingly haphazard places in a piecemeal urban context.

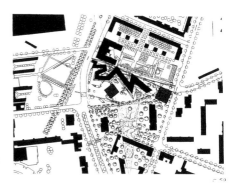

188

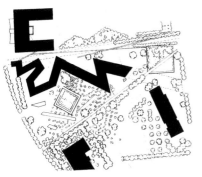

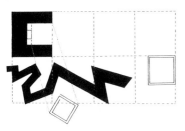

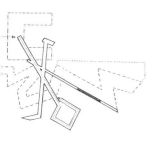

above to below:
Square frames shut out the chaos and create inside an order very much their own.

Plan configuration. An invisible order informs the placement of the gardens. Among the rose bushes in one angle of the museum is the E.T.A. Hoffmanngarten (the tilted square), scooped out of the ground plane. The dimensions of the square equal those of the courtyard of the Collegienhaus, the existing Baroque museum building (top left corner). The direction of the Collegienhaus is echoed by that of the Paradiesgarten (right). This garden is shot through by a long line crossing the entire site.

Plan configuration. A subterranean system of passages stitches the autonomous components together.

organization is nowhere to be found, everywhere walls and spaces have something to hide.

TWO GARDENS. Nestling between the shards of the design are two enclosed gardens, a suggestion of order in a shambolic context. The internal order of the gardens and the chaos of the surroundings do relate, though heterotopically. An underground line beginning in the existing museum, the Collegienhaus, ducks beneath the Jewish Museum to terminate in the E.T.A. Hoffmanngarten. From there, a ramp spirals up to street level. Another line joins together the two housing districts flanking the museum grounds. Just before leaving the grounds, this line crosses the otherwise out-of-bounds Paradiesgarten.

With a ramp around its perimeter, the E.T.A. Hoffmanngarten further consists of a square filled with 49 tightly packed columns set in an orthogonal grid. There thus emerges a second plane as a negative image of the ground plane six metres below. Libeskind energizes and complicates the static form by introducing the spiral ramp, tilting the wall planes and giving the floor a ten-per-cent slope. The grid of columns creates a labyrinth of paths one metre wide, with the garden lifted into space as a temenos. Grapevines and ivy adorn the walls and columns, oleasters atop the columns provide a green canopy. The space defined by the ramp and tilted walls is symbolic of the unstable situation in which the Jews found themselves before and during the World War II. The 49 columns (seven times seven) derive from the use of numbers in the Kabbalah, the mystical religious Jewish system. The tension between the incomprehensible and appalling reality and faith in an underlying order is expressed in a space that is as much confusing and labyrinthine as it is static and involuted.

Clusters of Robinia that have grown up spontaneously among the rubble of war are the basic premise of the Paradiesgarten. This world in miniature is delineated by a small channel and a thick hedge. Hidden among the foliage is a source of water, a spiral spring hewn from stone. A row of poplars on the north side joins this garden to the Baroque garden, and the east-west link across the park sliced diagonally through the Paradiesgarten. This diagonal disrupts both the symmetry of the square and the enclosure. Generating a division into two parts, one open, the other sporting a thick cluster of Robinia against a screen of poplars. The design is superimposed on the natural situation without impairing it. So now we have two visual layers within the enclosure. By retaining the existing situation of wasteland and weeds and placing it in an organizing framework, Libeskind is again illustrating that the horrors of reality are part of a greater scheme.

PROGRAMME AND MEANING. The Biblical ideal of paradise, shut off from the outside world by a thick hedge, links arms here with the symbol of the power of unsullied nature, a power traditionally excluded from paradise. The outside world is transported to the inner world, where it is hermetically sealed and endowed with mystical properties. In Eastern symbolism, the spiral spring binds space and time with its doubly woven form. Here the spring emerges by

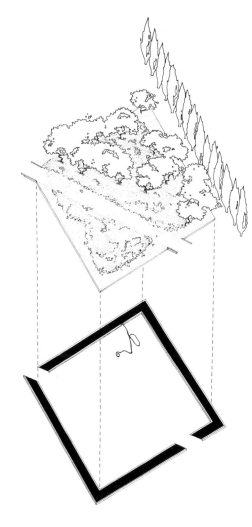

a tree, thereby symbolizing the mythical origins of the river in paradise from where it flowed into the world and into time and space.

SYNTHESIS. In a fragmented setting such as this, the garden suggests wholeness. In the gardens, however, this wholeness is in turn qualified by a deformation in the Hoffmanngarten of the static basic form, and b the Paradiesgarten's relationship with the landscape.

above: Spatial form and appearance of the Paradiesgarten. Mythical symbols underlie the planting.

left: The Hoffmanngarten, the building and the city.

Brion cemetery garden

Commissioned to design a new cemetery as an extension to the local one, Carlo Scarpa staged a great number of scenes within a boundingwall. Here the hortus ludi gets a new lease of life. The wall takes centre stage in the design. It is defensive yet one can look over it from inside; it excludes and at the same time holds its disorderly contents together; and it accepts departures from the everyday.

AN ISLAND OF THE DEAD AMIDST FIELDS OF MAIZE. On a broad plain at the foot of the Veneto lies the village of San Vito d'Altivole, with beyond it the cemetery. Village and cemetery are linked by a long avenue partly bordered by cypress. Slicing through the cemetery, this axis ends at the Brion family plot, an L-shaped area wrapped around the old cemetery.

Enclosed by a massive concrete wall, the ensemble is an isolated object on the plain. The concrete objects and the trees that protrude above the wall betray a varied inner world. The two parts of the ensemble – cemetery and garden – are self-sufficient entities, linked by a stair in a concrete box at the end of the axis, that terminates at a window looking out over the garden. Both the village and the surrounding farmlands resonate in the garden as stage scenery.

The garden lies like an island in a sea of maize, with the avenue of cypress a bridge to the inhabited world, the village. The cemetery garden in some ways resembles a city, within whose bounding wall buildings rise like church spires. These buildings are linked by 'streets', with a 'square' for the chapel and the garden beyond that. A game played between the old wall of the cemetery and the new one of the garden sees to it that each of the four sides presents a different view of this 'city'.

Following the route we can perceive a sequence, from the broad open area to steadily smaller and more enclosed spaces. Beginning in the village, the long line stabs through the cemetery and on into the garden where it fragments on the lawn to end at the only internal space, the chapel.

above: Treviso, painting by F. Bertelli. In its maizefield setting, Brion cemetery garden is much like a walled city of towers, streets, squares and districts.

centre: Carlo Scarpa, Brion cemetery garden, San Vito d'Altivole, 1969-1978.

below: Plan configuration and geomorphology. A gateway in the landscape marks the large open space of the maizefields. This expansiveness is related to the containment of the chapel in a spatial sequence of ever smaller spaces with a diversity of enclosures and differences in height. 1. Cemetery garden / 2. Old burial ground / 3. Avenue of cypress / 4. San Vito d'Altivole

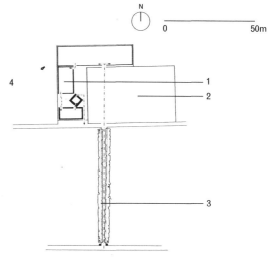

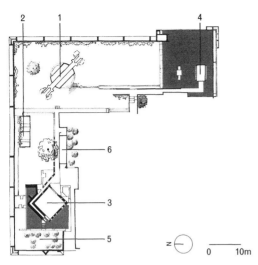

Widely spaced pavilions, trees, paths, lakes and lawns are pulled together by a solid wall. 1. Arcosolium / 2. Family vault / 3. Chapel / 4. Water pavilion / 5. Sacro Bosco / 6. Hidden garden

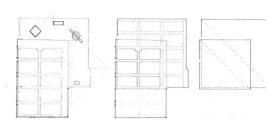

Plan configuration. Geometric orders underlie the seemingly haphazard composition. The shape of the ground plane corresponds to that of the square of the original cemetery and the module derives from the arrangement of the graves. The location of the objects is fixed by an imaginary plan for the cemetery projected over the true plan at an angle of 45 degrees.

AN ASSEMBLAGE OF SCENES. The L-shaped plot of the new garden is composed of two strips, each split into two using differences in height and oblique lines. This fourfold division relates to a series of free-standing objects: the chapel, a family vault, the Brion tomb and a pavilion. In this composition the tomb figures uppermost because of its pivotal position in the garden. Curved concrete elements, water channels and plants further distinguish the ground plane.

Given its L-shape and the myriad objects, walls and trees, it is impossible to take in the garden at a stroke. The most open part is at the pivot, which is also raised emphasizing the view to be had from it. Involuted sunken spaces occupy the ends of the garden. The horizon is continually vacillating between present and absent. The raised section of garden acts as a balcony, opening up a view over the wall of the village, making it part of the plain. It is at this very place too that the tomb is sunk. Encounters between garden and horizon, and introvert and extravert, are intensified at this pivotal point.

The axis begun by the avenue of cypress ends at a window consisting of two entwined circles. The sight line proceeds through the window in a straight line to the garden wall, where the route splits: turn right and a path leads to the separate world of the pavilion in the water, turn left and the route ends at the plateau. From there a second T-shaped system of paths accesses the other part of the garden. Behind the chapel we discover a cluster of cypress, rounding off the seemingly haphazard route with the same planting that began it.

The objects ostensibly scattered at random throughout the ground plane in fact comprise a scenographic composition. Movement through the garden strings the scenes together. The pavilion is an island in the water-lily pool, where you get a view across the cemetery landscape from a sitting position only. The tomb is a grotto in the mead, a concrete canopy over a tiled 'cave' symbolizes the tomb that the early Christians made in the catacombs for important personages, the arcosolium. Between the cemetery and the new Brion family plot lies a secret garden, where a lone maple set before a concrete screen has everything of a Japanese print. The family vault is a catacomb, the chapel a temple lifted above the water. Movement through the cemetery, which has proceeded in concert with an increasingly sunken ground plane, ceases at the sacro bosco behind the chapel. The horizon too has sunk progressively from view behind the wall. Views and containment are related to movement, standing and sitting.

The sculptures, deriving from numerous cultures – Islamic, Roman, Romanesque, Venetian, Japanese – consist of contrasting forms, directions and materials, crude elements and refined details (mosaic and stepped concrete edges). Cypress, a weeping larch, conifers and garlands of ivy intensify the elegiac atmosphere.

Clockwise from top left: gateway, entrance, arcosolium, chapel. The beginning of the avenue of cypress is marked by a gateway. The burial ground and cemetery garden are linked by an entrance building, a complex composition of walls and views through. The arcosolium sits on a raised area, from where the church of San Vito d'Altivole is visible over the wall. Stepping stones access the introverted chapel which is configured as an island in the pool.

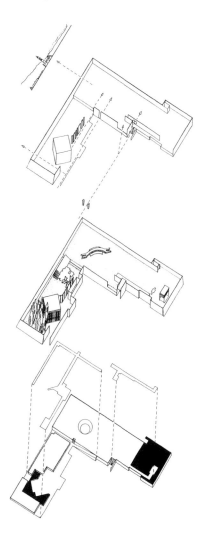

above: The cemetery garden is a garden of contemplation. The design forces the visitor to slow down, such as at the water pavilion where views, in this case across the water-lilies to the arcosolium, can only be had from a sitting position.

left: Spatial form and route. Differences in level and planar divisions into grass and water divide the garden into four parts identified by the chapel, the family grave, the arcosolium and the water pavilion. Two distinct systems of pathways stitch the components to each other and to the world beyond (each system is related to one of the two entrances). Walking through the garden brings a constant change of view between one framed by gateways and windows and a wide panorama across the wall. This wall is resolutely present in the smaller spaces.

PROGRAMME AND MEANING. This garden is not only a place for burial, it is an homage to the Brion family, who have done so much for the villagers. So the fact that their memory is enshrined in a contained space but at the same time qualified by the view out is quite deliberate. Life and death, contemplation and the pleasures of the senses, garden and landscape are drawn together.

SYNTHESIS. Here, so many individual scenes are stitched together into a frame story. The scenes are visually held together by the uniform materiality of concrete and grass and spatially by the sturdy boundary wall. This gathering together of oppositions is expressed by the inversions encountered everywhere. The introverted cave of the arcosolium is the central point of the composition, and is sited at the most outward-looking place in the cemetery. Heavy and light trade places by having the solid pavilion hover above the water, clear lines are suddenly cut short, secondary places in the composition are pointedly detailed. Set against this ambivalence is the certainty of the landscape and the wall. The fullness and exuberance of the garden suggest a completeness. By these means, earth (landscape) and sky are brought both visually and spatially into the garden.

Jardin des Bambous

'There is no point in designing a detail that acts counter to the totality, but neither did I want to design something that would underpin Tschumi's plan … . That is why I've made a hole in the ground, a new independent space.'

Alexandre Chemetoff 198

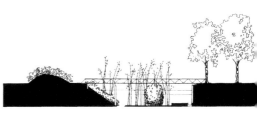

Alexandre Chemetoff (with Madeleine Renan and the artists Daniel Buren and Bernard Leitner), Jardin des Bambous, Paris, 1987. For all its capricious form, the garden has the same profile throughout its length: an earthen wall, a bamboo covered slope, a gully, a bamboo covered ground plane, a raised strip with a pattern of pebbles, a gully, a heat-collecting wall and an avenue of plane trees.

A GARDEN IN THE PARK. The Parc de la Villette in Paris is a graphic composition of superimposed lines, planes and points. One of the lines is a promenade cinématique, strung off which are several gardens. As it meanders through the centre of the park, the promenade cinématique defines a plane together with two straight avenues and their point of intersection These three lines are decisive for the organization of the Jardin des Bambous, or bamboo garden. The serpentine line reverberates in Chemetoff's sunken garden as rippling planted plots. One of the avenues is brought into the composition courtesy of a retaining wall running parallel to it with a number of channels meeting the wall at right angles. Even the sewers discovered to be crossing the site were incorporated in the scheme.

By burying the Jardin des Bambous the plan has become a space. The plane-tree lined avenues and a meandering dyke comprise an unbroken framework within which the sunken green mass is contained.

The fragmentary park has a wide diversity of images on offer, a theatrical make-believe world that extols the chaos of the city. The Jardin des Bambous seeks to escape this chaos but also to critique it. The garden is a world of its own, distinct from the city and from the park, welded into a single entity by the exuberant growth of bamboo. It also shows us something of the network necessary to creating and maintaining the dream world of the park.

The promenade cinématique presents a filmic succession of images with which to experience one's movement through the park. In this sequence, each garden is composed as a 'still'. In the case of the Jardin des Bambous, its sunken position gives rise to two layers in the routeing. If the aerial walkways crossing the garden suggest the visual aspect of experiencing a film, the ground-level route through the garden generates a feeling of intense physical involvement. The footbridges counter the openness of the park with the intimacy of the garden.

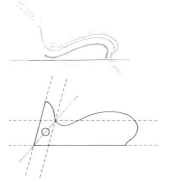

above: Plan configuration. These lines are the most important components in organizing the garden.

below: Plane trees enfold the sunken garden.

left: Plan configuration and context. The form is a result of an 'accidental' convergence of lines.

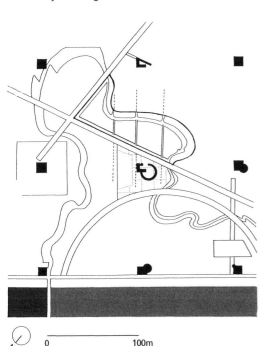

THE GARDEN: A SUNKEN BAMBOO LANDSCAPE. The formal ordering system for the garden is the 120-metre-long retaining wall and the path that accompanies it. Against these we can set the sinuous forms of the planted areas. The straight frames make a sharp angle, faintly endorsed by the undulating frames, with the pivot of the ensemble marked by a circle. The composition is the result of individually extrapolating the lines from the park (the avenues, the grid of follies), so that various autonomous geometric layers are overlaid: the system of paths, the zoning of bamboo species and the water system.

The clarity of the straight line and suggestiveness of the undulating line are fairly literally rendered in the spatial build-up of the Jardin des Bambous. On the side to the wall you can look along the entire length of the garden. Because of the serpentine boundary

0   100m

it is impossible to survey the garden in its entirety, giving the impression that it is endless, an effect reinforced by the dense dark stems. This confrontation is intensified by the water system which emphasizes both the serpentine meanderings and the unequivocal line of the wall. There are two enclosed spaces within its bounds that mark the beginning and the end of the oblong garden. Both are linked to the world above by a narrow stair.

The route through the garden is firmly controlled. A cylindrical space and a stair constitute the monumental entry to the garden, which ends abruptly at the boundary wall. From here on, the route, a path skirting the wall, is designed as a theatre gallery with the forest of bamboo supplying the action onstage. Any sense of distance between gallery and garden is then extinguished where a sewer pipe hangs so low over the path that you have to lower your head. A second path winds through the wilderness; again, it is so narrow as to necessitate pushing the foliage aside to proceed. Both paths end in the second enclosed space, a place to pause before ascending a narrow stair to the exit.

The illusory world of the bamboo landscape as sacro bosco alludes to far exotic climes. Contrasting with the blaze of impressions in the park, this is a place dedicated to ambience, warmth, climate, quiet and 'du ciel retrouvé' (the recovered sky). The sunken garden is protected against the wind; the south-facing wall acts as a climate facade, absorbing the heat and storing it. This keeps the garden several degrees warmer that its surroundings. At the same time, an acoustic microclimate obtains that shields the space from exterior noises. Taped frog noises amplified by the cylinder and the sound of running water, temper any sounds from outside. Water channels, drippers and anti-evaporation devices keep the air damp. The water enters the garden through the south-facing wall, the pressure of the high water table forcing it to seep through, as well as pouring in from the cascades on either side of the stair. Inside, a perimeter trough circulates the water. The exotic, restrained ambience of the bamboo in its bed of white pebbles contrasts with the state-of-the-art wall and the accompanying path of plain gravel.

PROGRAMME AND MEANING. Away from the action and adventure of the park, the garden is a haven of tranquillity. The cylinder acts as an intermediary, where visitors get a foretaste of the peace of the garden while being distracted by curious froglike gurglings. The informal space at the end of the gallery, kept clear of the lines of movement, offers a moment of repose.

In the garden are some forty species of bamboo, a situation made possible by the experimental climate control. Emphasis on the details, the 'unimportant things' such as the difference between, say, Phyllostachys flexuosa and Pleiobastus linearis, makes us forget the world outside and provides the feeling of repose only an enclosed garden can bring.

'A manner of dreaming, a form of cultivation hidden in the folds of the countryside and of history; an "agricultural theatre".' (Alexandre Chemetoff, 1989) In the garden the designer counters the flighty world of film characterizing the Parc de la Villette with the more intense experiential world of the theatre. Watching and experiencing are played off against one another, particularly along the two routes. Through the change in climate we can even physically feel the crossover to this more intimate response to nature.

SYNTHESIS. The Jardin des Bambous is a garden bristling with contradictions. Illusion against making the real visible, enclosure against boundlessness, simplicity against multiformity, a clearly organized strip next to a labyrinth, a scooped-out hollow that shows us the sky. The wall underlining the sense of enclosure is at the same time the binding element bringing the context into view. The bamboo, evoking the illusion and autonomy of an oasis, suggests instead an expansiveness. Even the relationship between form and function is reversed. The hermetic circle introduced at the entrance to the garden is in fact only a component of the route, whereas the residual area at the end of the gallery is the social space of the ensemble.

In the Parc de la Villette, infinite natural space is represented by the grid of follies and the serpentine lines. The Jardin des Bambous complements this expansiveness by proffering an enclosed, even sunken, garden. The vertical lines of the bamboo underscore the relationship with the sky. What is more, the garden visualizes the condition of horizontal expansiveness with row upon row of bamboo, which give concrete form to this abstract notion.

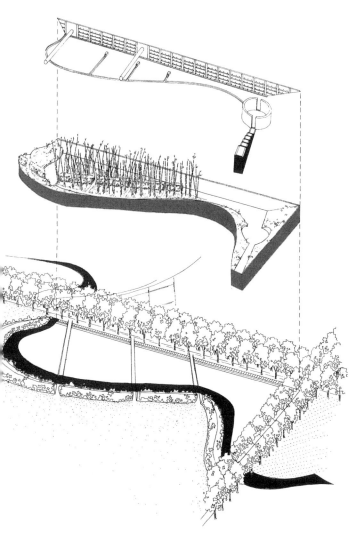

Spatial form and appearance. By making a hole in the ground the garden is removed from the chaotic world of the park. In it, a carpet of bamboo of every sort provides a 'natural' world with the technical elements occupying a separate layer.

The enclosed garden as kaleidoscope

Inside the walls of the 'kaleidoscope garden', an illusory, ideal world is projected that contrasts with its surroundings. There, the local landscape is shouted down by the universal baggage of the idealized image. Thus we see the monumental lawn of the Parc André-Citroen set against the hermetic world of the series of gardens, the chaotic tissue of a Parisian suburb against the simplicity of the Square des Bouleaux. The well-formed geometric shapes of the gardens are islands in the fractured landscape of the Berlin museum. The lush growth of the Brion family cemetery counters the open expanse of farmland, the hidden forest of the Jardin des Bambous is played off against the technical world of the Parc de la Villette. This game of oppositions can be played to bring out the urban condition, the artificial as a means of making the real visible.

In the fifteenth-century Japanese Zen garden of Ryoan-ji, we see the ultimate natural illusion, an extreme reduction of the cosmos. Bounded by two temples and two walls is a rectangular surface of ten by thirty metres covered by fine gravel raked in a severely ordered pattern of ripples. Fifteen irregular stones are arranged in five groups of five, two, three, two and three respectively. No matter where you stand there is always one stone you cannot see. There are no trees or flowers, the only growth being moss on the stones. This moss symbolizes the passing of time in an otherwise timeless setting. The balance between rocks and gravel represents the balance between the complementary elements of nature: mountains and water, active and passive. The pines behind the wall inject into this image a reference to the landscape outside the garden. The transcendental (the enclosed garden as heavenward telescope) and the immanent (the enclosed garden as field glass) come together in the idea of nature as a view through a kaleidoscope.

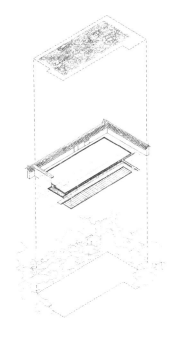

above: Katsumoto, Ryoan-ji, Kyoto c. 1450 (restored by Soami, 1499). The 'stone garden' consists of carefully raked white gravel and five clusters of stones. These groupings alternate between horizontal and vertical, held in check by the fifth, static group. Together with the linear pattern of the fine gravel this composition suggests a movement from east to west, like the flow of a river

left: The garden seen from the veranda on the north side against a backdrop of pines. This second horizon puts the autonomous world into perspective and forges a link with the real landscape.

The hidden city

'In Eudoxia, which spreads both upwards and down, with winding alleys, steps, dead ends, hovels, a carpet is preserved in which you can observe the city's true form. At first sight nothing seems to resemble Eudoxia less than the design of that carpet, laid out in symmetrical motives whose patterns are repeated along straight and circular lines, interwoven with brilliantly coloured spires, in a repetition that can be followed throughout the whole woof. But if you pause and examine it carefully, you become convinced that each place in the carpet corresponds to a place in the city and all the things contained in the city are included in the design, arranged according to their true relationship, which escapes your eye distracted by the bustle, the throngs, the shoving. All of Eudoxia's confusion, the mules' braying, the lampblack stains, the fish smell is what is evident in the incomplete perspective you grasp; but the carpet proves that there is a point from which the city shows its true proportions, the geometrical scheme implicit in its every, tiniest detail.'

Italo Calvino, 1972

The urban landscape of today is dominated by infrastructure. A source of major problems, infrastructure can also be a source of potential and therefore a key task for designers. Take Utrecht Central Station, the number one rail interchange in Holland. A radical design has been made for it and the shopping complex interwoven with it, that is to improve connections with the central city. In our fourth design experiment an enclosed garden is lifted up on to the station roof, giving this locus of high-powered circulation a social space, a static enclosure where inner-city dwellers can read the paper, or where travellers can

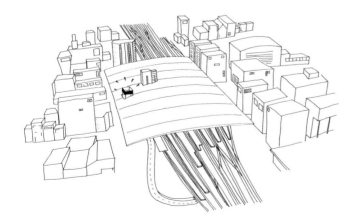

A design experiment. The enclosed garden is lifted up above the roof of Utrecht Central Station from where it looks down on the hectic goings-on at this interchange.

catch their breath before rejoining the flow, and take a detached view of the world they came from. The space is reached up a flight of stairs wrapped in see-through gauze. During your ascent you can take cognizance of the inner city and the giant canopy oversailing the station. Up in the enclosed garden the sounds of arriving and departing trains, the pulse of the city, can be heard through loudspeakers. After nightfall the reflecting pool is lit up to present a landmark visible for miles around.

The glass bottom of the pool acts as a magnifying glass that isolates activities below in the station, metaphor of the city, and shows them to the visitor. In Paris the Jardin des Bambous likewise shows the understructure of the city as well as an idealized image of nature. There the exposed sewers and the concrete wall give an idea of the local water management. The city's hidden structures are summarized in the enclosed garden. If we could express the hidden structure of our cities in a carpet as in Eudoxia, would it enable us to solve the real-time problems of unbridled growth? Might we be able to read the solutions there? Would enlarging the railway system with a magnifying glass in the bottom of an aerial pool give us some sort of insight into the urban wilderness?

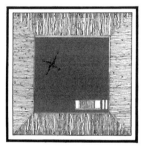

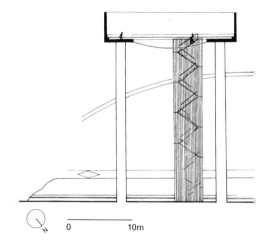

0   10m

From inside the station, one takes a stair which finally emerges from a reflecting pool in the centre of the space, circumscribed by a path of bamboo sticks. Sitting on comfortable wooden benches set against the walls, visitors observe the pool out of which they see new arrivals emerging. The convex transparent bottom of the pool gives through the ripples in the water a distorted view of the mundane reality of the station.

A sunken garden in Geneva

Hidden away from the bustle of the Swiss capital is this entrance to the underground auditorium of the Louis-Jeantet research institute, an enclosed garden doubling as a landscape filter. The existing villa housing the institute is lifted on to a plinth out of which the garden, the villa's negative image, has been scooped. The auditorium is excluded from this formal series of villa – garden – street, being linked to the street by a zig-zag line cutting through the plinth and the garden. A dark cavelike opening in the garden wall gives entry to the auditorium.

The entrance cum garden is surrounded by a ha-ha of two narrow interlocking U-shaped channels. A ramp poking out of the plinth is the only way the auditorium and the garden reveal their presence to the city.

The ground plane is of strips of black slate in a carpet of pearlwort with a haphazard pattern of tenuous flowering cherry, the whole framed by water and concrete walls. The sound of

TER Landscape Architects, Fondation Louis-Jeantet, Geneva, 1993. The garden is scooped from the building's plinth as an incision slicing all the way through the urban layer into the earth below.

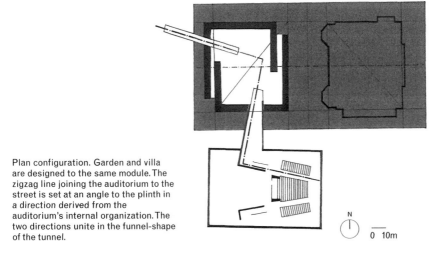

Plan configuration. Garden and villa are designed to the same module. The zigzag line joining the auditorium to the street is set at an angle to the plinth in a direction derived from the auditorium's internal organization. The two directions unite in the funnel-shape of the tunnel.

N

0 10m

gently splashing water in the channels atop the walls percolates down the stairs and through the walls to channels below. The noise of traffic abates and is replaced by birdsong. At night the lighting situation is reversed, natural light descending during the day being replaced by artificial light from below.

The garden does duty as a decompression chamber, filtering the sounds of the city, reducing its speed and its welter of imagery. Here the *historical layers* of the place are visualized in the spatial layers of the villa on its plinth and the auditorium in the ground. That the former is lifted up and the latter buried can be observed in the garden. Resolving an urban issue of accessibility with an abstract representation of nature generates all sorts of unexpected relationships. An illusion of nature, day-to-day activities and the historical layers of the city all consort in this enclosed garden.

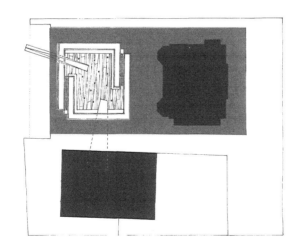

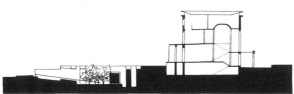

In the garden, the circulation route is interrupted and movement dispersed among the spread of trees. The thickness of the wall is emphasized by the two stairs that lead through the heart of the wall to the plateau, and by the two tunnels. A red square with a rotating gateway marks the entrance to the auditorium.

Freshwater pavilion

The paradox of endlessness in enclosure is unconnected with the concept of the enclosed garden as elaborated in this hermetically sealed pavilion. In the vast reaches of the North Sea and the Oosterschelde tidal basin lies the former construction island of Neeltje Jans. As part of an educational and recreational programme for this island, two architectural practices designed between them a water pavilion shaped like a half-buried drop of water and dividing into a freshwater and a salt water section. Complexity, dynamism, artificiality and alienation as indicative of the modern life-feeling: the freshwater pavilion registers all of these. In this section all impressions from the world outside are excluded and a new, virtual world created in their stead, with no references to horizon, sky or earth. This 'fluid' architecture takes over the motor system of the human body. Instead of calming and comforting, the hermetically sealed space accelerates and energizes the body, which has to organize its own equilibrium and is itself the centre of the universe.

In the original design for the pavilion there is a single reference to the outside world, a diaphragm in the skin of the pavilion. A basin beneath the diaphragm captures the mirror image of the sky. When it rains, the rainwater falls through the diaphragm into the basin. The falling drops of rain and the water's surface materialize as a vertical coordinate and a horizontal coordinate, a temporary balance organ in a space otherwise entirely lacking equilibrium. In this theoretical case, the space in the pavilion is reunited with that outside.

NOX Architecten, freshwater pavilion, Neeltje Jans, 1997. In the original design of 1995 the pavilion had a diaphragm in its skin with below it a water basin. 'The most vertical and the most horizontal (the water) are preserved here. ... Instead of a horizon this building has a well.' (Maurice Nio and Lars Spuybroek, 1995)

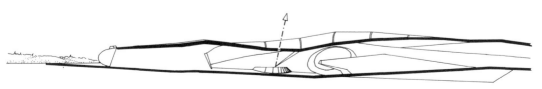

Longitudinal section through the freshwater pavilion with water basin and diaphragm.

Invenzioni capric di Carceri, plate VII, engraving by Giovanni Battista Piranesi, 1760. A shadowy world of constant movement.

The square concrete 'box' of fifty by fifty metres and twenty-five metres high lies between parking garages (6000 places on four levels), motorway and TGV station (100 trains a day), at the rear of the station, where it makes the connection with the outlying districts.

Espace Piranésien

'The hydra-headed monster of complexity can only be subdued in the enclaves of which the entire undertaking [Euralille] is composed.'

Harm Tilman, 199▮

Giovanni Battista Piranesi is the author of extraordinary architectural fantasies. *Invenzion capric di Carceri,* the series of prison engraving published in the mid eighteenth century, is an almost abstract play of forms in which space is turned on its head, so to speak. 'The carceri compel the spectator to undergo an optical journey of frenetic motion by means of a succession of stairs, ramps, bridges, balconies, catwalks and galleries – a nervous continuum with no point of stability or rest throughout.' (J. Wilton-Ely, 1978) This shadow world of continuous movement, endlessly rising stairs that suggest ever new lines of development and which are never resolved, has been put into practice in the Espace Piranésien in Euralille.

Between the inner city and a suburb of Lille lies Euralille, the transferium designed by Rem Koolhaas and the OMA architectural practice in connection with the forthcoming TGV link. One of the elements in this complex ensemble is the Espace Piranésien. A new shopping centre and the TGV station link arms with the central city and the old station, with the infrastructural lines stretching out behind them. In the midst c this tumult of infrastructure and buildings is an open core, a square box. The point of congestion is not a building but a void, comparable with the role of the hortus contemplationis in a monastic ensemble. It organizes the complex functionally too, being the crossover point where trains, cars and métro trade occupants. On an urban level it is a link between the inner city and the periphery.

Lifts, six escalators, a wide assortment of stairs, platforms and a tube station are gathered together in a three-dimensional frame. The lines of infrastructure converge at a condensation point whose wall planes crystallize it into a spatial unit, the 'garden'. Whereas the concrete walls and lift shafts are solidly built, the jutting glass and steel roof seem to float above street level. Never-ending stairs generate a strong upward thrust. This vertical alignment is underpinned by the reflecting pool, the light exclusively from above, and the stacking of horizontal layers.

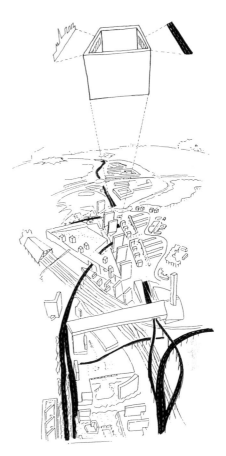

OMA'S PARADISE. Piranesi's fantasies materialize in this enclosed garden as a reflection of the dynamics of today's metropolis. Within the static square framework the complexity is pumped up by a multiplicity of directions and layers. In showing the construction and the movement flows (infrastructure), the true complexity and impossibility of the infrastructure is revealed to the city's population (see Rem Koolhaas, 1993). Just as the cosmogram hidden in the monastery complex is an all-explicating emblem of a hierarchical world-image, and the prison as referred to by Piranesi is deployed time and again as a simplified microcosm of society, so the Espace Piranésien extols as a hidden city the complexities of the urban fabric. Yet for all that, this paean to urban chaos has its counterpart in representations of nature: pool, cascades (escalators, spiral stairs) and grotto (the deep recesses).
The Espace Piranésien is a transferium for pedestrians, an interchange for escalators, lifts, spiral stairs, a tube station, a taxi rank, entrances, exits and accesses. From this slow-

Espace Piranésien. A hole in the ground hides Euralille from view, to elucidate one by one each of the elements of that complex ensemble.

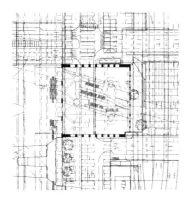

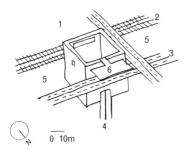

0 10m

above: Plan of the box as a component of the infrastructural constellation.

below: Espace Piranésien in context.
1. Central city / 2. TGV / 3. Motorway /
4. Métro / 5. Parking / 6. Square

right: The thickness of the walls is explicit in the entrances and in the openings bringing daylight into the parking garages. Inside the static framework the complexity is pumped up. The programme divides into the following levels. 0: métro, lift and escalator / 1: plateau, lift and escalator / 2: entrance beneath motorway / 3: plateau, lift and escalator, entrances to parking garages, entrance to station / 4: lift and escalator, rear entrance (pedestrian precinct above motorway), taxi ranks.

moving, small-scale and individual system, windows and balconies give a glimpse of the rapid, large-scale and multitudinous system of rail and motorway networks.
As a converging point for infrastructural lines, the transferium is a metaphor for the dynamic and unbounded condition of the urban landscape, the city abstracted to a tangle of movement. But even this abstraction overwhelms and confuses. The enclosed garden reduces the surroundings to a microcosm in which the transferium, the city and the world are all represented. Seen in the reflecting pool, the city is abstracted still further into a two-dimensional surface that reflects three-dimensional space.

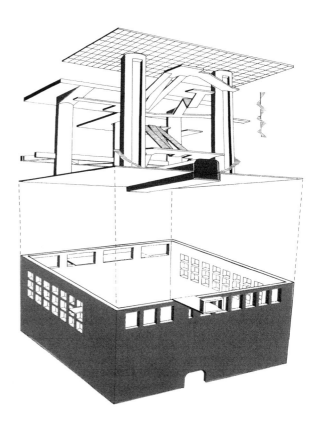

The enclosed garden as magnifying glass

The city of today has many gardens, but gardens that engage in dialogue with current and future urban processes are few and far between. The Espace Piranésien assimilates the context of the transferium, thereby becoming an inseparable component of that transfer-machine, an illustration of the leap in scale that is one of the most sweeping spatial changes of the past century. A transformation from city to metropolis, from a day at the beach to a holiday in Gran Canaria, from pocket calculator to electronic superhighway, from station to transferium. In this context the enclosed garden is no longer a component of equal standing such as the hofje or the square which entered into a harmonious relationship with the network of urban spaces. It is a special item, like Gulliver in Brobdingnag, like the hortus conclusus in the overwhelming natural landscape of the Middle Ages.

In the 'magnifying-glass garden', the complexity of the context, rather than being excluded, is gathered together as an inverted idyll. Here the dynamic of the city is heightened, its many-layered state exposed. It is inside its walls that the city's fragmented condition is accentuated. Seen through a magnifying glass, fragments become self-sufficient, conflicts and hiatuses intensified.

In Desvigne and Dalnoky's Villa Medici project, natural processes such as sedimentation and erosion are brought under control architecturally. Geometric patterns of channels and dams guide the accretion and dispersal of sand, so that the natural dynamic, the landscape's history of becoming, is played off as a permanent 'source' against the speed and changeability of urban life.[5] In the enclosed garden as magnifying glass, urban processes are brought under control architecturally and the transience of the city put on display by focusing on a part of its quotidian context. The box can of itself act as a generator of urban processes by either organizing or activating them.

In contradistinction to the telescope, the kaleidoscope and the field glass, the magnifying-glass garden exalts the city. But even this is the idealizing of a theme, as is the representation of a paradisiacal nature. This box makes a selection of elements and aspects and displays them, while itself withdrawing from the city. The Jardin des Bambous, the Espace Piranésien and the sunken garden in Geneva all disappear below street level. Representing the city, proceeding from an acceptance of reality, is as much a process of mystification as representing nature as a paradise. Hidden urban workings are made manifest at hidden places.

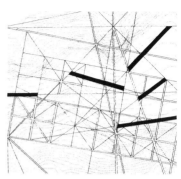

Michel Desvigne and Christine Dalnoky, Villa Medici project, 1987. Geometric forms (grids and bars) bring out the permanent state of transformation informing the landscape in the hills of Rome. This is expressed in the water that periodically descends from higher placed channels to violently wash away the (planned) deposits of sand at the dams, whereupon the process begins anew.

5. Tiberghien 1987.

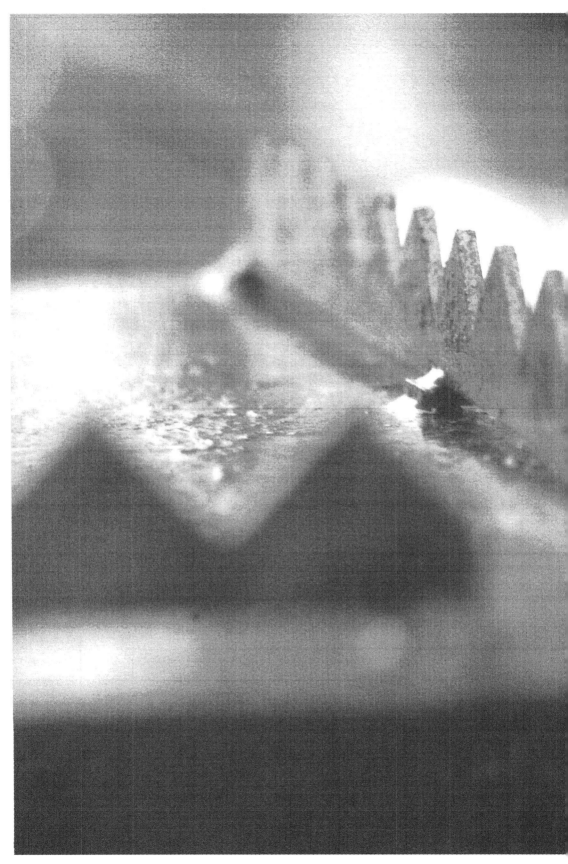

A landscape with no horizon

'Landscape architects can play a dominant role in urbanism by
applying themselves to realizing distinguishable textures at the
macro scale and to creating gardens. Gardens in the most
traditional sense: walled oases with a mystical, condensed
nature, an extreme control of details, a caring upkeep. A place of
seasons, imaging and contemplation.
In a country that is getting fuller all the time, where the individual
expression of houses and gardens is uppermost, pleasure in
large-scale authenticity is more essential than ever. Indeed, this
is how city-dwellers can get their bearings on reality. ... Nestling
in the urban static can be found beneficient gardens, the
Vondelparks [citypark of Amsterdam] and the Keukenhofs [Dutch
tulip exhibition garden]. These are what we must work on.'
Adriaan Geuze, 1996

Anatomy of the enclosed garden

The enclosed garden is both a landscape without a horizon and a room without a ceiling. It is landscape expansiveness and domestic size brought together within a single space. The image of the landscape as we encounter it in the garden is reduced and presented on a tray. The enclosed garden responds in all kinds of subtle ways to its setting, although this is itself invisible.

In it, the paradox of the garden has come to be expressed in architectural terms. The polarities coincide now instead of being set side by side. The garden is as much open as closed, inside as outside – the illusion of paradise and the reality of daily life come together.

In the medieval enclosed garden, the hortus conclusus, the horror vacui led as if naturally to this compression of extremes. And this remained, even after the fear was vanquished and the landscape conquered. If the guise of the enclosed garden changed, its qualities remained essentially the same. From our analyses of the examples, a series of characteristics can be distilled that define the enclosed garden as a landscape-architectural type, and act as a springboard to further transformation and reworking.

CONDENSED SPACE. The enclosed garden reflects a bounded (medieval) notion of space: a hollow related to its core and to its walls, held clear of everything outside it. Condensation of the space is brought about by two opposing spatial concepts.

The vertical endlessness of the sky is emphasized by intensifying the containment of the space. The walls are palpably present and show their solidity. A gallery placed before them doubles the enclosure and makes it three-dimensional. Perforations in the envelope, such as recesses and doors, can strengthen the containment by showing the thickness of the walls.

On the other hand this same containment is put into perspective. In the restricted space all possible means are deployed to suggest a great expanse. Thus, the gallery of the Patio de los Leones is a field of columns, and the reflecting pool of the Patio de los Arrayanes brings the endless space of the skies into the garden.

LIMITED SIZE. The interaction between the walls, and that between them and the ground plane is decisive for the sense of enclosure. The enclosed garden is small, like an interior. The lower limit of its size is determined by the size of a person. Walls directly abutting the garden vary in height between three and six metres. Within these limits, the height can be directly compared with one's own. If it is less than three metres, too much of the outside world is visible to sustain the containment, if more than six there is no relationship with one's own height. The gallery serves as a height reference. The minimum surface area can be arrived at using the same yardstick. If their distance from the wall is less than twice their own height, those in the garden can no longer see the edge of the surface under a normal angle of vision (27 degrees). So from this we can fix a minimum size of 4 m x 4 m. To calculate the volume of the space, the floor surface area is related to the height of the wall; assuming a half-cube to be the minimum volume, the floor surface area for a minimum height of three metres is 6 m x 6 m.

The upper limit of the enclosed space derives from Renaissance experiments with dimensions. Those of the Cortile del Belvedere at the Vatican, a hundred metres by three hundred, take the containment generated by the walls and transform it into openness, an effect reinforced by perspective manipulations.

Materials can make a space seem larger or smaller. The patio of the German Pavilion in Barcelona is twelve metres long, 6.5 metres wide and 3.5 metres high, but appears larger thanks to the polished colourless walls and the reflecting water. The Jardin des Bambous in the Parc de la Villette in Paris is a hundred and twenty metres long and five metres high. Its width of twenty metres narrows to four and widens again to thirty. But the irregular shape and luxurious planting render its true size illegible. Although the surface of this garden is ten times that of the patio of the German Pavilion, they share the same degree of containment. Abstraction makes the patio seem more expansive, while condensing the Jardin des Bambous increases its sense of enclosure.

On the following eight pages, you can take cognizance of the limited size of the examples analysed in this book and compare them using the Romanesque garden of the Santes Creus monastery as a reference.

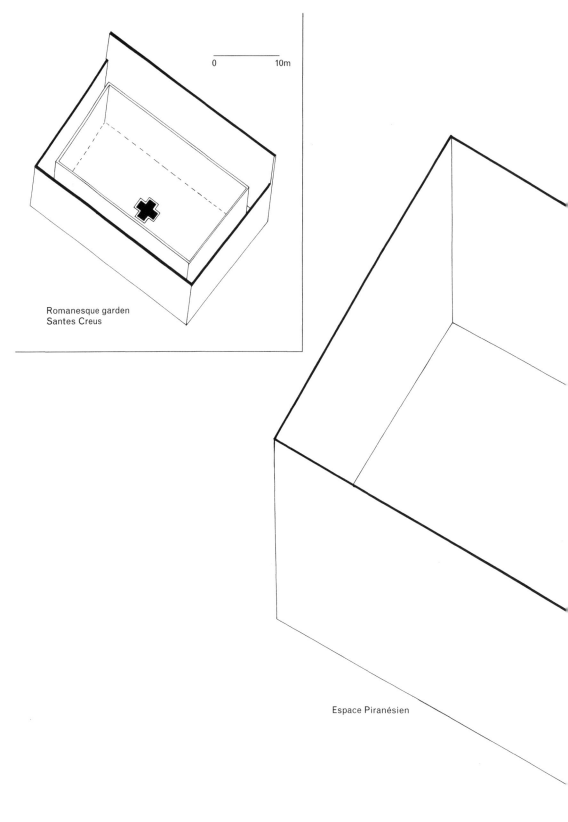

0   10m

Romanesque garden
Santes Creus

Espace Piranésien

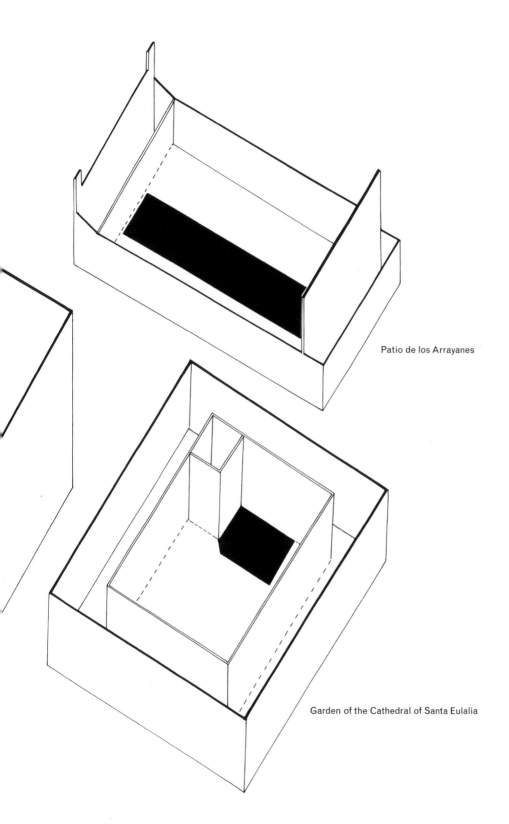

Patio de los Arrayanes

Garden of the Cathedral of Santa Eulalia

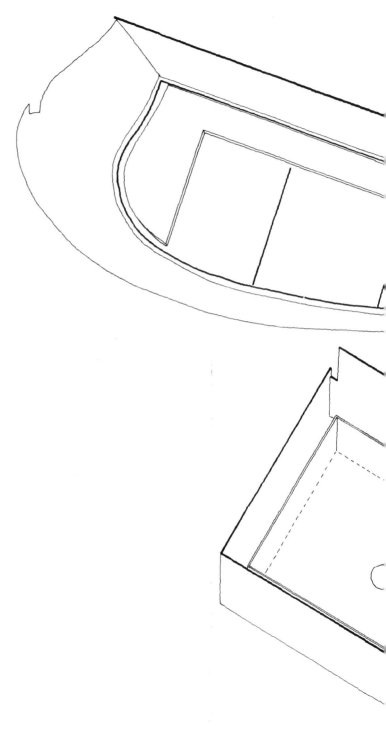

Garden court of the Mariavall conv

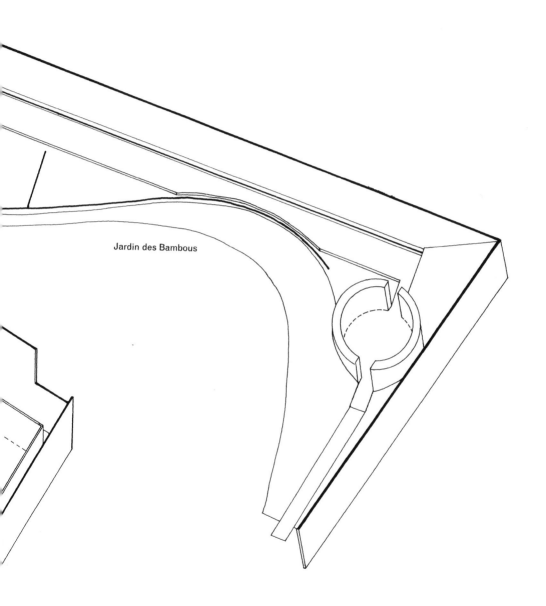

Jardin des Bambous

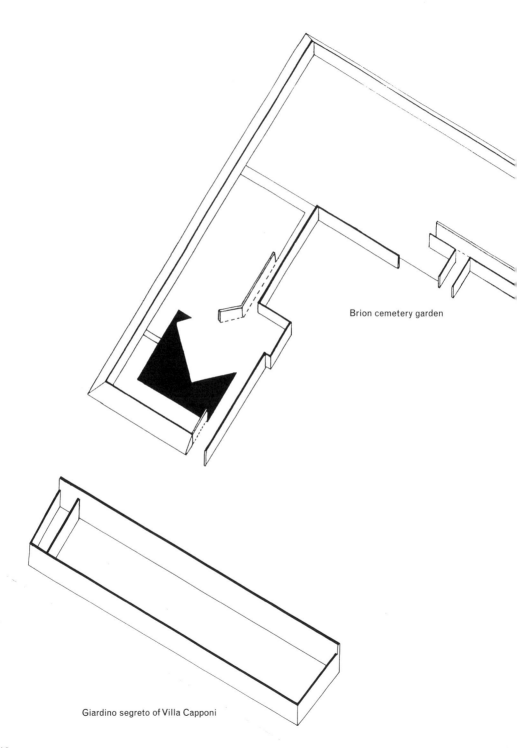

Brion cemetery garden

Giardino segreto of Villa Capponi

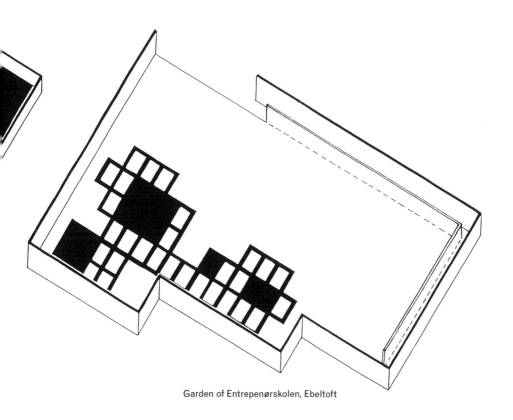

Garden of Entrepenørskolen, Ebeltoft

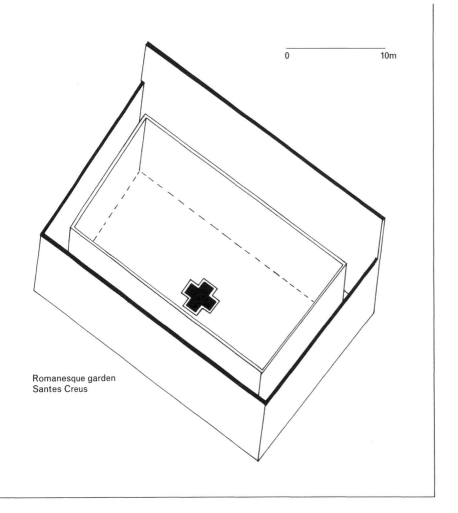

0   10m

Romanesque garden
Santes Creus

Patio of the German Pavilion

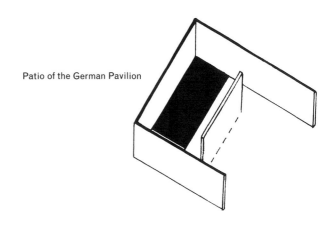

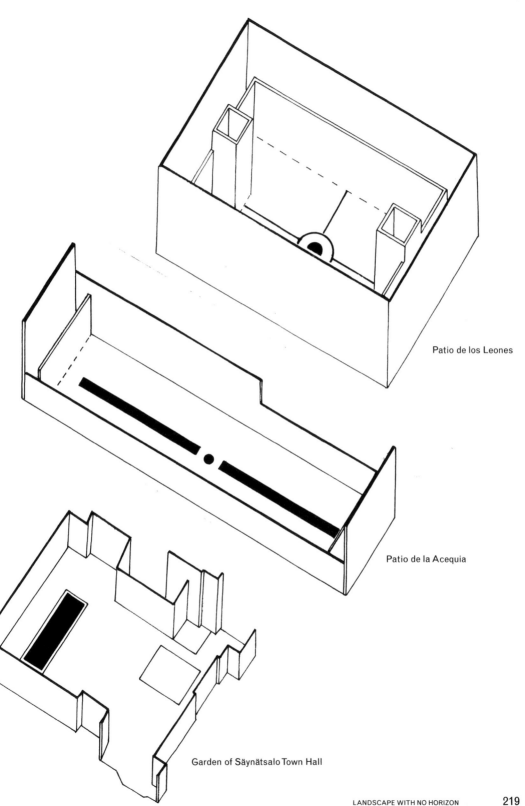

Patio de los Leones

Patio de la Acequia

Garden of Säynätsalo Town Hall

EMBLEM OF NATURE. 'When we find a hill in the woods, six feet long and three feet wide, shovelled up into the form of a pyramid, we become serious, and something inside us says: Somebody is buried here. That is architecture.'[1] The symbolism of the memoria (architecture as an emblem of nature) transcends the reality of half a cubic metre of earth and tells us about life and death as universal givens. The hortus conclusus with its symbolic representation of nature does the same. It gives a reproduction of the world in the closed geometrical system of a half-cube and an axial cross.

The iconography of water and greenery in the hortus conclusus is a ritual of magic and illusion enacted using an extreme form of abstraction. 'The smaller the tree, the further away it is from nature. The less the resemblance to reality, the more magical the effect.'[2] Nature is placed under a magnifying glass, and stripped down until only the essence remains.

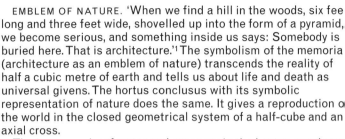

CONNECTION WITH THE SKY. In the enclosed garden, the horizon is replaced by a slice of sky. The tensionality between the ground plane and the celestial plane generates a vertical alignment in the garden. Thus, we see the stairs in the Espace Piranésien in Lille turning about an imaginary vertical line towards the sky, in the same way as the dancer does in the patio of the German Pavilion. Both lines begin in a reflecting pool that visualizes the sky on the ground.

Because the walls shut out all other images, it is not the natural processes visible on the earth's surface that we see there but the natural rhythms legible in the sky: the rising and setting sun, the waxing and waning moon, the glittering stars.

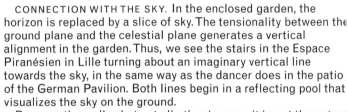

SENSUOUS WORLD. The wall not only excludes the visual aspect of the surroundings, it shuts out noise, wind, bitter cold, fierce sun and the stench of exhaust fumes. Inside, the wall captures the fleeting scents of flowers. The diverse textures of screens and columns, plants and water invite one to touch, to feel. The quiet, which the murmur of water and rustle of leaves only seems to intensify, is a delight to the ear. In the enclosed garden the sensuous world of the garden is made more sensuous still.

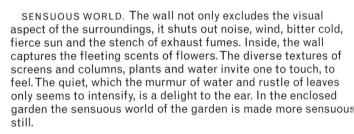

1. Loos, 1962.

2. Stein 1987.

NO PROGRAMME. Each clearly defined function would impair the freedom that typifies the garden. It is the very emptiness of the enclosed garden that acts as a screen on to which one can project one's imagination, as a frame which viewers can fill in themselves. Through the absence of a programme the enclosed garden is a 'pause for breath' in the city. The garden court of the Mariavall convent in Sweden is an empty box, an expanse of grass with grey walls and a gallery. If you imagine this garden projected on to the visual and programmatic welter of the condensed city and the urban landscape, then the contrast between the two worlds would endow the garden's emptiness with the quality of freedom. Freedom from the obligations and regulations imposed by the city.

RELATION TO THE CENTRE. A square ground plane is the simplest geometric form there is. All directions are reduced to the two basic coordinates of the flat plane and the distance from the sides to the centre is the same everywhere. There is a hierarchic relationship between the edges and the centre so that all other elements within the garden can be defined from their position in this force field; their place in respect to the edge and in respect to the centre.

The Romanesque garden of the Santes Creus monastery in Spain has many outer layers: a wall, a gallery, a circle of cypress and a cruciform fountain. These layers of skin form as many echoes of the actual centre: the fountain designating the vertical axis joining it to the sky, the 'axis mundi'. An empty centre can just as easily fix the form of the plane or space such as in the Patio de los Arrayanes in the Alhambra, where the ground plane consists of a reflecting pool and the empty centre generates a vertical coordinate.

KEYHOLE PERSPECTIVE. The enclosed garden shuts itself away from the landscape yet at the same time gathers the landscape around it. A window gives a view out of that landscape. Only a glimpse is visible, but of precisely that part which provides the key to an understanding of the landscape and of the garden's place in it.

The Alhambra is an impermeable fortress, yet one tiny window in the main space relates it to the landscape. The ensemble lies on the rim of a valley hugged by hills. That single window faces along the axis of the Patio de los Arrayanes and is preceded by a sequence of openings. Thus it seems, in an accelerated perspective, that the distance from the garden is greater than it really is. In the centre of the view rises the farthest hilltop, the outer limit of the visually controlled landscape.

CYCLIC ROUTE. Movement in the enclosed garden produces an image no different from that when standing still. The persistently identical enclosure – even the corners of the gallery are not particularized – emphasizes the repetitiveness of the image: column, intercolumnium, column. The beginning and end of the route are strung together into a walk about a fixed central point. This encircling movement distinguishes the field in the centre, which is not accessed. This field is unhitched from the edge by a colonnade, a step or a threshold and is elevated to a temenos. Thus, the route in relationship to the central area makes manifest the act of observing.

There is an abrupt transition between the linear route outside the garden, one end of which the garden terminates, and the cyclic route inside. The door marking the changeover from outside to inside is eminently visible from outside, to identify the garden as one in a series of spaces. Movement within the garden has no further need of the outside world, and so on the inside the door is hidden.

TIMELESSNESS. In the enclosed garden the progress of time is irrelevant. The chronology of past, present and future is extinguished, and eternity and the moment seem to coincide. There, linear time cedes to cyclic time. Instead of a succession of images marking the passing of time there are only the constantly repeating rounds of day and night, spring, summer, autumn and winter, an endless cycle. Static space materializes stationary time. Time and space are one.

The materiality of the garden again is an illustration of these two sides to timelessness: cyclic time and changelessness. In the Patio de la Acequia the cycles of the year are represented by flowering annuals that look the same every summer, and fruit trees with their evident seasonal changes; in the convent garden of Mariavall, it is grass and concrete that provide an immutable backdrop to the changing light and climate.

The enclosed garden as urban landscape requisite

The landscape, once the 'outside' of the town, threatens to be deprived of this role because these days inside and outside are in fact impossible to tell apart. The landscape is fragmenting; what used to be black and white is now a grey haze. The pattern of the ground looks likely to lose its meaning, and both the legibility and the physical differentiation of the landscape are diminishing. On the other hand, existing cities are compacting. Is the new landscape to be a chaos, an unstable and discontinuous urban field of fragments?

Urban growth and the accompanying loss of landscape spatiality can be parried by intervening at the scale of the landscape. But this can also be done by means of surgically precise interventions, small open spaces that return the experience of space and landscape to the urban fabric. With the increasing concern for public urban space, there is a danger that, however paradoxical it sounds, an excess of urban space will ensue, quantity instead of quality. In every new residential development a park and a square are always stock items, despite the low density. Is that really necessary? The number one shopping mall in the Netherlands (Amsterdam's Kalverstraat) is only six metres wide. Shouldn't we be more economical with our public realm and create concentrated spaces instead of the umpteenth misplaced square or unused park?

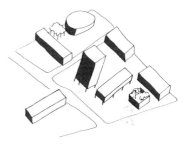

What can the hortus conclusus mean as a classical landscape-architectural type in a new landscape where space gets splashed about regardless and is crammed full of objects? How can the enclosed garden pick up on such present-day phenomena in the (urban) landscape as levelling out, fragmentation, scaling-up and consolidation?

Influenced by the context, the type transforms into ever new forms. In the analysed examples, we can distinguish a number of types of transformation that can be deployed in the urban landscape, each in its own way and each to bring out another aspect. These applications of the enclosed garden are illustrated by the following design experiments, montages of a classical garden implanted in the urban landscape of Amsterdam, or of new gardens in peri-urban Rotterdam.[3]

3. The design experiments described in the chapter 'Current transformations' are largely directed at giving shape to the garden design as a visual means of tackling the contemporary context. Because they unavoidably react to that context in the process, they are returned to the spotlight here to illustrate how the enclosed garden can be made to spatially relate to the urban landscape.

BOX OF EMPTINESS. Rembrandtplein ————————

LINK. Oosterbegraafplaats (cemetery) ——————
VANISHING POINT. Martin Luther Kingpark ——————————————————————

BLACK HOLE. Watergraafsmeer ——————

STANDARD ELEMENT. Bijlmermeer ——————

OASIS. A2 Motorway ——————

BOX OF EMPTINESS. In the condensed city the enclosed garden is a tantalizing substitute for the landscape, a suggestion of space where this is lacking. The compactness of the enclosed garden is just what makes it so effective in densifying cities and sprawling urban landscapes, where space is such a scarce commodity.

In the entertainment centre of Amsterdam, on Rembrandtplein, a door permits escape from the thumping beats, consuming masses and flashing neon signs. Condensing the limited outdoor space at the rear of the shops and houses actually serves to create space. Just as in the Patio de los Arrayanes (right), two simple walls and two galleries enfold a space for seclusion, a void with a reflecting pool. A long and indirect route acts as a filter between city and garden. In the patio the pool exactly mirrors the double-height gallery at one end and the old brick facade at the other.

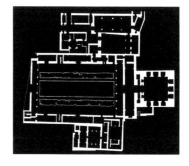

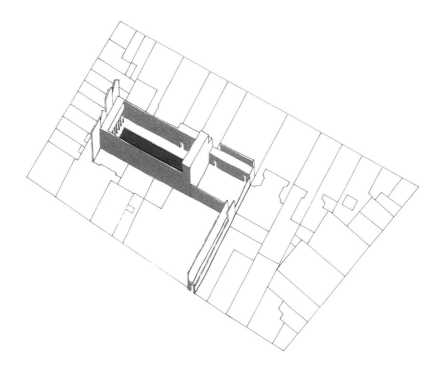

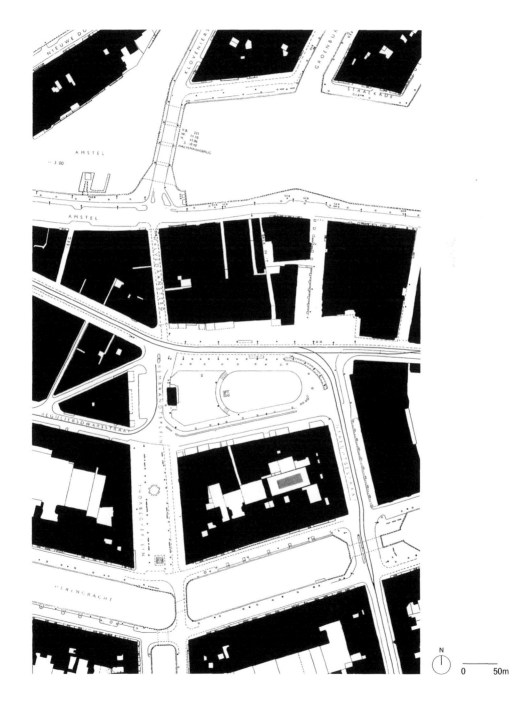

N

0   50m

OASIS. Placing the garden in an open landscape instead of in the condensed city gives it the opposite meaning. No longer is the space in the spotlight, but the element defining it, the enclosure. The large dimensions of the landscape are pitted against the intimacy of the space within the walls.

Superimposing the Patio de la Acequia in the Duivendrechtse Polder south-east of Amsterdam makes manifest the surrounding landscape as if in a camera obscura. The patio holds both the polder and the motorway up to scrutiny as two visualizations of endlessness. Like the oasis in the desert, it is as much a fixed point in endless space as a point of repose along the route (the desert itself is not a place to linger, one can only pass through it). Two buildings joined by a strip of fenestration draw the attention from the motorway to the garden, one brief moment of stillness and beauty. The route to the garden alternates views of the garden and the polder, drawing these two into the most natural of relationships. Journey's end is a view from the garden across the pastures.

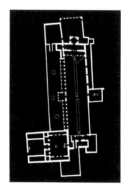

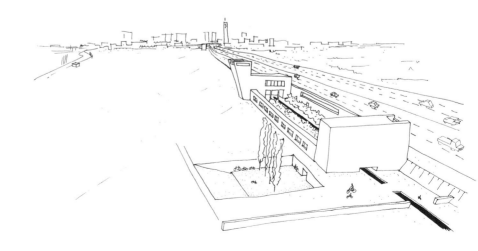

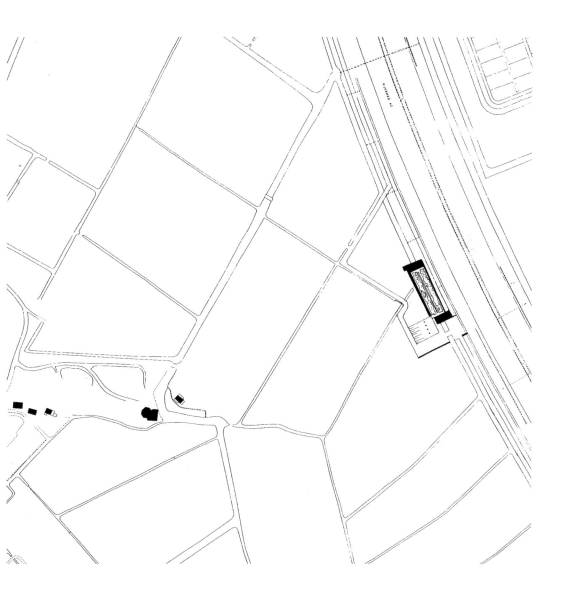

N

0 10m

LINK. At the place where two divergent landscapes meet, the enclosed garden can provide the link, a gateway effecting physical and visual transition.

On the south side of Amsterdam is the Oosterbegraafplaats, a large cemetery lying like an island between two residential districts. Forming a new access to the cemetery is a transformation of the Espace Piranésien in Lille, a concrete box of fifty by fifty metres filled with lines of infrastructure. Here the infrastructure is reduced to a link between the two entrances and the pool in the box magnified to dramatize the canal interceding between district and cemetery.

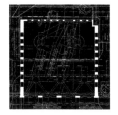

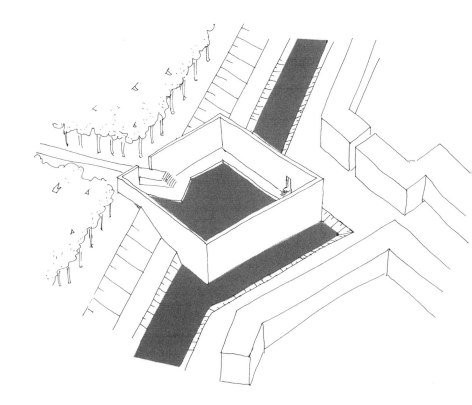

N

0 ___ 10m

STANDARD ELEMENT. In the standardized design of, say, Roman settlements and seventeenth-century Dutch expansion areas, the enclosed garden was one of the basic building bricks. When the modern movement rediscovered serial urban design, it was promptly dispensed with. This tied in with the resulting disappearance of spatiality and privacy in the outdoor space.

An invisible grid containing box-shaped gardens between the high-rise and low-rise in the typical sixties district of Bijlmermeer effectively upgrades the existing standard lots and imposes a new order that welds neighbourhoods on unequal footing into a single ensemble. Back gardens are done away with, so that the unbroken space round the tower blocks penetrates the low-rise areas. Seen from outside, each box is an inconspicuous part of the whole, seen from inside each box is the only one anywhere. The boxes can be hired by groups or individuals and filled with vegetable patches, cycle parks, floral paradises, picnic tables and pens for animals.

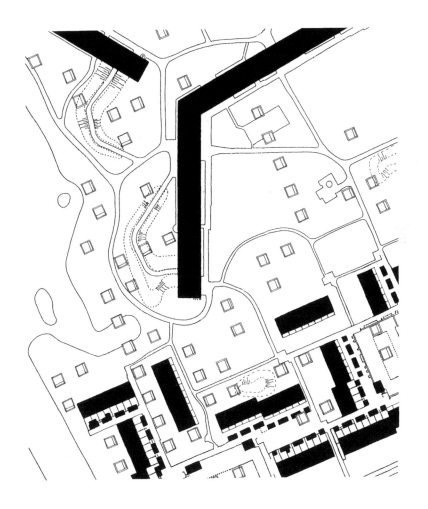

BLACK HOLE. A black hole is a hypothetical
cosmic body with such an intense gravitational
pull that nothing can escape from it, not even
light. All nearby matter is sucked by the pull of
gravity into the 'event horizon' of the hole where
it disappears. Everything inside the black hole
originated outside it. But its departure therefrom
is permanent and once it passes the event
horizon it only satisfies the laws obtaining
inside.

In an urban landscape as undefined and
unordered as, say, the southern edge of
Watergraafsmeer in east Amsterdam the
enclosed garden (the Jardin des Bambous)
withdraws from the landscape by taking up a
position below ground level. There it creates its
own context, making use of the now largely
hidden structures of the reclamation (see larger
context below). The two original bearers of the
structure, the encircling canal to the south and
drainage ditch to the west (dotted line), join
with the new flow lines of the motorway to order
the garden. In the garden however they present
quite another composition than that above the
'event horizon' of ground level.

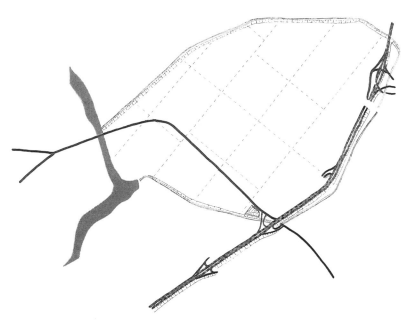

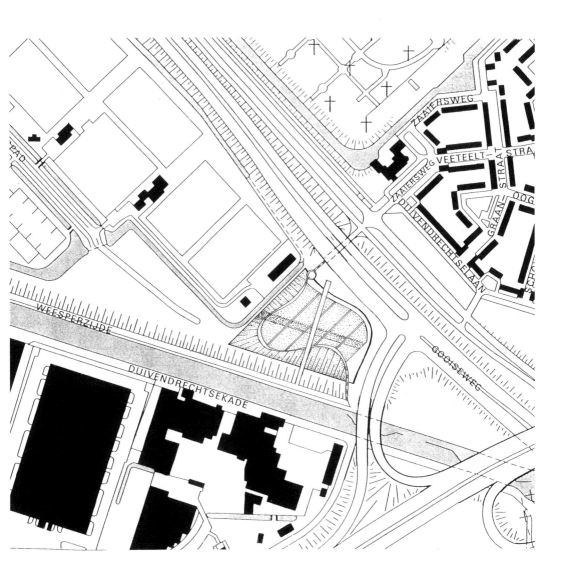

ZAAIERSWEG

WEESPERZIJDE

DUIVENDRECHTSEKADE

GOOISEWEG

ZAAIERSWEG

VEETEELT—

STRAAT

STRA

GRAAN

OOG

DUIVENDRECHTSELAAN

SCH

PAD

N

0   10m

VANISHING POINT. A latently present spatial sequence from a major landscape space – a valley, a polder, a plateau – to smaller spaces can be made visible by an enclosed garden. As the last and smallest space, the garden articulates the series architecturally as the vanishing point of the composition.

The urban periphery of Amsterdam, which remained more or less tangential from the Middle Ages to the nineteenth century and at the beginning of the twentieth suffered a series of bulges and indentations, now threatens to disappear. But the disappearance of a clear borderline need not mean that the distinction between inside and out should vanish as well. It can become more subtle and ambiguous. Along the river Amstel, this transition has enjoyed a layered state for centuries. Inserting the Roman Villa Giulia with its three courtyard gardens into the sequence of polder, personal allotments, cemetery, swimming pool and park formally embeds the landscape in the city.

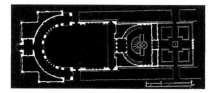

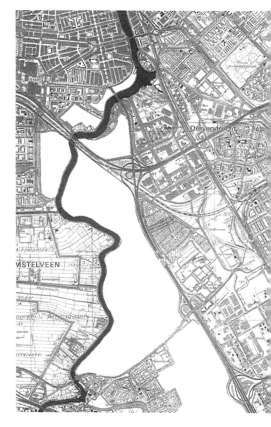

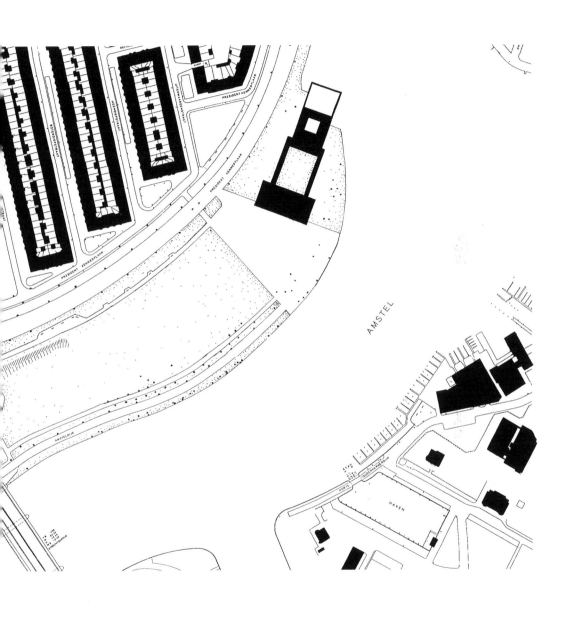

N

0 — 10m

OBSERVATORY. Hillegersberg ———————

DISPLAY CASE. Kralingen Transferium ———————

DISPLAY CASE. Just as a glass cabinet is only one more item of furniture, so the enclosed garden in the urban landscape is only one of the many features. The garden seeks not to introduce a new order, straighten out the landscape or emasculate the chaos as local greenspace, parkways and buffer zones attempt to do. On closer inspection a glass cabinet is a display case showing another, illusory world. The garden invites discussion of the disappearing landscape by parading a combination of natural order, endless space and its own image of nature.

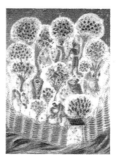

One such display case is the design for a miniature paradise amidst the bare expanse of the transferium at Kralingen (see page 182). A rolling mead of fragrant flowers, climbing plants, fruit trees and reflecting water present an idyllic image of nature. An impenetrable concrete wall, which you need to walk round to reach the entrance, screens off the garden from the surroundings. The steps lead to the parking garage below, and the ramp to the garden, raised as this is above the bustle on the asphalt.

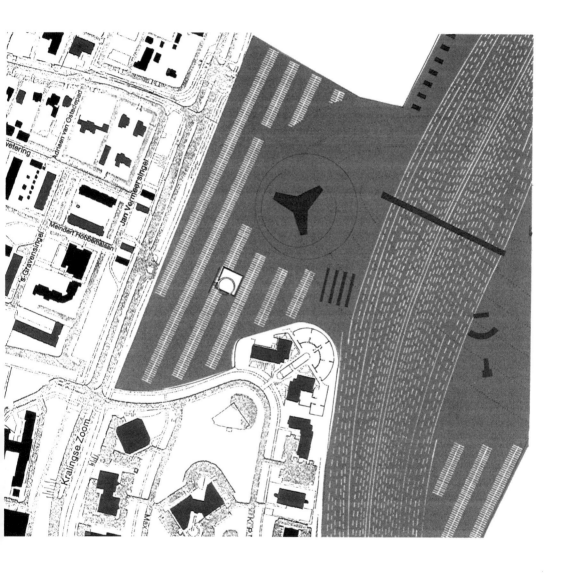

N

0   100m

LANDSCAPE WITH NO HORIZON   241

OBSERVATORY. By orienting an opening in an enclosed garden on to a salient point in a landscape, the landscape dimension is brought face to face with the containment of the garden. This way, a fragment of landscape can be fixed and something of the legibility of the original landscape transferred to the changeable and undefined urban landscape where cohesion and spaciousness are scarce.

In the northern periphery of Rotterdam, an enclosed garden embedded in an opening in the acoustic baffle gives on to a vulnerable landscape. The motorway, the view over the river Rotte and the intervening polder are fixed and related to one another. A concrete wall screens the garden from the motorway. A second screen captures the panorama in an elongated window, a balcony acting as intermediary between the polder and the garden.

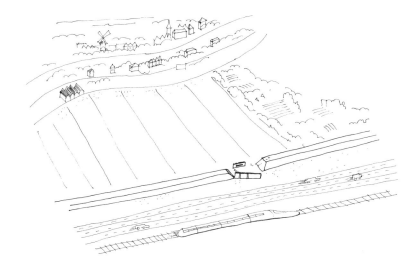

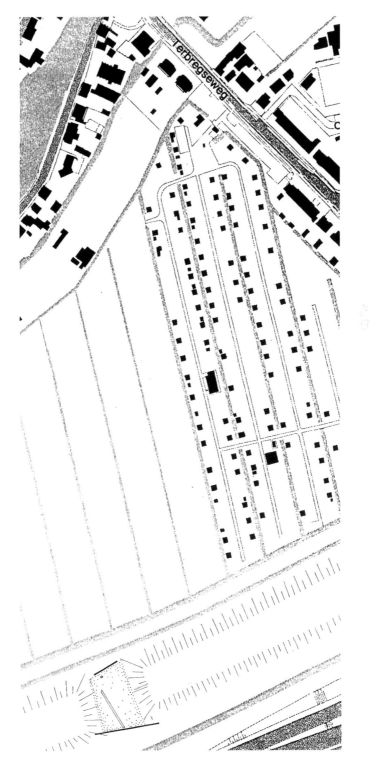

The range of the enclosed garden

In all areas of society we can see a reconsideration of the landscape taking shape. Garden fairs, nature holidays and the welter of recent literature on the subject show the landscape's growing popularity. It is also being recognized more and more as an indispensable given for urban design, and the search is on for points of application: what do we understand by landscape, how can it be read, how are we to deal with it? The enclosed garden has always been bound up with the landscape, being modelled on the landscape and therefore able to provide insight into it. This alliance also enables the relationship to be reversed, namely the landscape modelled on the garden. The formal tool kit of the enclosed garden can be translated to the macro scale of the landscape. Furthermore, interaction between the enclosed garden and the (urban) landscape can provide us with a wealth of possibilities for injecting new life into urban and landscape designs.

Deliberate confrontation between the smallness of the enclosed garden and the great size of the landscape can, for one thing, clarify the structure of our (urban) landscape. At present we can see a scaling-up on so many fronts: the city has become an urban region, the office a business park, the link between cities a boundary-hopping network of motorways, the public park a park system. The contrast with explicitly designed small public spaces could make spatially manifest the major dimensions of the landscape, which these days are still more a matter of statistics than anything else.

Enclosed gardens can have a catalytic effect on their surroundings. Small, carefully crafted external rooms at the right place can act as a kind of urban acupuncture whose impact reaches much further than the site in question. We see one such strategy applied by Oriol Bohigas in Barcelona, and by Bernardo Secchi in Kortrijk in Belgium. These deploy concrete interventions such as the designing of squares, buildings and boulevards to suture the tissue of the city.

As for the large-scale design tasks of today there is inspiration to be drawn from the tool kit of the enclosed garden. One quality of the enclosed garden is to couple programmatic freedom with spatial specificity. Brought to bear in the designs of urban landscapes, this would imply a radical about-turn: from merely adding together so many clearly defined programme components to a field fixed in its spatial composition yet able to admit a galaxy of programmatic configurations.

Other inroads might be the paradox of open and closed, or the complementary status of place and route. Or the paradox of the enclosed garden between lack of context and contextuality. Water purification plants, new residential neighbourhoods, sports complexes and business parks are often cut off from their surroundings, the only physical link being an access route to the city or the motorway. Might the very lack of context of such places not become a quality when seen against an architectural intervention in the landscape beyond? A window on a salient element of landscape, a second horizon, an urban balcony, a vertical feature making the connection with the celestial sphere, a scenographic route. By setting fragmentation against the continuity of the landscape, a major step will have been taken towards gaining architectural mastery of our urban landscape.

Isamo Noguchi, A California Experience,
Los Angeles, 1982. The different landscapes of
California assembled within four walls.

Glossary

anger a forest clearing made by grazing cattle.

appearance the totality of sensory impressions that together with the plan configuration and spatial form (qqv) fix the form of a design. These impressions consist of image-types and their references, materials and their textures, smells and colours, and impressions penetrating the garden from outside.

arbour a shady garden seat often sheltered by an openwork structure covered with climbing plants.

arcade from the Late Latin arcata (arched). A linked row of arches placed linearly to form a transparent wall.

Arcadian pertaining to Arcadia, the idyllic pastoral world of ancient Greek literature and metaphor for a happy and uncomplicated life.

archer's walk a raised path along the inside of a garden wall from where sentries can survey the surroundings for potential intruders, comparable with a castle wall.

atrium Hellenistic and Roman town houses often had two inner courts, the atrium and the peristyle (qv). The atrium was the formal reception room and was usually quite near the front of the house. It was surrounded by an inward-sloping roof supported on four pillars. At its centre was a rectangular opening (originally a smoke-hole) with below it a rainwater basin or impluvium.

axis mundi literally, 'world-axis', the imaginary vertical line joining the earth's surface with the heavenly vault. The line spans between the central point of the world – i.e. where the coordinates of the earth's surface intersect – and the zenith (qv). The axis is represented by a (cosmic) mountain, a tree, a fountain or another such vertical element.

Baroque garden see formal garden

belvedere literally, 'beautiful view'. An observation point (terrace, loggia, pavilion, turret etc) set on an eminence or high in a building.

berceau from the French; a tunnel of trelliswork covered with climbing plants.

bosquet a grove or shrubbery planted in a solid block as a formal wall for the main spaces in a garden. It often contains a recess, a shut-off space to contrast with the extraverted main spaces. Gardens based on an interplay of symmetrical and monumental space-organizing axes lined by bosquets were introduced in the French Baroque, the best-known example being the gardens at Versailles.

cabinet de verdure analogous to the small room (Fr. cabinet, literally 'little cabin') in a building, the *cabinet* de verdure is a small compartment (as opposed to the large salle de verdure) in a bosquet (qv) or between hedges.

casino a pavilion serving as a resting-point for the eye in the garden composition.

centrifugal tending away from a centre.

centripetal tending towards a centre.

chahar bagh literally 'quartered garden'. The oldest Persian gardens (c. 2000 BC) were square and divided into four equal parts by water channels. This pattern remained the basis of all Persian gardens throughout the centuries.

clearing an open space in the wilderness; one of the two natural archetypes of the hortus conclusus (qv), the other being the oasis (qv). The philosopher Martin Heidegger uses Lichtung, the German word for clearing, as a metaphor for Being.

cloister garth a quadrangle surrounded by a covered walk (see cloister walk).

cloister type a building type consisting of four bar-shaped volumes set round a square enclosed garden. A covered walk (see cloister walk) stitches the four volumes together, and serves also to relate the building to the garden.

cloister walk in a monastery, the walk surrounding the cloister garth or hortus contemplationis (qqv). It serves to link both the garden with the building as well as the building's four wings. It is generally sheltered by a lean-to roof projecting from the buildings. The cyclic route of the symbolic processions following the cross that are enacted in the cloister walk, underlines the latter's ritual character as depicting the experience of cyclic time.

concentric organization plan configuration based on a central point. In a concentric organization of space it is the central point that generates the volume. Cf. centralized organization about a prominent central space.

containment see enclosure.

contemplation a state, or the act, of attentive consideration (from the Latin contemplare). Templum means firmament, but also the space marked off by the augur in which to observe the flight of birds for divining purposes. Hence contemplate essentially means studying part of the sky.

context There are three meanings of the notion of context that bear some relationship to the hortus conclusus (qv): 1. context as a social, time-related given: the chaotic world from which the hortus conclusus turns away, or the overarching order the latter reflects; 2. context as the (urban) landscape as it exists: the hortus conclusus relates directly or indirectly to the landscape; 3. context as fantasy: the ideal landscape or the ideal city of which the hortus conclusus is part.

cortile originally a courtyard in an Italian palazzo. It later joined the urbanist's repertoire.

cosmic orientation 'To satisfy his inner sense of orientation, man needs to situate himself in space.' (Arnheim, 19, 21) There are three categories of references with which one can orient oneself: cosmic, territorial and temporal orientation (qqv). The opposition between earth and sky gives man the primitive feeling of being on earth, a distinction between above and below, vertical and horizontal, light and dark. In addition, the sun's path from east to west, and that of the pole star from north to south, is a given with which we can get our bearings. The word orientation derives from 'orient', the east where the sun rises.

cosmic space space which refers to the boundless universe by rendering absolutely the coordinates of the three dimensions, by eschewing references to earthly, tangible things and by stressing void over mass.

cosmogram the emblematic rendition of the cosmos.

cosmos Greek for 'order'. The Platonists used this term to describe the idea behind nature. This is how the term is understood in this book, rather than in the current meaning of universe.

curtain the term is related etymologically to 'garden', and so originally meant 'enclosure'. The wall between two bastions in fortifications is called a curtain. A curtain can also be described as a movable enclosure.

divine model (divine order) In pre-rational civilizations the physical world was regarded as reflecting the universal order, the only summum bonum. This divine model can be expressed in an arrangement by size, number and weight and the specifying of enclosure, sort and durability.

Eden, Garden of According to the Christian tradition man's earthly existence began in the Garden of Eden, a paradise where complete harmony prevailed. Since his expulsion from Eden man has looked back on it with longing, so that the Garden of Eden became the model for those Western European gardens designed as earthly paradises.

enclosure the relationship the observer has with the space he occupies is determined by the palpable presence and solidity of the surrounding walls shutting out the external world. Enclosed or contained is somewhere between open and closed. A space is 'closed' as soon as its height prevails over the breadth, and 'open' when one seems likely to lose contact with the walls.

Eros spatially bound, sensuous, earthly, hidden. The polarity (qv) is Oceanos.

exedra from the Greek ex (out) and hedra (seat). Architecturally it is a concave wall terminating a space. Its chief qualities for landscape architecture are the view and its spatial meshing with the landscape, comparable with a loggia. In Renaissance gardens the exedra takes on meaning for the garden as a whole by terminating the main axis which is thrown back on itself, so to speak, by the concave wall. The containment of the wall and the openness of the view are set in direct opposition.

existential space the stable image of the surroundings as constructed by man using cultural archetypes, socially and culturally conditioned structures and individual ideas.

fenêtre en longueur one of the 'five points of a new architecture' formulated by Le Corbusier: a long horizontal window that cuts off the sky and the ground from the landscape to bring a lack of depth to the view through it.

formal garden (also Baroque garden) the garden of seventeenth-century country seats, based on an absolute concept of nature and space. Garden and horizon are tied together by a single monumental space-organizing axis, a condition enabled by manipulating the perspective.

free plan configuration a plan configuration fixed not by the geometrical relationship between walls and volumes but by the plane which organizes the elements it contains into a dynamic composition. 'The walls of the "plan libre" are as free as the organizing contours of the "living free spirit"' (Polak 1984, 15).

free space a free space is autonomous with regard to its surroundings. It has an internal organization, and image and meaning are independent of the context which is excluded from the space. This space has a cosmic orientation (qv). A 'constrained' space by contrast enjoys an open relationship with the surroundings, and has a territorial orientation (qv).

gallery a covered passage with a building on one side and a windowed wall, arcade (qv) or colonnade on the other. It acts as a sheltered walk joining the spaces around (the Italian galleria also means tunnel).

garden the most condensed unit in which the historical, functional and spatial complexities of the landscape are made manifest.

gathering according to Norberg-Schulz a place's identity is determined by the fundamental distinction between sky and earth. The meaning of the natural surroundings is condensed wherever these two are brought together. The hortus conclusus is part of the earth because of the buildings around it, and part of the sky because of its airy ceiling. In it the landscape is 'gathered' and made manifest, freeing its meaning from its physical context and giving an image of the world (imago mundi).

genius loci literally 'genius of the place'. The Romans read a place as if it were a human face, an external revelation of the inner spirit. Like each person, each place has its own spirit. This notion was revived in eighteenth-century England, where Alexander Pope wrote: 'Consult the Genius of the Place in all; That tells the Waters or to rise, or fall... '. He regarded nature as an inner force that strives for perfection but is thwarted in this by all manner of misfortunes. To consult the genius of the place is to try to gain insight into the potential natural perfection of a place, and where necessary help it to manifest that perfection.

giardino segreto literally 'secret garden', although the garden is usually not actually hidden away. The giardino segreto is a component of the fifteenth-century Italian Renaissance villa, a transformation of the medieval hortus conclusus which steadily became less enclosed as time went by (the giardino segreto of the Villa Gamberaia is over two hundred metres long).

glorieta (also gloriette) a literal translation into Spanish of the Arabic word al-aziz meaning resplendent, glorious. Originally this was a garden pavilion in the heart of the walled garden. In the Mudejar-style gardens of Moorish Spain it is a green room of clipped trees, usually cypress.

grotto from the Greek krypte meaning crypt, vault. The grotto derives from the nymphaeum, a natural cave dedicated to the nymphs. The Romans copied the idea and built artificial versions which they decorated with stucco-work, mosaic and shells.

ha-ha a suddenly encountered gully constructed on the edge of eighteenth-century landscape gardens to separate these from the fields beyond and keep cattle from straying in.

herber from the Latin herba: grass, aromatic plant. In the medieval sense the term means a small garden, the herb garden, or an ornamental enclosed flowery mead set in a larger garden.

heterotopia The term comes from early texts by the philosopher Michel Foucault, most particularly his book Les Mots et les Choses, 1966. He describes heterotopias as possessing 'the curious property' of juxtaposing 'in a single real place several spaces, several sites that are in themselves incompatible', the only relationship between them being proximity. Heterotopia fragments and relates simultaneously. Foucault compares this method of juxtaposition with that of '"a certain Chinese encyclopaedia" in which it is written that "animals are divided into: (a) belonging to the Emperor, (b) embalmed, (c) tame, (d) sucking pigs, (e) sirens, (f) fabulous, (g) stray dogs, (h) included in the present classification, ..."' etc.

historical layering the visible presence of the history of a place, in that the residue left by one transformation becomes part of the next.

horizontal alignment the imaginary line between a fixed point and the horizon.

horizontal expansiveness boundless space in the horizontal plane, as suggested in, say, the German Pavilion in Barcelona.

horror vacui literally 'fear of the void'. This term is often used to describe the medieval world of thought and is materialized in the shelter and safety of the bounded settlements, bounded fields and bounded gardens.

hortus botanicus the garden as a collection of plants whose aim was to acquire and display knowledge. The plants are ordered according to a particular system that can differ from one such garden to the next. This classification can be taxonomical (i.e. a hierarchical ordering of species based on biological characteristics), geographical or functional. This hortus was originally designed in the shape of a hortus catalogi.

hortus catalogi a garden in which the plants are arranged in rectangular beds. The first vegetable and herb gardens were laid out in this geometrical configuration to make them easier to tend; it was later adopted almost unaltered for the botanical and ornamental gardens. The parterre (qv), which played a major organizing role in the Renaissance (rational) and Baroque (formal) gardens, is a derivative of the hortus catalogi.

hortus conclusus medieval enclosed garden, whose paradox is to manifest the landscape in all its complexity and exclude that landscape at the same time. It is at once internal and external.

hortus contemplationis a garden of contemplation. Informed by a centripetal (qv) plan organized by the surrounding buildings as, it presents a clear spatial and geometrical whole. A gallery provides it with a double outer wall. See cloister garth.

hortus ludi a delectable garden, the garden of delights as a profane reading of paradise. This bounded flowery mead was given over to play (ludus), courtship, rhetoric, philosophy, dance, music, poetry, but also to games such as vaulting, blind man's buff, chess and casting dice.

intention when different layers and

levels of planning convey the same idea then they are said to share the same intention. There is no absolute intention, as it always occurs somewhere between the two poles of freedom (the microcosm (qv)) and restraint (a fragment of a larger entity). A free space (qv) has a line joining it to the sky (vertical alignment (qv)), a constrained space one joining it to the horizon (horizontal alignment (qv)).

labyrinth an infinite complex route in a finite simple matrix – a square or circle – that symbolizes the arduous path (the path of life or indeed death, the path to paradise).

labyrinthine space the counterpart of rational space (objective relationships expressible in measures and proportions). Labyrinthine space expresses an awareness of image-related experience. It can be opaque or transparent, as long as there are no straightforward, rationally grasped spatial relationships.

landscape garden originating in eighteenth-century English country estates. It presents an ostensibly haphazard disposition of clumps of trees and architectural features in a free expanse of grass and water. It is in fact meticulously crafted into series of scenes, with garden and landscape conceived as a single spatial ensemble. (Also pictorial garden.)

lavabo from the Latin verb lavare, to wash. A basin in which the celebrant washes his fingers after the offertorium, while he says 'Lavabo inter innocentes manus meas' (I will wash my hands among the innocent).

lavatorium outbuilding attached to the cloister or pavilion in the centre of the cloister garth (qv) and containing the washbasin. The building can be circular, square or polygonal, the basin circular or polygonal and equipped with countless waterspouts.

Lichtung see clearing.

locus Latin for place. In this definition the place is considered an artefact with its own internal order, as opposed to topos (qv) which regards it as part of the landscape context.

locus amoenus literally a delightful spot, a shining field of flowers surrounded by trees and with a crystal stream, first described by Virgil in his Bucolics (42-37 BC). This is the image medieval and renaissance man used as

a model for the paradise garden.

loggia from the German word Laube, shelter or canopy. A shady niche or recess in the facade, acting as an internal balcony to bring the view to the villa.

Mannerist garden Mannerism describes the style that follows upon the zenith of every major movement in the arts, in which rationality cedes to emotion, and purity to affectedness. Here it specifically denotes the Mannerism of the Renaissance, exemplified by an affected and complex garden of a sixteenth-century Italian villa, composed as a dynamic succession of visual experiences.

maze a garden form with narrow paths between tall hedges, its intricate meanderings intended to confuse the visitor who has to get to the centre and then out again.

microcosm a condensed version of the macrocosm or great world. Man and in fact all living things can be regarded as a microcosm. So too can the hortus conclusus (qv). A microcosm is an introverted, enclosed and centripetal (qv) spatial unit, a cohesive composition of sensory impressions.

mirador from the Spanish mirar, to watch. A prospect tower resembling a belvedere, a generally greenery-clad pavilion or platform.

mount an artificial hill in the garden that enables its occupants to view the landscape without needing to leave the garden. After the Middle Ages the mount became a component of the plan configuration (qv), its function instead being to overlook the garden itself. The embroidered parterres in the garden were in fact designed for observation from above.

oasis a fertile spot in an inhospitable flat expanse; one of the two natural archetypes of the hortus conclusus (qv), the other being the clearing (qv).

Oceanos universal, timeless and unfixed to place and sensory perception, spatial in the sense of unbounded expansiveness. The polarity (qv) is Eros (qv).

palazzo Italian palace built in towns, customarily consisting of a rectangular block enfolding a cortile (qv) with a symmetrical facade to the street.

panorama garden garden belonging to

fifteenth-century Italian villas, in which the panorama across the landscape and the city is assimilated as part of the composition, which is predicated on harmony, clarity and quiet.

panoramic composition open unbounded spatial composition that seems to continue beyond the horizon. The landscape garden is one example.

paradise from the Persian word pairidaeza, meaning park or orchard. It is the ideal image of a blissful garden, a place of eternal peace in the hereafter to compensate for a wretched and temporary existence on earth. In the hortus conclusus (qv) earthly attributes are excluded and replaced by a tangible paradise.

parterre literally 'on the ground'. A formal terrace planted with flowers or grass. It can also be a geometrical pattern of clipped box hedges with gravel or shells between.

patio a garden courtyard of houses in Mediterranean areas. The form derives from Moorish architecture. It is an external room providing coolness and shade and is the functional and physical centre of the house. Hence the floor is most usually paved.

patte d'oie three (sometimes four or five) allées or avenues converging at a sharp angle in a shape comparable to the foot of a goose, hence the name.

perimeter walk a path following the boundaries of a landscape garden (qv) with places to sit and viewing points. The perimeter walk can be compared with the gallery (qv) of the hortus conclusus (qv). Both link the route and the view, thereby defining the outer limits of the garden. The difference is that the perimeter walk strings together a number of scenes whereas the gallery illuminates one image from different sides.

peristyle In Hellenistic and Roman times town houses and villas often had two inner courts, the atrium (qv) and the peristyle (or peristyle garden). Set behind the atrium, the peristyle was a courtyard garden with a colonnade all round. This was the setting for informal family life: eating, making music and playing games.

plan configuration the basic form of the design which it defines together with the spatial form and the appearance (qqv). It is the rational system of measures and proportions that examines the interference between

the design and the natural givens of the site.

polarity the form of an architectural object can be described with the help of opposing concepts or polarities. Examples include Eros and Oceanos (qqv), free and constrained, closed and open.

portico an open or partly enclosed roofed space forming the entrance to a building, usually the centrepiece of the classical facade. The roof is borne aloft on columns.

rational garden (also Renaissance garden) a garden belonging to fifteenth- and sixteenth-century Italian villas. The design is based on a rationalized concept both of controlling and perspectivelly manipulating space, and of nature as an object of research and admiration. Rational gardens divide into two types: the panorama garden and the mannerist garden (qqv).

Renaissance garden see rational garden

sacro bosco literally, holy wood. This is an element of the Renaissance garden that refers to the ancient Greek and Roman tradition of honouring one of the gods by dedicating a particular tree or grove to them. As a result of this symbolic charge it is sometimes applied unrelated to the Renaissance garden context, as in the Brion cemetery garden.

scenographic route route composed as a filmic succession of scenes.

spatial addition the combining and stacking of autonomous spaces.

spatial division the subdivision of spaces into inferior spatial components.

spatial form space conceived as an entity of plastic form. It may be articulated and experienced as dynamic and in motion. 'Our glance glides horizontally over the plan, then rises vertically along the wall, washes across the ceiling and finally sinks down again. These containing lines combine into an impression of space.' (Brinckmann, 1924) The spatial form fixes the design together with the plan configuration and the appearance (qqv).

square a clearing in the city planted with trees. It might be the forecourt to a building set back in an otherwise unbroken elevation.

stabilizer a point or space which fixes

the urban context through its static nature.

stoa a covered promenade along an agora or other public space, and the primary setting for public life when Greek culture was at its height (800-400 BC). The stoa was bordered on one side by a wall, and on the other by an arcade on a base. The gallery (qv) is a derivative of the stoa.

suburb a dwelling form wholly based on car ownership, in which the idea of living in natural surroundings is translated into a community of as many detached houses as possible per hectare. These are spread in a free-form composition. Proceeding from a need for equality and openness, the garden as self-contained unit is replaced by a necklace of front gardens generating a collective lawn.

tapis vert French for 'green carpet'. A taut lawn whose purpose is to pull together the various components in a garden composition.

temenos a physically enclosed sacred place, deserving of a respectful distance.

temporal orientation besides cosmic and territorial orientation (qqv), reference to the passing of time can also help us get our bearings. Spring, summer, autumn and winter dictate the rhythm of our behaviour, and the changes in temperature that the seasons bring, make us aware of our bodies. The rhythm of day and night provides two utterly different experiences of space. The presence of the past in ancient stones, streets and trees give us insight into the continuity and perpetual change of our surroundings, and into life itself.

territorial orientation the visible landscape – plains and hills, valleys and mountains – in other words the topography and geography, gives us the most direct information about our position on the planet. The horizon is the intangible boundary. Differences between close by and far off, foreground and background, central point and periphery, act to relate elements to one another. Inside and outside also generate a fundamental distinction between spaces.

topology from the Greek topos: a place and logos: a discourse. The transformation of an autonomous geometric pattern through the influence of topographical properties of the place, without the cohesion of the pattern being broken.

topos Greek for 'place'. Originally the term referred in particular to a place within the mythological landscape. As distinct from locus (qv), topos is imbedded in the landscape and is dictated by, among other things, the contours, climate, planting, water and soil type.

transferium a node or interchange of distinct infrastructural lines where users of one transport mode can transfer to another, hence the name.

trellis, trelliswork a latticework structure of willow, later also of iron, either overarching or as a screen and supporting climbing plants, particularly roses.

turfed bench, turfed seat a raised bed planted with grass and herbs serving as an aromatic seat.

urban landscape hybrid landscape in which the distinction between city and environs is erased.

vacuole a tiny globular cytoplasm-filled cavity in the protoplasm of a living cell. The space of the hortus conclusus (qv) can be compared with a vacuole in that it is sealed off from the outside world, a void scooped from the built surroundings.

vertical alignment the imaginary line joining a fixed point on earth and the zenith (qv). This alignment gains a strong symbolic charge in the axis mundi (qv).

vista a framed view.

vista garden a seventeenth-century French formal garden (qv). It marks the peak in the development of the central-perspective axis, where the horizon is gathered into the garden by means of an all-dominating vista.

way of the cross a series of sculpted or painted depictions of episodes from Christ's via dolorosa, often proceeding uphill to the cross that forms the termination and goal of the procession, individual pilgrimage or journey of penitence. The ritual character is determined by the linear progression towards this culmination point.

zenith from the Arabic samt (short for samt-ar-ras, literally direction of the head). The highest point on the celestial sphere directly overhead, where an imaginary line perpendicular to the earth's surface bisects the celestial sphere. The point terminating one end of the axis mundi.

Bibliography

A ROOM WITH NO CEILING
Desvigne, M. and C. Dalnoky, untitled, in Vandermarliere, K. (ed.), *Het Landschap. Vier internationale landschapsontwerpers*, De Singel, Antwerp 1995, 176-213.
Erp-Houtepen, A. van, *The Garden as an Enclosure. Changing Attitudes towards the Fence in English Gardens 1620-1820*, unpublished doctoral thesis, Rijksuniversiteit Leiden 1986.
Eijck, A. van, *Ecology in Design* 1978.
Frankl, P., *Die Entwicklungsphasen der neueren Baukunst*, Berlin 1914. Translated as *Principles of Architectural History*, MIT Press, Cambridge (Mass.) 1968.
Jong, T.M. de, *Culturele variatie*, Monografieën Milieuplanning / SOM23, Delft 1994.
Komrij, G., *Alles onecht. Keuze uit de gedichten*, De Arbeiderspers, Amsterdam 1984.
Lewis, C.S., *The Lion, the Witch and the Wardrobe*, The Bodley Head, London 1950.
Norberg-Schulz, C., *Genius Loci. Towards a Phenomenology of Architecture*, Academy, London 1980.
Norberg-Schulz, C., *Existence, Space and Architecture*, Praeger, New York 1971.
Polak, M., *Het kreatief ontwerp in architectuur en stedebouw, een psychodynamisch-kritische benadering*, Delft University Press, Delft 1984.
Polak, M., O. Das et al., *Ruimtelijkheid in het ontwerp*, Publikatieburo Bouwkunde, Delft 1989.
Reh, W. and C.M. Steenbergen (eds.), *Architectuur en landschap. De techniek van de rationele, formele en picturale enscenering*, Publikatieburo Bouwkunde, Delft 1992.
Reh, W. and C.M. Steenbergen, *Architecture and Landscape. The Design Experiment of the Great European Gardens and Landscapes*, Thoth, Bussum 1996.
Steenbergen, C.M., *De stap over de horizon. Een ontleding van het formele ontwerp in de landschapsarchitectuur*, Publikatieburo Bouwkunde, Delft 1990.

THE HORTUS CONCLUSUS AS LANDSCAPE-ARCHITECTURAL MODEL
Ackerman, J.S., 'Ars sine Scientia nihil est. Gothic Theory of Architecture

at the Cathedral of Milan', in *Art Bulletin* (1949) 31, 84-116.
Bekkers, P., 'De geruisloze blik', *De Volkskrant*, 4 October 1991.
Berghs, H., 'Martin Heideggers bijdrage aan een filosofie van het wonen en het milieu', in Nagel, B. (ed.), *Maken en breken: over produktie en spiritualiteit*, Kok, Kampen 1988, 28-63.
Comito, T., *The Idea of the Garden in the Renaissance*, Rutgers University Press, New Brunswick New Jersey 1935.
Cowell, F.R. and J. Cowell, *The Garden as a Fine Art*, Weidenfels and Nicholson Ltd., London 1978.
Crisp, F., *Mediaeval Gardens*, London 1924, reprint by Hacker Art Books, New York 1966.
Fumagalli, V., *Als de hemel zich verduistert. De geschiedenis van het middeleeuwse levensgevoel*, Wereldbibliotheek, Amsterdam 1992.
Heidegger, M., *Sein und Zeit*, Niemeyer, Tübingen 1972. (offprint from *Jahrbuch für Philosophie und phänomenologische Forschung Vol. VIII*; Edmund Husserl, 1927.)
Hennebo, D., *Gärten des Mittelalters*, Artemis Verlag, Munich/Zurich 1987.
Hyams, E., *A History of Gardens and Gardening*, J. M. Dent & Sons Ltd., London 1971.
Jellicoe, G., S. Jellicoe, P. Goode and M. Lancaster (eds.), *The Oxford Companion to Gardens*, Oxford University Press, Oxford/New York 1991.
Jong, T.M. de, *Culturele variatie*, Monografieën Milieuplanning / SOM23, Delft 1994.
Komrij, G., *Over de noodzaak van tuinieren, Huizinga-lezing 1990*, Uitgeverij Bert Bakker, Amsterdam 1991.
Laan, Dom H. van der, *De architectonische ruimte. Vijftien lessen over de dispositie van het menselijk verblijf*, E.J. Brill, Leiden 1977.
Leach, E., *Culture and Communication*, Columbia University Press, New York 1976.
Le Goff, J., *La civilisation de l'Occident médiéval*, Arthaud, Paris 1987.
Le Goff, J., 'Le jardin dans la ville médiévale', *Temps Libre* (1984) 9, 71-74.
Lemaire, T., *Filosofie van het landschap*, AMBO, Baarn 1970.
Marel, H. van der, *Filarete's Sforzinda 1461-1464*, unpublished doctoral thesis, Technische Universiteit Delft 1985.
Masson, G., *Italian Gardens*, Thames and Hudson, London 1961.

Moore, C.W., W.J. Mitchell and W. Turnbell, *The Poetics of Gardens*, MIT Press, Cambridge (Mass.) 1988.
Moynihan, E.B., *Paradise as a Garden in Persia and Mughal India*, George Braziller, New York 1979.
Nuttgens, P., *The Story of Architecture*, Phaidon, Oxford 1983.
Pinder-Wilson, R., 'The Persian Garden', in Macdougall, E. B. and R. Ettinghausen (eds.), *The Islamic Garden. Dumbarton Oaks Colloquium on the History of Landscape Architecture IV*, Dumbarton Oaks Trustees for Harvard University, Washington D.C. 1976, 69-85.
Prest, J., *The Garden of Eden. The Botanic Garden and the Re-Creation of Paradise*, Yale University Press, New Haven 1981.
Solmsen, F., *Aristotle's System of the Physical World*, Ithaka, New York 1960.
Steenbergen, C.M., *De stap over de horizon. Een ontleding van het formele ontwerp in de landschapsarchitectuur*, Publikatiebureau Bouwkunde, Delft 1990.
Stein, R. A., *Le monde en petit. Jardins en miniature et habitation dans la pensée religieuse d'extrême-orient*, Paris 1987.
Stuip, R.E.V. and C. Vellekoop (eds.), *Tuinen in de Middeleeuwen*, Uitgeverij Verloren, Hilversum 1992.
Tzonis, A. and L. Lefaivre, *Het architektonisch denken en andere architectuur-theoretische studies*, SUN, Nijmegen 1991.
Zilsel, E., 'Copernicus and Mechanics', *Journal of the History of Ideas*, I, 1940.
Zuylen, G. van, *Paradise on Earth. The Gardens of Western Europe*, Harry N. Abrams, New York 1995.

LANDSCAPE TRANSFORMATIONS
Ackerman, J.S., *The Villa. Form and Ideology of Country Houses*, Thames and Hudson, London, 1990.
Adams, W.H., *The French Garden*, George Braziller, New York 1979.
Appleton, J., The Experience of Landscape, Wiley, London 1975.
Baker, G., *Le Corbusier, an analysis of form*, Van Nostrand Reinhold Co Ltd., Hong Kong 1989.
Bijhouwer, J., 'Gebouw en tuin', *De 8 en Opbouw*, 9 (1938) 22, 209-213.
Comito, T., *The Idea of the Garden in the Renaissance*, Rutgers University Press, New Brunswick New Jersey 1935.
Cornford, F.M., 'The Invention of space', in *Essays in Honour of Gilbert Murray*, London 1936, 215-235.

Cowell, F.R. and J. Cowell, *The Garden as a Fine Art*, Weidenfels and Nicholson Ltd., London 1978.
Ganay, E. de, *André le Nostre 1613-1700*, Editions Vincent, Paris 1962.
Gothein, M. L., *Geschichte der Gartenkunst, Zweiter Band. Von der Renaissance in Frankreich bis zur Gegenwart*, Eugen Diederichs, Jena 1926.
Harbison, R. and G. James, *The Italian Garden*, Harry N. Abrams, New York 1991.
Hunt, J.D. and E. de Jong (eds.), *The Anglo-Dutch Garden in the Age of William and Mary/De Gouden Eeuw van de Hollandse tuinkunst*, Taylor & Francis/Thoth, London/Amsterdam, 1988. Special double issue of the *Journal of Garden History*.
Jellicoe, G., S. Jellicoe, P. Goode and M. Lancaster (eds.), *The Oxford Companion to Gardens*, Oxford University Press, Oxford/New York 1991.
Kask, T., *Symmetrie und Regelmässigkeit. Französische Architektur im Grand Siècle*, Birkhäuser, Basle/Stuttgart 1971.
Kern, H., *Labyrinthe. Erscheinungsformen und Deutungen 500 Jahre gegenwart eines Urbilds*, Prestel Verlag, Munich 1982.
Lemaire, T., *Filosofie van het landschap*, AMBO, Baarn 1970.
Loudon, J.C. (ed.), *The Landscape Gardening and Landscape Architecture of the Late Humphrey Repton Esq.*, Longman & Co., London 1840 (facs. repr. 1969).
Louwerse, D., 'De wederopbouw en de vormgeving van het stedelijk groen', in Smienk, G. (ed.), *Nederlandse landschapsarchitectuur. Tussen traditie en experiment*, Thoth, Amsterdam 1993, 23-32.
Lovejoy, A.O., *The Great Chain of Being*, MIT Press, Cambridge (Mass.) 1936.
Masson, G., *Italian Gardens*, Thames and Hudson, London 1961.
Moore, C.W., W.J. Mitchell and W. Turnbell, *The Poetics of Gardens*, MIT Press, Cambridge (Mass.) 1988.
Mul, J. de, *Het romantisch verlangen, in (post)moderne kunst en filosofie*, unpublished doctoral thesis, Faculteit der Wijsbegeerte, Erasmus Universiteit, Rotterdam 1990.
Murray, P., *The Architecture of the Italian Renaissance*, Batsford, London 1963.
Polak, M., *Het kreatief ontwerp in*

architectuur en stedebouw, een psychodynamisch-kritische benadering, Delft University Press, Delft 1984.
Reh, W., *Arcadia en Metropolis, het landschapsexperiment van de Verlichting*, Publikatieburo Bouwkunde, Delft 1996.
Reh, W., *Reconstructie en Perspectief, deel B: Het landschapsarchitectonisch denken*, Staringcentrum-DLO, Wageningen 1993.
Reh, W. and C.M. Steenbergen, *Architecture and Landscape. The Design Experiment of the Great European Gardens and Landscape*, Thoth, Bussum 1996.
Schwartz, M., 'Our culture and the Art for Public Places', in Vlug, J. et al., *International IFLA Conference 1992. Focusing on the Interface between Landscape Architecture and the Visual Arts*, Thoth, Amsterdam 1992.
Shepherd, J.C. and G.A. Jellicoe, *Italian Gardens of the Renaissance*, Alec Tiranti, London 1966.
Steenbergen, C.M., *De stap over de horizon. Een ontleding van het formele ontwerp in de landschapsarchitectuur*, Publikatieburo Bouwkunde, Delft 1990.
Tzonis, A. and L. Lefaivre, *Het architektonisch denken en andere architectuur-theoretische studies*, SUN, Nijmegen 1991.
Von Simson, O., *The Gothic Cathedral. Origins of Gothic Architecture and the Medieval Concept of Order*, Bollingen Series XLVIII, Princeton University, Princeton New Jersey 1962.
Warnau, H., 'Landschapsarchitectuur en de moderne stroming in de bouwkunde', in Smienk, G. (ed.), *Nederlandse landschapsarchitectuur. Tussen traditie en experiment*, Thoth, Amsterdam 1993, 33-40.
Watson, A., *Agricultural Innovation in the Early Islamic World: The Diffusion of Crops and Farming Techniques*, MIT Press, Cambridge (Mass.) 1973.
Wegner, J., *De Europese stad in het Middeleeuwen*, Publikatieburo Bouwkunde, Delft 1993.

URBAN TRANSFORMATIONS

Bakema, J. 'De vrije vorm', in *De 8 en Opbouw*, 12 (1941) 8, 106-107.
Barrucand, M. and A. Bednorz, *Moorish Architecture in Andalusia*, Benedikt Taschen Verlag, Cologne 1992.
Boekraad, C., 'Oscillatie of parabool. Nieuwe interpretaties van Mies van Der Rohes architectuur', *Archis* 2 (1987) 3, 11-21.

Champigneulle, B., *Paris. Architectures, sites et jardins*, Editions du Seuil, Paris 1973.
Dezallier d'Argenville, A.J., *La Theorie et la Pratique de Jardinage*, Charles-Antoine Jombert, Paris 1760.
Doesburg, T. van, [article] *Neue Schweizer Rundschau* (1929) 8, 630.
Gothein, M. L., *Geschichte der Gartenkunst, Erster Band. Von Ägypten bis zur Renaissance in Italien, Spanien und Portugal*, Eugen Diederichs, Jena 1926.
Grisebach, A. von, *Der Garten, eine Geschichte seiner künstlerischen Gestaltung*, Verlag Von Klinkhardt & Biermann, Leipzig 1910.
Hegemann, W. and E. Peets, *The American Vitruvius. An Architects' Handbook of Civic Art*, The Architectura Book Publishing Company, New York 1922.
Imbert, D., *The Modernist Garden in France*, Yale University Press, New Haven/London 1993.
Jellicoe, G. and S. Jellicoe, *The Landscape of Man. Shaping the Environment from Prehistory to the Present Day*, Thames and Hudson, London 1975.
Jong, E. de and W. Reh., 'De Tuin en de Stad. De Amsterdamse grachtentuin in vogelvlucht' in Veenendaal, E. et al. (eds.), *Amsterdamse Grachtentuinen. Keizersgracht*, Waanders Uitgevers, Zwolle 1997, 15-48.
Kostof, S., *The City Assembled. The Elements of Urban Form Through History*, Thames and Hudson, London 1992.
Lörzing, H., *Van Bosplan tot Floriade. Nederlandse park- en landschapsontwerpen in de twintigste eeuw*, 010 Publishers, Rotterdam 1992.
Migge, L., 'Kritik am Landschaftlichen Park der Jahrhundertwende – heute noch aktuell?' in *Der Hamburger Stadtpark und die Neuzeit*, Hamburg, 1909.
Moël, M. le, *L'Architecture privée à Paris au Grand siècle*, Commission des travaux historiques de la Villa de Paris, Paris 1990.
Moos, S. von, *Turm und Bollwerk, Beitrage zu einer politischen Ikonographie der Italienischer Renaissance*, Atlantis, Zurich 1974.
Murray, P., *The Architecture of the Italian Renaissance*, Batsford, London 1963.
Polak, M., O. Das, K. Rijnboutt and J. van Zwol, *Ruimtelijkheid in het ontwerp*, Diktaat BK 245 differentiatie Architectuurgrammatica, Faculteit der Bouwkunde, Delft 1989.

Pollan, M., *Second Nature*, 1991.
Prest, J., *The Garden of Eden. The Botanic Garden and the Re-Creation of Paradise*, Yale University Press, New Haven 1981.
Rowe, C. and F. Koetter, *Collage City*, MIT Press, Cambridge (Mass.) 1978.
Schulze, F. (ed.), *Mies van der Rohe. Critical essays*, Museum of Modern Art, New York 1989.
Scott, F., *The Art of Beautifying Suburban Home Grounds*, 1870.
Sijpesteyn, C.H.C.A., *Oud-Nederlandsche Tuinkunst. Geschiedkundig overzicht van de Nederlandsche tuinarchitectuur van de 15e tot de 19e eeuw*, Martinus Nijhoff, The Hague 1910.
Sutcliffe, A., *Paris. An Architectural History*, Yale University Press, New Haven/London 1993.
Summerson, J., *Georgian London*, Barrie & Jenkins, London 1988.
Taverne, E., *In 't land van belofte: in de nieuwe stad. Ideaal en werkelijkheid van de stadsuitleg in de Republiek 1580-1680*, Gary Schwartz, Maarssen 1978.
Vroom, M.J., *Outdoor Space, Environments designed by Dutch landscape architects since 1945*, Thoth, Amsterdam 1992.
Zucker, P., *Town and Square. From the Agora to the Village Green*, Columbia University Press, New York 1959.

CURRENT TRANSFORMATIONS
Braudel, F., *Ecrits sur l'histoire*, Flammarion, Paris 1969.
Bruin, R. de and K.-E. Löfqvist, *Ett klosterbyggen i tiden*, Fyrkanten Arkitekter, Höganäs 1994.
Calvino, I., *Invisible Cities*, Harvest, San Diego/New York, 1974. (Translation of *La città invisibili*, Einaudi, Turin 1972.)
Chemetoff, A., 'Parc de la Villette in Paris', *Anthos* 28 (1989) 1, 21-27.
Chemetoff, A., 'Le jardin des bambous', *Architecture d'Aujourd'hui*, (1989) 262.
Desvigne, M. and C. Dalnoky, untitled, in Vandermarliere, K. (ed.), *Het Landschap. Vier internationale landschapsontwerpers*, De Singel, Antwerp 1995, 176-213.
Dijk, H. van, 'Fluid, animated baroque. The water pavilion on Neeltje Jans', *Archis*, 10 (1995) 11, 18-25.
Guinee, A., 'Kwaliteit die van ontworpen buitenruimten architectuur maakt', *Blauwe kamer Profiel,* 6 (1996) 4, 30-37.
Heuvel, W.J. van, 'De architectuur van

Friis en Nielsen', *Polytechnisch tijdschrift* (1974), 681-688.
Keyzer, K. de et al., 'Wil de echte Aalto opstaan?', *Forum* 31 (1986) 1, 271-282.
Kittredge, W., *Owning it all*, Graywolf Press, St. Paul 1987.
Koolhaas, R. and B. Mau, *S,M,L,XL*, 010 Publishers, Rotterdam 1995.
Koolhaas, R., *Urban Operations*, 1993.
Koster, E., 'Dom van der Laan's Arcadian Architecture', *Architectura & Natura Quarterly*, 1 (1992) 1, 32-48.
Laan, Dom H. van der, *De architectonische ruimte. Vijftien lessen over de dispositie van het menselijk verblijf*, E.J. Brill, Leiden 1977.
Lamarre, F., 'Genève l'emprise du vide', *D'Architectures* 1 (1996) 62, 60-61.
Los, S., *Carlo Scarpa Architect*, Benedikt Taschen, Cologne 1993.
Louwerse, D. and H. Meyer (eds.), *De stad, een landschap*, Publikatieburo Bouwkunde, Delft 1992.
Lucan, J., *OMA – Rem Koolhaas*, Princeton Architectural Press, New York 1991.
Moore, C.W., W.J. Mitchell and W. Turnbull, *The Poetics of Gardens*, MIT Press, Cambridge (Mass.) 1988.
Neuenschwander, E. and C. Neuenschwander, *Finnische Bauten; Atelier Alvar Aalto 1950-1951*, Verlag für Architektur, Erlenbach/Zurich 1954.
Padovan, R., *Dom Hans van der Laan. Modern Primitive*, Architectura & Natura Press, Amsterdam 1994.
Reh, W., 'Voorbij de videoclip', in Smienk, G. (ed.), *Nederlandse landschapsarchitectuur*, Thoth, Amsterdam 1993, 79-93.
Schildt, G., *Alvar Aalto. The early years*, Rizzoli, New York 1984.
Shriver, P.E. et al. (eds.) 'Entrepenørskolen, Ebeltoft', *Arkitektur*, 12 (1968) 6, 271-282.
Theroux, P., *The Kingdom By the Sea, A Journey Around the Coast of Great Britain*, Hamish Hamilton Ltd., London 1983.
Tiberghien, G.A., *Jardins Elémentaires. Michel Desvigne*, Edizioni Carte Segrete, Rome 1987.
Tilman, H., 'Vruchtbare reductie van de complexiteit. De stedebouw van Euralille', *De Architect*, 25 (1994) 12, 22-31.
Tolkien, J.R.R., *The Fellowship of the Ring*, part 1 of *The Lord of the Rings*, Unwin Paperbacks, London, 3rd edition, 1978 (1st edition 1968; first published separately 1954).
Uyttenhove, P., 'A conductor of modest

intentions. Christian de Portzamparc's project for Masséna, Paris', *Archis*, 11 (1996) 7, 66-69.
Vandermarliere, K. (ed.), *Het Landschap. Vier internationale landschapsontwerpers*, De Singel, Antwerp 1995.
Vermeulen, P., 'An open place in the woods', *Archis*, 10 (1995) 3, 48-49.
White, T., *The Once and Future King*, William Collins Sons and Co. Ltd., Glasgow 1958.
Wilton-Ely, J., *The Mind and Art of Giovanni Battista Piranesi*, Thames and Hudson, London 1978.
Wortmann, A., 'Variationen zum Thema Atriumhaus', *Baumeister*, 92 (1995) 8, 28-33.
Zeeuw, P. de, C. M. Steenbergen, I. Bobbink and H. Veenenbos, *Stadslandschap Amsterdam, Landschapsarchitectonische kwaliteiten en potenties tussen Dam en Spaarne*, Publikatieburo Bouwkunde, Delft 1996.
Zwinkels, C., 'Diversiteit en kwaliteit kenmerken recente Deense architectuur', *De Architect*, 17 (1986) 9, 92-97.
Zwol, J. van, 'De specifieke rationaliteit van Aalto; een studie naar de ontwikkeling van zijn werk', in Polak, M. et al., *Ruimtelijkheid in het ontwerp*, Diktaat BK 245 differentiatie Architectuurgrammatica, Faculteit der Bouwkunde, Delft 1989, 84-115.

A LANDSCAPE WITH NO HORIZON
Geuze, A., 'Het vermeende succes', *De Architect*, 27 (1996) 2, 42-49.
Loos, A., *Sämtliche Schriften Bd. 1. Ins Leere gesprochen 1897-1900; Trotzdem 1900-1930*, Herold, Vienna 1962. Translation of 'Architecture' (1910) quote taken from M. Risselada (ed.), *Raumplan versus Plan Libre*, Delft University Press, Delft 1988.

GLOSSARY
Arnheim, R., *The Dynamics of Architectural Form*, University of California Press, Berkeley 1977, 21.
Brinckmann, A.E., *Plastik und Raum als Grundformen künstlerischer Gestaltung*, Piper, Munich 1924.
Sheridan, A., *Michel Foucault. The Will to Truth*, Tavistock Publications, London 1980.
Warchauer, M., 'Heterotopias, panopticons, and Internet discourse', in *University of Hawai'i Working Papers in ESL*, 14(1), 1995, pp. 91-121.

Index

Credits

This book has been made possible through the generous support of the Netherlands Architecture Fund, Stichting Fonds Landbouw Export Bureau 1916-1918 and Rens-Holle Stichting.

Digital models: Bastiaan Kwast
Cover photography and chapter headings: Katharina Türler
Translation from the Dutch: John Kirkpatrick
Design: Erik Wong and Annelies Frölke
Lithography and printing: Snoeck-Ducaju & Zoon, Gent

© 1999 The authors and 010 Publishers, Rotterdam
[www.010publishers.nl]
ISBN 90-6450-349-4

Second revised edition, 2001.

Originally published in 1998 as 'De omsloten tuin. Geschiedenis en ontwikkeling van de hortus conclusus en de herintroductie ervan in het hedendaagse stadslandschap'. (ISBN 90-6450-348-6)

Our thanks go first of all to Clemens Steenbergen for his patience and invaluable criticism, Wouter Reh for his persistent good advice, Bastiaan Kwast for his enthusiasm, Erik de Jong for his thoroughness and critical eye, Meto Vroom for slipping in useful comment, and Paul van der Ree for a less serious angle just when we needed it.
Thanks are also due to Caroline for sharing her command of Spanish with us, to Niek for his wide knowledge of the Alhambra, to Jaco for his willingness to give advice whenever asked for it, and to Sebastiaan for his contribution to the illustrations. And of course to all those who have supported us throughout five years of research, the travelling companions, willing ears, collaborating minds, helping hands and tireless makers of coffee, our thanks and appreciation.

To the sisters of the Jesu Moder Maria convent in Mariavall, we owe a particular expression of thanks for their hospitality, as also to Rik van der Laan and the Alvar Aalto Foundation for their willing assistance, and to all the other organizations, wardens, priests and gardeners who kindly gave us access to their premises.